Fish Diseases and Water Chemistry

AQUARIOLOGY

Fish Diseases and Water Chemistry

Dr. John B. Gratzek, Dr. Richard E. Wolke, Dr. Emmett B. Shotts, Jr.,
Dr. Donald Dawe, and George C. Blasiola

Tetra Press

Tetra Press
Aquariology: Fish Diseases and Water Chemistry
A Tetra Press Publication

Gratzek, Dr. John B.,
Aquariology: fish diseases and water chemistry; edited by Dr.
John B. Gratzek with Janice R. Matthews

L.C. Catalog card number 91-067994
ISBN number 1-56465-108-8
Tetra Press item number 16858

1. Gratzek, Dr. John B.   2. Matthews, Janice R.

Tetra would like to gratefully acknowledge the following sources
of photographs and artwork:
For the chapters "Getting Started," "Maintaining Aquaria," and
"Infectious Diseases" © Dr. John B. Gratzek; for "Physiological
Mechanisms of Fish Disease" © Dr. Richard E. Wolke; for "Diseases of Marine Fishes" © Dr. George C. Blasiola. Additional
illustrations were provided by Tetra Archives, except as otherwise noted.

Printed in Hong Kong.

First edition
10 9 8 7 6 5 4 3 2 1

Production services by Martin Cook Associates, Ltd., New York

Table of Contents

Diseases of Ornamental Marine Fishes *(continued)*

Checklists, Quarantine Procedures, and Calculations of Particular Use in Fish Health Management

Contributors

Index of Scientific Names

Subject Index

Foreword

The successful keeping and reproduction of ornamental fish in a confined environment is the foundation of the tropical, goldfish, and pond fish hobby which is enjoyed by millions of people throughout the world. Information, education, and knowledge for ornamental fish keepers to be successful is an obligation for those companies engaged in providing products for home aquariums and outdoor fish ponds.

Tetra is extremely pleased to have undertaken the educational Aquariology Series of books to enhance successful ornamental fish keeping. *Fish Diseases and Water Chemistry* is an excerpt from the Aquariology Master volume, *The Science of Fish Health Management*. To maintain healthy fish and a proper environment, *Fish Diseases and Water Chemistry* is an important and continual reference.

The Aquariology Series should be the basis for any library of ornamental fish keeping books. Here is a complete listing for your reference:

The Science of Fish Health Management
Item #16855 ISBN # 1-56465-105-3

Fish Breeding and Genetics
Item #16856 ISBN # 1-56465-106-1

Fish Anatomy, Physiology, and Nutrition
Item #16857 ISBN # 1-56465-107-X

Fish Diseases and Water Chemistry
Item #16858 ISBN # 1-56465-108-8

Alan R. Mintz
General Manager
Tetra Sales (U.S.A.)

Getting Started with Aquaria

John B. Gratzek

The simplest definition of an aquarium is a container capable of holding water in which fish and other aquatic organisms can live over a long period of time. Aquariology is the study of keeping fish in aquaria. It explores the reasons for keeping fish and requires a knowledge of the biological characteristics of fish, as well as of such aspects of their husbandry as feeding and nutrition, reproduction, water quality management, sources and control of stress, and disease control.

This book is written with the hope that it will provide both basic knowledge for the beginning aquarist and more specific information for advanced aquarists, producers of ornamental fish, and those wishing to keep fish as laboratory research subjects.

Choosing Appropriate Equipment

Selecting the aquarium: Obvious considerations will determine the size of the aquarium. Available space in a particular room, the size and type of fish you wish to keep, and the cost are factors which will influence your decision. In general, larger aquaria for a given number of fish will result in fewer problems than smaller aquaria with the same amount of fish. Pollutants accumulate more slowly in a larger tank, increasing the interval between required water changes. A

larger aquarium also has the advantage of flexibility—providing space for several species of smaller fish or one or two very large fish. Additionally, a larger aquarium will provide the space for planting an interesting variety of living plants.

For the beginning aquarist, it is recommended that the aquarium be no smaller than 10 gallons (38 liters) and preferably larger. A 30-gallon (114-liter) aquarium would be an ideal size for the novice. If lightly stocked, a tank of this size provides sufficient volume of water to dilute out accumulated fish wastes. At the same time, it affords ample room for fish growth and addition of new residents. For breeding purposes, a larger aquarium will provide space for particularly territorial fish as well as escape room for small fish.

Wholesalers in the pet-fish trade prefer to use aquaria between 25 and 30 gallons (95 to 114 liters) in size. To facilitate netting fish, as well as cleaning, tank height is minimized. Retailers usually employ a series of 10- to 15-gallon (38- to 57-liter) aquaria to display freshwater fish; larger aquaria house saltwater fish and the larger freshwater species.

Aquaria are sold in many shapes, from rectangular to hexagonal or cylindrical. If due attention is paid to water quality, fish will do fine in any of them. Very deep aquaria may be difficult to clean; additionally, plants may not do well in very deep aquaria because of poor light penetration to the aquarium bottom.

A sturdy stand must be selected and carefully balanced to prevent the weight from shifting once the aquarium is filled with water.

It is a good idea to clean a new aquarium to remove fingerprints and to make its glass surfaces as clear as possible before filling it with water. A small amount of dishwashing detergent dissolved in lukewarm water is perfectly acceptable for cleaning aquarium glass, provided that the aquarium is *thoroughly* rinsed with warm water afterward to remove all traces of cleanser. Scale which has collected at the water line of used aquaria can be removed with commercially available preparations designed for the removal of lime deposits. Weak acid solutions such as vinegar may also be used to remove lime deposits. Some soaking time is necessary for removal of scale regardless of what preparation is used. An alternative method is to scrape scale away with a razor blade.

Supporting the aquarium: The stated capacity of an aquarium is somewhat more than the actual volume. For instance, a standard 10-gallon (38-liter) aquarium with inside measurements of 19.25 inches (38.9 centimeters) long, 10 inches (25.4 centimeters) deep, and 11 inches (27.9 centimeters) wide will hold about 9.16 gallons (34.7 liters). Addition of gravel, rocks, or inside filters will further reduce the water volume.

One gallon of water weighs 8.34 pounds; consequently the water in a "10-gallon" aquarium—about 9.16 gallons—would weigh about 76 pounds. (The water in a "38-liter" aquarium would weigh about 35 kilograms.) Gravel adds still more

weight. If a filled aquarium is either moved or placed on a stand which is not level, the resulting twisting stress on the glass is likely to result in breakage and leaks.

Aquarium stands constructed from metal or wood are available in a wide range of styles. Stands which include a cabinet below the aquarium have the advantage of hiding equipment such as air pumps and canister filters, and can be used for storage. For research purposes where many tanks are used, double-tiered racks constructed of 2-by-4-inch lumber (standard construction studs) bolted together can be easily constructed. A rack need not have a complete solid surface to support the aquaria; placing either end of the aquaria on a 2-by-2 or 2-by-4-inch board is adequate. Racks can be built so that the long axes of the aquaria are side by side. This configuration allows an investigator to utilize space more efficiently.

Providing cover and lighting: Most aquaria are manufactured so that various types of covers or hoods fit them snugly. If a cover is not used, evaporation can be a problem. As water evaporates, the concentration of dissolved minerals and organics (uneaten food, plant detritus, fish wastes, etc.) will tend to rise. A cover will keep the air directly over the water closer to the temperature of the water, minimizing heat loss and maximizing the efficiency of the heater. The cover also prevents fish from jumping out of the aquarium, an otherwise very frequent occurrence.

Most aquarium hoods have spaces provided for the installation of artificial lighting. Either ex-

For research purposes, an arrangement such as this one at the University of Georgia's College of Veterinary Medicine works well.

There are many lighting, filtration, and heating systems available on the market. Fluorescent light fixtures are common and varied.

clusively incandescent or fluorescent illumination can be used. In some specially designed units, a combination of both types is provided. Incandescent fixtures are less expensive than fluorescent ones, but incandescent bulbs will use more electricity and will give off more heat than fluorescent bulbs, which burn "cooler" and will not substantially affect the water temperature. Another distinct advantage of fluorescent lights is that they can be purchased in sizes which cover the entire length of the aquarium and consequently provide an even distribution of light for plant growth.

The aquarist has a wide choice of types of fluorescent bulbs which emit various spectra of light waves, some of which will stimulate plant life, including algae. If living plants are not used in the aquarium, bulbs are available which are more suitable for highlighting the coloration of a tank's fish than for stimulating plant growth. Full-spectrum bulbs for plant growth are available under a variety of trade names. The wattage required for optimal plant growth depends on the size of the

aquarium. In general, 1.5 watts per gallon of water is adequate. For example, a 30-gallon (114-liter) aquarium would require a single 40-watt tube or a pair of 20-watt tubes. The performance of fluorescent tubes will degrade over time. Their replacement as often as every six months is recommended by some experts to assure optimal conditions for plant growth.

For research purposes, individual aquarium lighting is not required unless the experimental protocol requires a definite photoperiod. Generally, outside rooms with windows will provide enough natural light to facilitate observing fish. In rooms where natural light is unavailable, establishing a photoperiod of between eight and twelve hours using normal room lighting is advisable.

Buying a heater: A desired water temperature can be easily maintained by using a thermostatically controlled immersible water heater. Without heaters, water temperature will fluctuate with room temperature.

Cold-water fish such as goldfish prosper over a wide temperature range. For example, goldfish will overwinter in iced-over backyard ponds. Most species of tropical freshwater fish as well as marine tropical fish do well at 75 degrees F (24 degrees C), but can tolerate temperatures 10 degrees F (6 degrees C) above or below that optimum at which the metabolic processes of the fish are at maximum efficiency. However, as temperatures drop lower than an acceptable range for a tropical variety, there is a depression of all body functions, including appetite, growth, and the immune system. Temperatures above the optimum range can cause stress by reducing the amount of available oxygen in the water, resulting in increased respiration. Increased respiratory rates can accelerate the development of disease problems relating to poor water quality or to the presence of parasites which affect gills. For special needs, where very cold water is necessary, refrigerated aquaria are available.

The wattage of a heater describes its power—the more wattage, the more heat will be delivered to the tank. Larger aquaria will require heaters of higher wattage, as will aquaria which are situated in cooler areas. As a general rule, use from 3 to 5 watts per gallon of water, depending on the room temperature. For example, if the room temperature is kept 8 to 10 degrees F (4 to 6 degrees C) lower than the desired aquarium temperature, as in a basement area, use a heater delivering at

Proper aeration of aquarium water will ensure the success of plant growth in the "natural aquarium."

least 3 watts per gallon. Buy an accurate thermometer to use when setting the heater's thermostats and for periodic checks of water temperature. Some brands of aquarium heaters have their thermostats set to regulate water at a specified temperature.

Both immersible and fully submersible heaters are available, as are low-wattage heating pads that are placed outside and under the tank being heated.

Buying an air pump: An air pump is a necessity for a modern aquarium and serves many functions. A simple diffuser stone positioned at the bottom of an aquarium serves to circulate water by the upward movement of air bubbles. As bubbles contact the surface of the water, the agitation increases the air–water interface, causing an increase in the rate of diffusion of atmospheric gases into the water and of dissolved carbon dioxide from the water. Air pumps can be used to move water through gravel beds, in conjunction with outside filters, and through cartridges containing water-softening or ammonia-removing resins. The "lifting" of water is accomplished by directing a stream of air bubbles through a tube. The upward buoyancy of the bubbles acts like a piston moving water through a tube. A variety of air pumps is available, and all generate some sound which should be evaluated prior to purchasing the pump.

Filters and filtration materials: All of the many varieties of filters available for use in aquaria can be categorized functionally as mechanical, biological, or chemical. Many combine two or more of these modalities in a single unit.

A mechanical filter functions by trapping suspended particulate matters which could include uneaten food, fish wastes, or any kind of biological or inert particles, in a filter matrix. The size of particle which a mechanical filter will remove and the time required for removal depend on the density of the filter material. Filter media include gravel, floss, foam, or inert particulate materials such as diatomaceous earth. These act as a mechanical barrier to fine suspended particles when adsorbed to a filter screen. Mechanical filters will eventually clog and their media will require cleaning or replacement. The time required for clogging is related to pore size. Filters with a pore size small enough to retain bacteria, for example, if installed in an aquarium without some sort of prefilter, would last a matter of minutes prior to clogging. In aquaria, mechanical filters are expected to remove large particles. Removal of particles as small as the free-swimming stages of most protozoan parasites by filters is possible. However, the pore size of the medium must be small enough to trap the parasites and there must be no possibility for the parasites to bypass the filter as the medium clogs. Some parasites have the ability both to swim and to change shape. This enables them to pass through filter materials, much like a water-filled balloon being forced through a small opening.

Biological filters oxidize fish waste products, primarily by changing ammonia to nitrates. The bacteria involved in this process, collectively known as nitrifiers, are common in nature and

Scanning electron micrographs (3000x) show one of the major effects of conditioning. Unconditioned gravel (top) is barren of life, but after conditioning (bottom), bacteria are visible on the gravel surface.

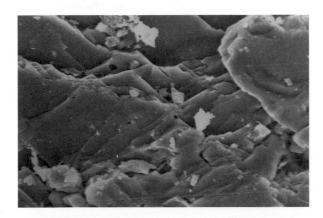

are introduced into the aquarium along with water and fish. They also are called chemo-autotrophic bacteria, because they require ammonia and nitrite ions for their growth. Bacteria of the genus *Nitrosomonas* utilize ammonia excreted by the fish as an energy source and oxidize it to nitrite ion. A second group of bacteria, belonging to the genus *Nitrobacter,* oxidizes nitrites to nitrate ion. These nitrifying bacteria initiate the conversion of nitrogenous wastes to free nitrogen. The second stage of the process, denitrification, is carried out by a different set of bacteria in the absence of oxygen. This makes it impractical to incorporate denitrification into home aquarium filter systems. Nitrifiers gradually colonize the surface of gravel, floss, foam filters, tubing, and any other solid surface, including the inner surface of the aquarium glass. (Note the scanning electron micrographs showing nitrifying bacteria on the surface of aquarium gravel.)

Chemical filtration entails passing aquarium water through some substance capable of changing the chemistry of the water. The type of change produced will depend on the substance included in the filter. Common chemically active filter media include:

1. Activated carbon. The physical structure of activated carbon includes a network of spaces responsible for adsorptive capacity. Activated carbon will adsorb a wide variety of organic substances, including color- and odor-producing substances. It effectively removes from solution dyes and chemicals used for treatment of fish disease problems, as well as dissolved heavy metals such as copper. It will remove neither ammonia nor nitrite ion from solution, nor will it soften water. Its primary use in home aquarium systems is to clarify water. Many manufacturers supply disposable inserts such as floss pads permeated with carbon particles or bags of activated carbon. Periodic replacement is necessary since temperatures required for reactivation of the carbon approach those attained in a blast furnace.

2. Ammonia-adsorbing clays. Also known as zeolites, these clays are sold in the form of chips. They require rinsing under a running tap prior to use in order to avoid clouding the aquarium's water. Many have the capacity to adsorb positively charged cations such as ammonium (NH_4^+) and can be used in filters. Since some zeolitic clays will also remove other types of cations such as calcium or magne-

sium, they also act as water softeners.

3. Ion-exchange resins. In some areas, water is "hard"; that is, it contains extremely high levels of calcium and magnesium ions. Frequently, the pH of such water is relatively high (7.8 to 9.0). Although a surprising number of fish can tolerate high levels of these minerals in water, many species will only breed under softer, more acidic water conditions. Thus many fish culturists prefer to adjust pH downward in their tanks. Doing so is difficult in the presence of calcium carbonates because the latter have a buffering effect. However, synthetic resins can be placed in a filter to soften water.

Resins which exchange sodium ions for calcium and magnesium ions are called cationic exchangers. When water is passed through this type of resin, a water test will indicate that the water has been softened. Many aquarists utilize softened water without problems for the fish. If softened water is used, the addition of a few grams of magnesium salts (Epsom salts) and calcium salts in the form of dolomitic limestone and/or oyster shell may be indicated.

The use of "mixed-bed" resins in a filter will essentially remove both cations (calcium and magnesium) and anions such as sulfates and carbonates. The resulting water is then said to be deionized. Fish cannot tolerate completely deionized water. However, partial deionization may be necessary in lowering pH in some hard-water areas.

4. Oyster shell or coral gravel. These media are usually used in a filter in areas where soft water has a tendency to become acidic abruptly. These materials contribute calcium carbonate to the

A corner filter, which works by the air-lift principle, is appropriate for a small aquarium.

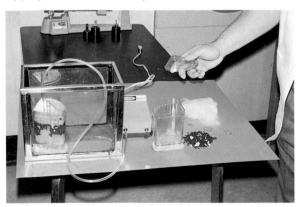

Attached to the side of the aquarium, this outside power filter has disposable inserts to facilitate the periodic cleaning that all such filters require.

water, increasing hardness and buffering capacity. In soft-water areas of the country, water in an unbuffered aquarium may decrease in pH to a point where fish are severely stressed or die.

5. Peat moss. Peat moss has been used in filters to soften water, usually for breeding purposes. It is likely that peat moss releases a hormone-stimulating substance into solution which induces spawning. Use of peat moss in a filter will impart a light brown color to water.

Choosing a filter: There is no good or bad filter. The various types available have distinct applications, depending on a variety of factors, including expense, tank size, number and/or size of fish kept in an aquarium, and whether the aquarium houses saltwater or freshwater fish. Practically every hobbyist, experienced retailer, or authority will have his or her own strong opinions on exactly what is best, but successful filtration always has both a mechanical and biological component. (Chemical filtration is required on a basis of need for special water requirements.)

These processes can be carried out using very simple or very expensive filter units—fish do not know the difference as long as the water quality is good. All filters provide for the movement of water through the filtering material, either by the air-lift principle or by electrically driven pumps. Filters may be located inside or outside of aquaria. All eventually tend to clog, resulting in reduced flow rates and inefficient filtration. All filter media, whether floss, foam pads, activated carbon, gravel, or plastic rings used for mechanical filtration, will eventually be colonized by nitrifying bacteria. The bacteria are firmly attached to the filter materials and are not removed by vigorous rinsing. Naturally, hot water, soaps, and various disinfectants will kill these bacteria and destroy the beneficial effects of biological filtration. All filters require periodic cleaning to remove debris which, although trapped within a filter matrix, is in fact still adding to the organic pollution of the aquarium water.

Since the mechanical and biological functions of filtration materials are so intertwined, it is recommended that when a filter is serviced, at least some of the media contained therein never be discarded. The easiest way to accomplish this is to include gravel, plastic, or ceramic rings in a filter along with disposable filter media such as activated carbon. Since activated carbon loses its filtering capacity after a period of time, placing it in a bag within the filter will simplify changing.

1. Corner filters. Included in many aquarium "beginner kits," an inexpensive corner box filter can be effectively utilized in smaller aquaria. Most corner filters are operated by the air-lift principle. Their filtration capacity is limited. For general filtration purposes, they function best when a small permanent sack of gravel or similar substrate is incorporated along with mechanical and chemical filter material (floss and activated carbon) to ensure that some bacteria-laden "conditioned" material remains after cleaning. Corner filters are frequently used in small aquaria for holding fish during a quarantine period or during a brief treatment period. Many aquarists interested in breeding fish use corner filters in their spawning setups.

2. Outside power filters. Most outside filters are constructed so that they can be easily hung from the rim of an aquarium. Various types of electrically driven filters are available, but most are driven by rotary impeller motors. However, an outside filter is defined only by location, and air-lift driven units are also available.

Outside power filters can be loaded with any type of filter material that meets the aquarist's needs. These generally include floss or foam pads, positioned to keep larger particulate matter from clogging activated carbon or other filter material. If gravel or other materials such as ceramic or plastic rings are included, the filter will in time develop a biological function. The waste-processing capacity of such units will be limited when

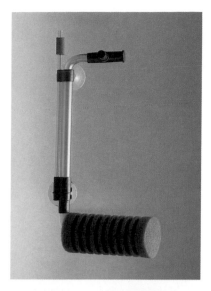

Outside power filters can be set up easily, and trapped debris rinsed periodically, with little disturbance of the enclosed environment. Foam (sponge) filters are also popular in situations where no gravel bed is to be used in the aquarium.

compared to an undergravel filter. However, aquarists wanting to avoid gravel beds for any reason will find such modified outside filters a useful alternative for use in breeding, fry rearing, or quarantine tanks.

All outside filters require periodic cleaning. Obviously, debris trapped in a filter remains in contact with the aquarium water. Depending upon the flow characteristics of the brand of outside filter being used, water may bypass the filter media as the filter clogs. This will result in less efficient filtration with little or no change in flow rate. By comparison, other filter types do not allow bypassing of water, so flow rate slows down as the filter clogs.

Cleaning outside filters is much easier if particulate media such as gravel, ceramic rings, or activated carbon are placed in separate net bags. Floss or foam pads should be cleaned whenever debris buildup is evident. Gravel bags need only

A thriving community of invertebrates will eventually develop within the filter system. This electron micrograph shows rotifers living upon a foam filter (260x).

tanks occasionally require isolation for treatment purposes, for maintaining biological filtration in quarantine tanks, and in tanks used for breeding fish.

Foam filters which have been in use for some time and which have developed a bacterial flora can be used to maintain and "seed" new aquarium systems with nitrifying bacteria. This is a simple way of avoiding the accumulation of ammonia and nitrites in freshly set-up aquaria that characterizes "new-tank syndrome."

Like all filters, foam filters will develop a thriving community of various invertebrates which provide food for fish in the aquarium. Many of these invertebrate forms are rotifers of various types. Rinsing foam filters under a stream of tepid chlorinated water will not kill the bacteria present, but may reduce the population of invertebrates temporarily. However, soaps, disinfectants, or deter-

Undergravel filters, the author's preference, come in many shapes and sizes. The simplest is a small flat plate (top) powered by a single air lift. For a larger aquarium, an undergravel filter with larger lift stacks powered by several air lifts (below) is ideal.

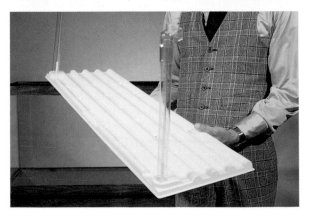

be rinsed under tepid tap water. Activated carbon should be replaced according to the manufacturer's suggestions.

3. Foam filters. Foam pads function very efficiently as mechanical filter media. They can be used in place of floss or floss pads in any type of filter. They eventually will develop a flora of nitrifying bacteria and function well as biological filters. Foam blocks must be rinsed periodically to restore their mechanical function. The most popular types of foam filters are powered by the air-lift principle. Larger units driven by rotary-impeller power heads are also available. Foam filters certainly are less efficient than outside power filters in their mechanical action, but will ultimately develop a good biological function as well. They are useful in systems where gravel is not required or desired as a biological filter bed. They also can be used either as a tank's sole filter or as a supplement to other kinds of filters. Single pads are suitable for smaller aquaria; multiple filters can be used in larger systems. Such filters are employed with considerable success for research aquaria at the University of Georgia for a variety of experimental uses. They are especially useful as adjunct filters in recirculating systems where

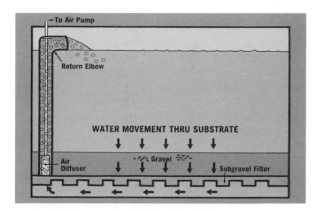

As water moves through the gravel into the undergravel filter plate, it carries oxygen to the nitrifying bacteria in the gravel. These bacteria process the fish wastes, converting ammonia to nitrites and eventually to nitrates. In this system, the entire gravel bed essentially acts as a biological filter.

gents may kill or inactivate all of the bacterial and invertebrate populations. Similarly, drying foam filters will inactivate bacteria and invertebrates. However, filters can be stored wet for several days without appreciably reducing their biological effectiveness.

4. Undergravel filters. Undergravel filters consist of a plastic plate equipped with one or more air lifts. At least 3 inches (7.6 centimeters) of washed gravel should be put over the plate. The air flow displaces water through the lift stacks, circulating water through the gravel bed. This brings both oxygen and organic wastes into contact with bacteria attached to the gravel. As long as this flow is maintained, the entire gravel bed of such a filter is biologically active. In a gravel-bottomed aquarium without water circulation, only the top centimeter or two is biologically active. Undergravel filter plates are sold in sizes adequate for the largest aquaria or for goldfish bowls. The flat plate types appear to be adequate for smaller aquaria. However, for larger aquaria, models with corrugated bottoms and larger-diameter lift stacks are likely to produce better water circulation. Undergravel units are widely employed in marine aquaria, where dolomitic limestone or coral gravel is used as the filter bed. As ammonia or nitrite poisoning is of special concern in marine tanks, the rapidity with which an undergravel filter removes these toxic substances makes it a natural choice for the marine tank.

At this writing, it appears that more and more aquarists are utilizing undergravel filtration for freshwater aquaria. Because undergravel filters act as both mechanical and biological filters, they need not be supplemented with other types of filters if (and this is an important "if"!) debris is periodically removed from the filter bed and water is changed regularly. The gravel bed is easily cleaned when water is changed by using a distended siphon tube to remove debris deep in the gravel bed. If water is changed on a regular basis, water can be kept clear without the use of activated carbon.

Of course, additional filters of any type can also be used with an undergravel filtration system. For example, an external power filter loaded with a filtering substance such as activated carbon, peat, or ammonia-adsorbing clays could be used to effect some desired change in water chemistry. Although undergravel filters are usually powered by air displacement, an alternate method is to place rotary impeller–driven units known as power heads on top of the lift stack. Placing a siphon tube from an outside power unit in a lift stack is a good way to operate an undergravel filter in conjunction with an outside power filter.

One disadvantage of undergravel filters is that some fish burrow into gravel or else actively move gravel about the bottom. This exposes the filter plate, creating breaks in the gravel which lead to a reduced water flow through the bed. This can be avoided by placing a plastic screen 3 to 4 centimeters (about 1.5 inches) below the surface of the gravel. Perhaps the chief disadvantage of undergravel filters is their immobility. There is no way to remove an undergravel filter from a tank that is being treated with therapeutic agents toxic to nitrifying bacteria, such as methylene blue, formaldehyde, or many antibiotics. Another frequently cited disadvantage is that rock formations reduce the effective surface available for water flow. From experience, I do not feel that rock formations cause sufficient blockage of the filtration surface to be of any consequence.

There is some controversy regarding the suitability of an undergravel filter for plant growth. It has been suggested that root movement which may be associated with the use of undergravel filters inhibits plant growth. However, experts in the field of hydroponics are able to grow a wide variety of plants without any root substrate and suggest that the aeration and micronutrients supplied to roots by an undergravel filter would bene-

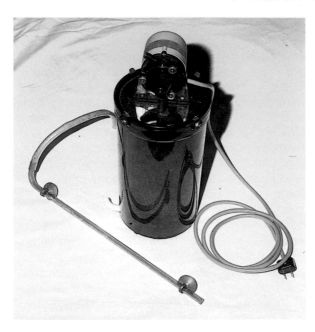

Canister filters are suitable for larger aquaria and can be loaded with a variety of filtering materials such as ceramic rings, ammonia absorbers, floss, and activated carbon.

fit the plants. Some recommend that when plants are to be used with an undergravel filter, the gravel layer should be increased to approximately 5 inches (13 centimeters). An alternative is to purchase plants which have been propagated in plant plugs containing fertilizers in a root-support growth medium. Plants can also be placed in small pots with good potting soil. It is important to place a layer of aquarium gravel over the soil in pots to stabilize it under water.

5. Canister filters. Canister filters take their name from their general shape. Their powerful motors pull water through a sealed container filled with various filter media. These filters are particularly useful in large or heavily stocked aquaria, which require a greater filtration capacity. Canister filters can be purchased in a variety of sizes. These units have two distinct advantages over other kinds of filters: they have enough volume to accommodate a series of filter substrates stacked in series, which greatly enhances their effectiveness, and they can be placed in a location remote from the aquarium. This latter feature is useful in display aquaria, for filters can be located in an adjacent work area.

Newer designs of canister filters are available in which the impeller is located at the bottom of the canister. This feature makes it very easy to prime the units and ensures that the impeller assembly never runs dry. Because of the increased size of the motor when compared to that of outside filters, some canister filters can be used in conjunction with inserts which will support a film of diatomaceous earth. These units can be used for water "polishing."

The disadvantage to canister filters is their higher cost in comparison to other types of filters. Another is that since outside canisters require tubing running to and from the aquarium, connectors must be carefully tightened and rechecked periodically lest leaks develop.

Buying gravel and ornaments: The aquaria in homes or for display purposes require a gravel base which, from an aesthetic viewpoint, mimics the bottom of a pond and provides a good base for rooting plants. For most freshwater aquaria, it is important to use quartzite or granite gravel, which will not contribute carbonate ions to water. There are advantages to using calcareous substrata in tanks housing fish that prefer hard alkaline water, such as African Rift Lake cichlids or most live-bearers.

The size range of the gravel particles should be approximately 4 to 6 millimeters (3/16th of an inch plus or minus 1/16th). The particle size is important for several reasons. If an undergravel filter plate is to be used, the spaces between gravel particles will allow free water flow and ample aeration for bacteria which will eventually colonize the surface of the gravel particles. The depth of the gravel bed will depend on whether or not an undergravel filter is used and whether live plants are desired.

Sand is not recommended as an aquarium substratum. The extremely small particle size results in packing and reduces water flow. Waste that breaks down in the resulting anaerobic conditions will generate hydrogen sulfide and other highly toxic substances. Aquatic plants also require a bed which will allow diffusion of nutrients to roots.

Marine aquaria usually are equipped with undergravel filters. Calcareous gravels, which contain carbonates, are recommended for such tanks. These include dolomitic limestone, crushed oyster shell, and coral gravel, materials containing high levels of carbonates. The slow release of carbonates in marine aquaria tends to

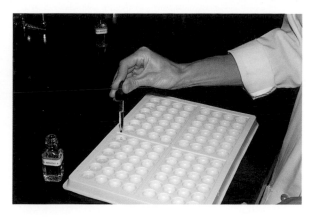

A multi-well tray allows many water samples to be tested at once.

buffer water towards the desired high (7.8 to 8.3) pH range.

Regardless of type, gravel intended for aquarium use requires removal of pulverized particles which can cloud tank water. Gravel should be rinsed under a tap while being stirred briskly, until the water runs clear.

Colored aquarium gravel is available. Although selection of color is largely a matter of human taste, white gravel reflects more light and may stress those species of fish which prefer dark areas in an aquarium.

Decorating an aquarium provides benefits both for the aquarist and for the fish. Many fish are territorial, and rock formations, plants, and a variety of other decorations will provide needed territorial landmarks and boundaries. Also, smaller fish may need to escape from larger species by taking refuge in small nooks provided by rock formations. A decorated tank also provides shade for those fish which prefer darker areas.

Not all objects are equally suitable for aquarium decoration. Coral, seashells, limestone, and marble will dissolve in fresh water and may increase the pH to an unacceptable level. Copper objects, galvanized metals, or steel can cause heavy metal poisoning, especially in areas where the water is soft and the pH is on the acid side of neutral. Rocks, driftwood, or gravel taken from streams or ponds should be soaked in a disinfectant such as chlorine bleach, then rinsed well, to avoid the introduction of snails and other unwanted invertebrates such as planarians and free-living nematodes.

The use of a background behind the aquarium serves to beautify the tank as well as to create the darker area preferred by certain shy species of fish. A variety of selections is available for outside use, including paints, paper with fresh- or saltwater motifs, and plastic materials constructed to create a three-dimensional illusion. Inside backgrounds constructed of a variety of waterproof inert materials are also available.

Buying water test kits: The serious aquarist should invest in test kits which will enable him or her to measure pH, hardness, ammonia, and nitrite levels. For saltwater aquaria, a hydrometer and copper test kit are also recommended. Most test kits sold for application in aquaculture are easy to use. They are based on color changes in the sample being tested, which is then compared to a color standard. Some kits are supplied with liquid reagents which over time may deteriorate. Others provide powdered reagents, which may be more stable over time. If it is necessary to test many aquaria, these kits can be used in conjunction with a tray containing many wells, each containing a water sample from a tank to be tested. This method provides a quick overview of water conditions in many aquaria.

Setting Up the Aquarium

Choosing a location: We will assume that you have purchased or built a stand which will support the weight of the fully set-up aquarium. If the tank is not level or appears to be unstable, it may be a good idea to shim the stand, or, alternatively, to fasten it to a wall to avoid accidental tipping. This can be done using an L-shaped piece of metal. The aquarium should be placed in an area where it is likely to be viewed, but not in an area where accessibility is limited. Regular maintenance will be much easier if it is possible to have working room above and behind the aquarium. Do not place the tank in direct sunlight. Otherwise, algae will rapidly accumulate and the aquarium may overheat. However, indirect light or even a short period of direct light in addition to the use of overhead lighting can be useful in stimulating plant growth. Placing aquaria close to air conditioning vents or over heat vents can complicate the task of regulating water temperature.

Equipping the interior: Once the aquarium is in the desired position, install the undergravel filter plate if this type of filter is going to be used.

Be careful not to displace gravel substrate while filling the tank with water. Rocks and plants can be more easily placed in tanks filled one-third to one-half capacity with water.

Then add washed gravel to a depth of 2 to 3 inches (about 5 to 8 centimeters) if an undergravel filter will not be used, to a depth of 3 inches (7.6 centimeters) if an undergravel filter will be used without live plants, and to a depth of 5 inches (12.7 centimeters) if such a unit will be used with

plants. For better plant growth, mix a soil additive or a proprietary slow-release fertilizer with the gravel. These products are available at pet-supply outlets.

After the washed gravel is added, fill the aquarium with water to about one-third of capacity; rock formations and plants are easier to set in place if some water is present. If an undergravel filter is being used, direct water over a shallow pan to avoid displacing gravel under it. Some aquarists prefer to slope the gravel slightly toward the front of the aquarium, which they claim facilitates removing debris from the aquarium.

Construction of caves and recesses makes for more interesting viewing while providing more timid fish with shelter. Do not use any type of rock which has the potential for releasing minerals, such as limestone, marble, or clays. Rocks collected from streams can be used. However, they should be thoroughly cleaned by brushing with water, rinsed, and dried prior to placement in the aquarium.

Plants, be they living or plastic, should be positioned with the taller-growing varieties toward the back of the aquarium and in a position to hide lift stacks, siphon tubes, or heaters which you will be adding. Because living plants require a favorable water quality in addition to plant nutrients and good lighting, some experts suggest waiting to add plants until after the aquarium has been established for a period of time. Presumably, in an established aquarium, nitrification would be in place and nitrates would be available for plant nutrients.

Although fish in ponds can tolerate water temperature fluctuations, in an aquarium there is no advantage to allowing such fluctuations, which can easily be avoided by installation of a heater. Heater placement will depend on the type purchased. Totally immersible types can be positioned horizontally at the level of the gravel, a location which may enhance plant growth. Models which are not totally immersible are usually clipped to the aquarium side; they require that the aquarium water level be kept at or above the level of the thermostat to avoid overheating of the water. With either type, promoting water circulation by positioning airstones at gravel level or using power filters for circulation will help ensure uniformity of water temperature throughout the aquarium.

Water temperature should be set prior to addi-

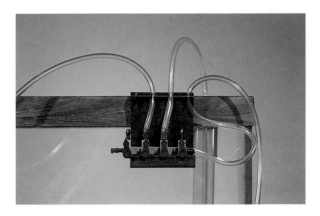

Loop the air line through notches in a tubing manifold to avoid the possibility of back-siphoning.

tion of fish to avoid any possible stress in the fish from drastic accidental changes in temperature. A good temperature for a wide variety of freshwater fish as well as plants is 75 degrees F (24 degrees C). Let the heater acclimate to the water for an hour prior to connecting the electricity. Then adjust it slowly in order to avoid possible overheating. A light will indicate whether the heating unit is on. For the first twenty-four hours, frequently check the temperature and adjust the thermostat as required to obtain the desired water temperature.

A few safety precautions should always be followed around tanks where a heater is in use. Never connect the heater unless the tube housing the heating element is immersed in water. Always disconnect the heater when changing water or lowering the tank's water level for any reason. Adjust the thermostat only when you have time to check the temperature of the water continually.

Providing aeration for the aquarium is the next matter of concern. Aquarium water is aerated by agitation of its surface by the outflow of power filters, a stream of bubbles produced by an airstone or by a stream of water splashed from the lift stacks of an undergravel filter. Gas exchange occurs at the surface of the water. Placement of an airstone toward the bottom of an aquarium will both circulate and aerate the water. Aeration of aquarium water provides oxygen required by fish, plants, and nitrifying bacteria. Aeration can always be increased by directing water flow from power filter outlets over the surface of the aquarium water. Undergravel filters have the built-in

advantage of "pulling" oxygenated water through the gravel bed.

When lines to airstones or lift stacks are attached to pumps located below the aquarium, there is a possibility of back-siphoning if the pump is accidentally disconnected or if there is a power outage. This can be avoided by positioning the air pump higher than the aquarium. If this is not possible, make sure that the air tubing to each outlet has a loop sufficiently high to avoid a siphon effect. Loops can be made by using the notches in a tubing manifold or by using plastic inserts in air tubing which prevent abrupt bending and the formation of anti-siphon loops. Check valves are also available, which can be placed in air lines to prevent back-siphoning problems.

A minimal agitation of the water surface from any type of aeration will generally result in oxygen levels of between 6 and 7 parts per million (ppm). Excessive agitation may disturb some more timid species such as discus fish. However, moderate circulation of water is tolerated by most fish and promotes plant growth.

At this point the aquarium should have gravel in place and be equipped with a filter, heater, and perhaps airstones. Fill the aquarium to the top with tap water. The air pump can be turned on immediately, but wait for a thirty- to sixty-minute period for the thermostat to adjust to ambient water temperature prior to plugging in the heater. The next step is to assure water quality that will support fish.

Dechlorinating the water: In many municipal water supplies, chlorine is added at the pumping plant to destroy bacteria pathogenic to humans. In tap water, dissolved chlorine concentrations usually measure between 0.2 ppm and 0.7 ppm, depending on the time of the year. Water for aquarium use must be chlorine-free, since even 0.2 ppm will kill fish by destroying gill tissues. Chlorine can be removed from tap water in three ways:

1. Aeration of water, resulting in diffusion of chlorine into the air. The use of a faucet-end aerator commonly found in households will aerate water and remove chlorine. Simply pouring water from one pail to another three or four times will also drive chlorine from solution. Letting tap water stand in pails for a few days also allows chlorine to dissipate gradually. This process can be speeded up by aerating the water with an air diffuser.

2. Passing water through activated carbon. Many of the faucet-end water purifiers sold to improve the taste of water are charged with activated carbon. Larger canisters available from water conditioning companies are also available for large-use situations such as would arise in a pet store.

3. Adding sodium thiosulfate to tap water immediately inactivates chlorine. Sodium thiosulfate is sold under a variety of trade names. One molecule of sodium thiosulfate will remove four molecules of chlorine. Based on this, 0.50 milliliters (10 drops) of a 1 percent solution of sodium thiosulfate would remove 0.5 ppm of chlorine from 10 gallons (38 liters) of city water. One drop per gallon of a 1 percent solution of sodium thiosulfate would provide a sufficient safety factor to avoid the consequences of fluctuations in chlorine levels.

Removing chloramines: In some municipal water plants, ammonia is added to react with chlorine to form chloramines, which then act as the disinfecting agent. The addition of sodium thiosulfate will neutralize both chlorine and chloramines. However, ammonia is released after the sodium thiosulfate combines with the chloramines, and this could be a problem to fish under conditions where there is little or no biological filtration.

In most home aquaria where biological filtration has been established, the routine use of sodium thiosulfate rids the water of chlorine; the remaining ammonia is quickly oxidized to harmless nitrates by the resident nitrifying bacteria. This assumes a very efficient biological filter and a relatively modest water change of no more than 25 percent of the tank volume at a time.

In newly established aquaria, or when most of the water has been changed at one time, sufficient nitrifying bacteria may not be present to oxidize ammonia. In these cases, sodium thiosulfate can be used in conjunction with ammonia-adsorbing media. The most readily available of these are certain clays (zeolites) sold under a variety of brand names. The ammonia-adsorbing chips should be placed in an outside or canister filter before making a water change to ensure that the ammonia released following dechloramination is quickly removed from the aquarium. An alternative method of neutralizing ammonia without using zeolites is simply to lower the pH of the water, if the tank's residents can tolerate it. At lower pH levels (6 to 7), the majority of total ammonia will be present as the nontoxic ionized form: ammonium (NH_4^+). In many areas of the country, pH can be lowered by adding buffers which are available in aquarium supply stores or by adding monobasic sodium phosphate, NaH_2PO_4.

Chloramines can also be removed from fresh water by the use of a high grade of unused activated carbon. Activated carbon which has been used may remove colors and odors, but will not remove chloramines.

In marine aquaria where pH levels are kept between 7.8 and 8.3, chloramine treatment with sodium thiosulfate would result in the generation of free ammonia. Zeolites are ineffective in removing ammonia from salt water, and lowering the pH in marine aquaria is not recommended. Before adding salt mix to tap water to make synthetic seawater, pretreat the requisite volume of tap water with sodium thiosulfate, then filter it through zeolite held in a household colander; alternatively, pass the tap water through virgin activated carbon prior to mixing it with salt.

If chloramines are present in locations where tap water is hard, with a high (7.8 to 9.0) pH, the ammonia resulting from treatment with sodium thiosulfate could injure fish if biological filtration has not been established. In such areas, pH may be difficult to adjust downward and water may have to be pretreated with sodium thiosulfate, then slowly poured through a pail containing zeolite chips before being used in the aquarium. (Holes in the bottom of the pail will facilitate this operation.) In any case, where chloramine removal is deemed necessary, treated water should be tested for total combined chlorine levels and ammonia to make sure that the treatment chosen was effective. Commercial products are also available that bind the ammonia produced by dechloramination into an organic complex that is harmless to fish. The complex is then metabolized by the biological filter.

Controlling pH: Water in various parts of the country may have different pH values, and in some cases the water may require some adjusting prior to addition of fish. Generally, fish can tolerate quite a wide pH range without problems. A pH of 6.5 to 7.8 for freshwater species is an acceptable range for maintenance of optimal health.

Purchasing and Adding Fish

Choice of fish: It has been customary to start new or unconditioned aquaria with hardy fish, supposedly more tolerant of ammonia and nitrites. There is no question that some varieties are less susceptible to nitrite intoxication than others. Our experience suggests that various species of tetras, such as the serpae tetra (*Hyphessobrycon callistus*), are less susceptible to nitrites than live-bearing fish such as swordtails, guppies, and platys. Common goldfish, zebra danios, and many barbs are also relatively hardy fish. If some form of conditioned filter—such as gravel from a conditioned aquarium or a conditioned foam filter—is added to a new aquarium, there will be less reason to fear the ammonia-nitrite problem.

A decision on what type of fish to eventually put into your aquarium is purely a matter of preference. However, you should be aware that some fish are incompatible with each other or with living plants. Different fishes also thrive in different water conditions. Some fish species may prefer brackish water. Others may do well in hard water with elevated pH, while still others may flourish in soft water with a lower pH.

A "community" tank exists when several species of fish are maintained together in an aquarium. In many cases, a few goldfish are included with species of live-bearing fish such as guppies or egg-laying species originating in South America. Such mixtures provide interesting visual variety but do not remotely reflect natural fish populations. If you are interested in goldfish, consider having an aquarium with nothing but goldfish. Alternatively, many aquarists like to create an aquarium with a few species of fish native to a particular part of the world. In many cases the schooling behavior of fish is not seen unless several fish of the same species are kept together.

How many fish in an aquarium?: In any new aquarium without an efficient biological filter system, just a few fish should be added initially. This introduction should be followed with regular water changes on a weekly basis for at least a month. As nitrifying bacteria develop in the filter material, more fish can be added.

The number of fish which an aquarium will support depends on several factors. A common rule which has been used by aquarists is that for every gallon (3.8 liters) of water, one may add 1 inch (2.5 centimeters) of length of freshwater fish or 0.5 inches (1.25 centimeters) of saltwater fish. Other aquarists suggest that the total inches or centimeters of fish which can be added should equal the number of inches or centimeters, respectively, which the aquarium measures along its long axis. A standard 10-gallon (38-liter) aquarium, for example, measures about 19 inches (48 centimeters) and thus could support nineteen 1-inch fish or twenty-four 2-centimeter fish.

It should be noted that some aquarists disregard all formulas and crowd their aquaria with fish. Their success is based on a good filtering system, a program of regular water changes, aeration, and due attention to nutrition and disease control. Nonetheless, it is generally better to have fewer fish in an aquarium to avoid deterioration of water quality and to minimize the risk of disease, which is enhanced by crowding.

Selecting healthy fish: Reputable retailers are not interested in selling an obviously sick fish, but often it is very difficult to detect fish which are carriers of a parasite and which with time will develop signs of disease. It is always prudent to select fish from aquaria where no disease has been evident over a period of time. Fish should be active, with a full underbelly. Signs of disease include clamped fins, lack of color, skin blemishes, white spots, excessive body slime, failure to eat, and inactivity. Some hobbyists will not purchase a fish (especially an expensive one) until they have observed it over a period of time in a retail shop. Particularly when evaluating marine fish, it is a good idea to ask a retailer if the animals in question have been routinely treated for parasites.

Quarantine: Quarantine refers to the isolation and observation of fish prior to introducing them into an aquarium. The objective of quarantine is to determine whether the specimen has a disease which could be transmitted to other fish. The assumption is that a serious disease is likely to develop during the isolation period. A quarantine period can vary in length, but fourteen days is common. In fish health management involving food fish, public aquaria, or fish used for research, fish may be routinely treated during the quarantine period. In cases where many fish are involved, a few fish may be killed and examined for parasites or chronic disease conditions. If disease is present, the fish are treated with a specific medication during the quarantine period. If a disease is detected which is either difficult or impossible to treat, a decision is made regarding the eventual use or disposition of the animals.

Quarantine of fish prior to their introduction into the home display aquarium is a rare, but nevertheless a recommended, practice. It is particularly advisable when adding new fish of questionable disease status to an established aquarium housing valued fish.

Adding fish to the aquarium: Although fish can live over a considerable range of water temperatures, sudden temperature changes can stress fish. It is a good practice to minimize stress by making sure that the temperature difference between the fish's transport container, usually a plastic bag, and the home aquarium is minimal (ideally less than 3 degrees F or 1.6 degrees C). In most situations, this can be done by floating the plastic transport bag in the aquarium water for ten to fifteen minutes. Keep the bag inflated during this period, since draping an uninflated bag over the side of an aquar-

Using a transport bag can allow you to introduce fish to the tank, while minimizing the shift in pH and temperature.

ium will minimize diffusion of oxygen by reducing water–air surface area.

Adding fish to the aquarium can be done in different ways, depending on the concentration of ammonia in the water of the transport container. Timely transport of a few fish in a plastic bag from a retail outlet to a home aquarium typically results in very low ammonia levels. However, on a commercial scale where hundreds of fish are transported, the ammonia levels in the transport water may be very high. Since the pH of the water in heavily packed bags is usually 6.5 to 6.8, the ammonia is in the nontoxic form. However, addition of fresh chlorinated water with a high pH (7.8 to 9.0) will serve to convert nontoxic ammonium to toxic ammonia, resulting in gill damage. This problem is particularly serious when marine fish are shipped considerable distances.

In most instances involving home aquaria, the practice of mixing aquarium water with the contents of the transport container, then adding the mixture to the aquarium, is unlikely to hurt the fish. Simply adjusting the pH of the aquarium water to approximately 6.8 to 7.0 will ensure that the ammonia levels remain low.

For wholesalers, retailers, and others who handle substantial numbers of fish crowded in bags, it is best to transfer the fish from the transport bag to the aquarium by the careful use of a net. The objective is to keep any polluted transport water and any associated disease organisms from entering the aquarium. Netted fish can be injured by contact and friction, especially if many fish are netted together. Netting injuries can be avoided by positioning a net just at the surface of a shallow container or pail filled with temperature- and pH-adjusted aquarium water. Fish in the transport bag are then "poured" into water but still contained by a net. A rapid transfer of fish into an aquarium can be effected with minimal contact of fish with the net.

Some wholesalers and brokers (trans-shippers) prefer to acclimatize fish by the slow addition of fresh water to the transport bag or to a container to which both fish and transport water have been transferred. In a matter of a few minutes, a total water change has been made and the fish can be transferred to aquaria without netting. This is an acceptable method provided that: (1) the pH of the incoming water does not differ from that of the transport water by more than 0.5 pH units in either direction and is not alkaline, (2) there is no great difference in water temperature, and (3) the water is dechlorinated.

It is always a good idea to determine the pH of the transport water, which generally will be between 6.5 and 6.8. Adjustment of aquarium water pH to between 6.8 and 7.0 prior to addition of freshwater fish is a sound and safe practice whenever the pH of the aquarium water is either much higher or much lower than the latter values.

Contrary to a widely held belief, most fish can tolerate rapid pH changes between the extremes of pH 6 and pH 9 if ammonia and other pollutants are not present. Fish in nature are often exposed to these variations without harm. Moreover, the author has experimentally shifted fish from pH 6 to pH 9 water without affecting their health. Nonetheless, overall it pays to err on the side of caution when contemplating pH changes in established aquaria. Both the direction and magnitude of pH changes must be evaluated, and this is a very complex subject. In addition, certain fish such as the neon tetra are quite intolerant of radical changes in water conditions. Thus, it is considered prudent not to alter pH by more than 0.5 units in a given twenty-four-hour period in a tank containing fish.

In the acclimation of marine fish, transport water should not be added to the aquarium, for the high pH of marine aquaria will ensure that toxic ammonia is present. After temperature equilibration, fish should be transferred to aquaria by careful netting or other appropriate methods, such as utilizing plastic containers with holes punched in the bottom as sieves. Fish can be caught easily, water allowed to drain, and the fish can be transferred quickly into the aquarium. As a rule, you can also avoid problems by refraining from adding transport water to aquaria.

Selected References

Baensch, H. 1983. *Marine Aquarists' Manual.* Tetra Press.

Hunnam, P.; Milne, A.; and Stebbing, P. 1982. *The Living Aquarium.* New York: Crescent Books.

Ladiges, W. 1983. *Coldwater Fish in the Home & Garden.* Tetra Press.

Randolph, E. 1990. *The Basic Book of Fish Keeping.* New York: Fawcett Crest.

Spotte, S. 1979. *Seawater Aquariums: The Captive Environment.* New York: Wiley-Interscience.

Vevers, G. (translator). 1973. *Dr. Sterba's Aquarium Handbook.* London: Pet Library, Ltd.

Maintaining Aquaria

John B. Gratzek

Once an aquarium has been established, successfully maintaining it becomes the aquarist's next job. This task will be simplified if one understands some important concepts about water, the "conditioning" period, and ways to circumvent or cure certain common problems in an established tank.

Understanding Water

A chemically pure molecule of water consists of two hydrogen atoms combined with one atom of oxygen with the common formula, H_2O. Such chemically pure water is found only after treatments such as distillation, reverse osmosis, or ion-exchange processing.

In its natural state, water quality varies considerably from location to location, depending upon which physical, chemical, and biological processes are predominant at a given spot. The composition of surface water from various geographical areas will vary with the acidity of rainwater. Once precipitation contacts ground, its chemical character will change depending on the composition and solubility of local geological formations and on the duration of contact. For instance, water flowing through a highly vegetated area such as a swamp would be expected to contain various organic components. As rainwater flows over soils and rocks, on the other hand, it becomes mineralized.

Groundwater from wells in a particular area may differ considerably in composition from surface water. Because of the demand for oxygen by decomposition processes, water will lose oxygen and gain carbon dioxide as it passes through surface layers of soil. Once it reaches the water table, minerals characteristic of the area will be added. For example, well water from a limestone area will be high in such dissolved solids as calcium and magnesium salts. Well water usually has low oxygen levels and frequently has a high iron content. The simple expedient of aerating well water prior to adding it to an aquarium will oxygenate it and convert the soluble ferrous form of iron to the insoluble ferric form. Consequently, iron will settle out as a rusty orange precipitate, and iron-free water will result.

Most aquarists utilize tap water for raising and propagating fish. Because regional and/or local health departments are responsible for the safety of water for human consumption, tap water routinely is treated with chlorine or chloramine to kill pathogenic microorganisms. Sodium fluoride is often added to prevent caries in humans. Alum is added occasionally to clarify water. In some municipal water plants, ammonia is added to react with chlorine to form chloramines, which then act as the disinfecting agent. This is done to prevent the direct combination of chlorine with naturally occurring organic compounds to form carcinogenic compounds.

The measurement of substances dissolved in water is usually expressed as parts per million and abbreviated as ppm. One ppm is equal to one milligram of dissolved material per liter of water (approximately 1.3 ounces in 10,000 gallons of water) and is abbreviated to mg/l. These terms are interchangeable. Some substances are best measured as parts per billion, abbreviated as ppb. One ppb is equal to one microgram per liter, abbreviated to μg/l.

Water Terminology

Many terms are used to describe the properties of water. While some of these terms are more appropriate to the description of pond, lake, or stream water, all are useful in describing changes which develop in an aquarium.

Biochemical oxygen demand: This is a measure of the amount of oxygen consumed by the biological process of respiration in a container of water at a specific temperature (20 degrees C or 68 degrees F) in the dark for a five-day period. By inference, the more oxygen used, the more organic materials (bacteria, algae, diatoms, organics) were present in the original water sample. The name of the test is often abbreviated to BOD. The BOD of fresh water is low; the BOD of water in an aquarium where the water has not been changed is high.

Chemical oxygen demand: The chemical oxygen demand (COD) is a measure of organic matter in water and provides a good estimate of the BOD. To measure COD, dichromate is added to a container of water. Results are expressed as the oxygen equivalent of the dichromate consumed during the oxidation process.

Both BOD and COD tests are used to monitor water pollution. Pollution by biological or organic substances such as the waste products of fish occurs because the decomposition of organic materials in a closed aquatic system utilizes oxygen. The end result of this waste processing by bacteria will be a decrease in pH of the water. In practical terms, a good aquarist will prevent the accumulation of organics by not overstocking aquaria, not overfeeding, and paying strict attention to proper tank cleaning procedures.

Total dissolved solids: This term describes the concentration of all dissolved mineral substances in water, such as carbonates, bicarbonates, chlorides, phosphates, and sulfates. Other elements in lesser concentrations could include nitrates, iron, copper, magnesium, and manganese. The biological significance of total dissolved solids is that fish cannot regulate their salt-to-water balance (osmoregulate) if the concentration of dissolved minerals is too high. Experience suggests that freshwater fish do well in waters which contain 400 ppm or less of total dissolved solids. However, in the case of such physiologically plastic species as desert pupfish, the upper limits for survivability may be as high as 5,000 ppm. Of practical importance to the aquarist is the possibility of osmotic shock when sensitive fish are moved abruptly from water with high dissolved solids to water with low dissolved solids.

Water hardness: The degree of water hardness is directly proportional to the concentrations of mineral ions in the water. Although other mineral ions such as iron, zinc, boron, copper, lead, and silicon may be present in trace amounts, calcium and magnesium are the dominant chemical species found in solution. Thus hardness is usually expressed in terms of the amount of calcium carbonate ($CaCO_3$) present in solution. Water hardness can be expressed as parts per million or by using one of several arbitrary scales of measurement. On the German scale, which is widely used by aquarists, the term "DH" refers to degrees hardness. One DH is equivalent to 17 ppm. A useful classification of "soft" versus "hard" water is given in the following table:

water quality	ppm
Soft:	0 to 75 ppm
Moderately hard:	75 to 150 ppm
Hard:	150 to 300 ppm
Very hard:	300+ ppm

From the aquarist's perspective, the most immediate practical aspect of water hardness is that softer water has less buffering capacity. This means that pH can drop abruptly in an aquarium filled with soft water, whereas pH tends to be stabilized in aquaria with hard water. Extremely soft water can pose other management problems for aquarists. It is erroneously believed by many hobbyists that distilled water or water passed through a reverse-osmosis filter is "pure" and therefore good for fish. This is not the case. Fish lose minerals (electrolytes) through urine and gills; minerals must be replaced for optimal health. Blood electrolyte balance is maintained by minerals in the diet and by adsorption of dissolved minerals through the gills. High mortalities associated with larval freshwater fish kept in very soft water can easily be attributed to mineral and electrolyte imbalances. As a group, fish can tolerate a wide range of water hardness levels, although each species has a preferred range of dissolved mineral concentrations. Levels of 50 ppm $CaCO_3$ sustain most freshwater fish without problems. A hardness level of 100 ppm is desirable for most Central American fishes, among them many popular live-bearers, and fish from Africa's Rift Lakes will live and prosper in water classified as very hard.

pH: In water, electrons often move from one atom to another to form charged entities called ions. The pH of water is a measure of the relative amounts of hydrogen ions (H^+) and hydroxyl ions (OH^-) present in solution. At a pH of 7.0, a solution is called neutral since there are an equal number of hydrogen and hydroxyl ions present. Various substances in the water can tip the balance between these ions. A pH value less than 7.0 signifies acidic conditions, in which hydrogen ions are more abundant than hydroxyl ions, while values greater than 7.0 signify alkaline conditions, in which hydroxyl ions predominate. Freshwater fish can live in extremes of pH from 3.8 to 9.0. However, in freshwater systems an optimum pH for the vast majority of species would be close to neutrality. In practice, pH values in closed freshwater systems should be kept between 6.8 and 7.8. Marine aquaria should be maintained between 7.8 and 8.3. While higher pH levels (7.8 to 8.5) are not intrinsically harmful to fish, such pH values will contribute to the toxicity of any ammonia present in the system.

Low pH values can develop in an aquarium through addition of acidic tap water, mistakes in adjusting pH with mineral acids, and biological degradation through bacterial respiration—especially when water is poorly buffered. Low pH values in freshwater aquaria can affect both the fish and the bacterial oxidizing system. At pH values below 5.5, the rate of oxidation of ammonia by bacteria (*Nitrosomonas*) is reduced, resulting in increased ammonium levels. pH values between 4.0 and 5.0 will in themselves have deleterious effects on the great majority of freshwater

and all marine fish. Histological studies of fish kept in low-pH water indicate that the gill epithelium is damaged, a situation which could result in reduced respiratory function and death from anoxia, and/or in dangerous blood chemistry changes.

Alkalinity and buffering capacity: Alkalinity of water refers to the concentration of basic substances such as bicarbonate (HCO_3^-), carbonate (CO_3^{-2}), and hydroxide ion (OH^-) present in solution. The amount of these bases present, as determined by titration, is referred to as total alkalinity and is expressed as ppm equivalents of carbonate. In general, total hardness measurements will be very close to measurements of total alkalinity, because calcium and magnesium generally are associated with the carbonate minerals which are the principal sources of alkalinity in water.

A buffer is a combination of an acid or base with a salt which, when in solution, tends to stabilize the pH of the solution. Water with high alkalinity is naturally more strongly buffered than water with low alkalinity. In nature and in aquaria where water is poorly buffered due to a low alkalinity, pH levels tend to decrease over time. This downward shift results from the gradual release of carbon dioxide from respiratory processes of aquatic animals, plants, and bacteria. As carbon dioxide is added to water, it reacts, forming carbonic acid (H_2CO_3). The pH drops because the carbonic acid is a source of hydrogen ions, which react with carbonate or bicarbonate. (An increase in hydrogen ions results in lower pH.) On the other hand, removal of carbon dioxide, as for instance by plants during photosynthesis, causes the pH to climb.

In practical fish-keeping terms, water becomes acidified in a closed aquatic system because respiratory processes increase hydrogen ion concentration. A pH "crash," where levels may fall as low as pH 3.8, can develop in soft waters when all the buffering capacity (bicarbonates plus carbonates) is utilized. Two simple expedients for replenishing the alkalinity (buffering capacity) of the water are to: (1) change a portion of the water and (2) add commercially available buffers. Bicarbonate buffers water against sudden changes in pH by combining with hydrogen ions to form carbon dioxide and water. (Refer to the section on buffers further on in this chapter for additional information on their use in aquaria.)

Chlorine: To destroy pathogenic microorganisms, urban water supplies are chlorinated by the addition of molecular chlorine (Cl_2) or calcium hypochlorite, $Ca(OCl)_2$. In water, dissolved (free) chlorine reacts to form hypochlorous and hydrochloric acids:

$$Cl_2 + H_2O \rightarrow HOCl + H^+ + Cl^-$$

In water with a high pH, the hypochlorous acid (HOCl) will dissociate into hydrogen and hypochlorite ions; with decreasing pH, the ions will shift back to hypochlorous acid. The hypochlorite ion is of particular importance because it in turn dissociates into a chlorine ion and atomic oxygen, which is a strong oxidizing agent and causes extensive gill damage to fish.

When molecular chlorine and hypochlorite ions react with water, they result in different proportions of chlorine, hypochlorous acid, and hypochlorite ion, depending on the pH of the water. These three chlorine-containing species are called the free chlorine residual, and all have disinfectant properties. However, all are toxic to fish. Chlorine and hypochlorite also react with nitrogenous organic compounds, including ammonia, to form chloramines, which are also toxic to fish. The term "combined chlorine residual" refers to chloramines. The term "total chlorine" is the sum of free chlorine plus chloramines. Residual chlorine levels should be 0.003 ppm or less to avoid damage to fish. Removal of chlorine compounds is discussed in the previous chapter.

Chloramines : Some city water supplies have high levels of organic compounds. These can interact with chlorine to form trihalomethanes, which have a cancer-producing potential. The solution to this problem has been to add ammonia and chlorine at the water plant to form chloramines, which have the ability to disinfect water but will not react with organic substances to form the carcinogenic trihalomethanes. While the production of chloramines is acceptable from a public health aspect, fish producers, hobbyists, and retailers in some cities where chloramines are produced have noted fish mortalities. Methods of chloramine removal are discussed in the previous chapter.

Dissolved oxygen: The amount of oxygen in water is affected by many variables. For example, warmer water will increase the metabolic rate of the fish and hence their demand for oxygen, but warm water will dissolve less oxygen than colder water. The solubility of oxygen (as well as other gases) also decreases with increasing salinity levels. The amount of surface area also affects oxygen exchange between air and water; creation of surface turbulence by aerators or by the outflow of water pumps will maximize this. In fish-production ponds, oxygen levels can fluctuate widely because of temperature variations, demand for oxygen by decomposition processes, and surface turbulence. In closed systems such as aquaria which have adequate aeration and water circulation, low oxygen levels are rare.

Oxygen levels are reported as parts per million. A dissolved oxygen level of 5 ppm would be adequate for tropical fish. Dissolved oxygen levels in a sampling of pet shops in the Athens, Georgia area ranged from 5 ppm to 8 ppm.

Elements associated with fish excretion and nitrification: While ammonia, nitrites, and nitrates are not normally associated with fresh water supplies, both are commonly found in aquaria for a finite period of time soon after the aquarium is set up. This period of high ammonia and nitrites, previously discussed, is referred to as the conditioning period or the run-in period. The basis of

Impurities in an aquarium lead to fish stress and disease. Understanding the nitrogen cycle and testing the water regularly for nitrites are important. Bi-weekly water changes by "hydro-cleaning" dirt and debris from the gravel allows nitrifying bacteria to cultivate; foam filters also are excellent for the cultivation of aerobic bacteria.

NITROGEN CYCLE

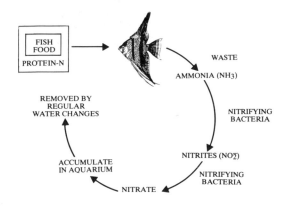

the problem is that when the aquarium is initially set up, there are insufficient numbers of ammonia- and nitrite-oxidizing bacteria (nitrifying bacteria) to utilize these nitrogenous products. Both ammonia and nitrites are toxic for fish; methods to avoid these problems are covered under a later section. When chloramines present in tap water are passed through activated carbon canisters, ammonia results from the dissociation of chloramines. If the carbon canister is not changed regularly, *Nitrosomonas* bacteria can colonize in the carbon canister, resulting in nitrite production. This problem would only occur in areas where chloramines are present in water and an activated carbon filter is used to remove chlorine. Regular testing for nitrites and/or frequent changing of the activated carbon would prevent this problem from developing.

Other elements in water: Copper in water can kill fish, but most cases of copper toxicity are the result of man-made problems rather than natural copper levels in water, which are rarely over 0.05 ppm. New copper pipes, especially in soft-water areas, could leach out enough copper ions to reach toxic levels for some species. Older copper pipes which have been subjected to oxidation present no problem. Addition of copper to control algae in ponds or for the control of certain diseases can lead to fish mortalities if dosage is not regulated.

In city water supplies, other heavy metals such as zinc or lead should not cause problems; however, zinc toxicities have occurred from placing fish in galvanized vats. Iron in water is not a problem to most aquarists, since it is only toxic in the ferrous (soluble) form which occurs when water is very low in oxygen and high in carbon dioxide—conditions which are not found in well-aerated aquaria. Aeration quickly oxidizes iron to insoluble forms (rust) which are not toxic.

Chemicals used for control of diseases of plants or animals are usually toxic to fish if present in high enough concentrations. Their levels in municipal water supplies are too low to cause public health problems or problems for the aquarist. Water from contaminated wells or rivers could contain a variety of toxins. Many state public health laboratories conduct testing of water for known contaminants. However, water taken from rivers in which various industrial chemicals have been spilled may result in prob-

lems for the aquarist—especially if sensitive fish are being raised or bred.

Using Water Additives and Conditioners

Many preparations sold under a variety of trade names may be useful to the aquarist interested in varying water conditions to meet specific needs. Some of these include:

Dechlorinating solutions: Most dechlorinating solutions sold contain sodium thiosulfate. A suitable solution consists of a 1 percent solution of sodium thiosulfate in water. At this concentration, 0.5 millimeters (10 drops) of the solution per 10 gallons (38 liters) of water will remove chlorine in most city water supplies with an ample safety factor. This reaction is almost instantaneous. In practice, dechlorination can be done as fresh water is added to the aquarium or even several minutes afterwards, since at tap-water levels the harmful effects of chlorine are not immediate.

Buffers: These are useful in areas with relatively low alkalinity or natural buffering capacity. Such waters are easily adjusted to any desirable pH. In waters with high alkalinity levels (highly buffered), pH adjustment is difficult. To lower pH, the water may have to be partially softened prior to adding a buffer. Since buffers are designed to keep the pH at a desired level, the amount of buffer added to water will not significantly change the pH but will only serve to keep the pH stable for a longer period of time or until the next water change.

pH adjusters: These consist of chemicals or solutions of chemicals which, when added to water, will either raise or lower the pH. There is some danger of lowering or elevating pH to dangerous extremes. pH adjusters may not hold pH levels as long as buffers will and may have to be added more frequently to maintain a desired pH level. Baking soda (sodium bicarbonate, $NaHCO_3$) will elevate pH. Normally, a solution is made and small amounts are added to the aquarium, with frequent pH testing to avoid excessively high pH levels.

Dilute solutions of phosphoric acid or hydrochloric acid have been used to reduce pH. In many areas of the country, the addition of monobasic sodium phosphate (NaH_2PO_4) to water will decrease pH. As opposed to acids, monobasic sodium phosphate is not dangerous to handle and can be purchased in aquarium retail outlets or chemical supply companies. In some areas of

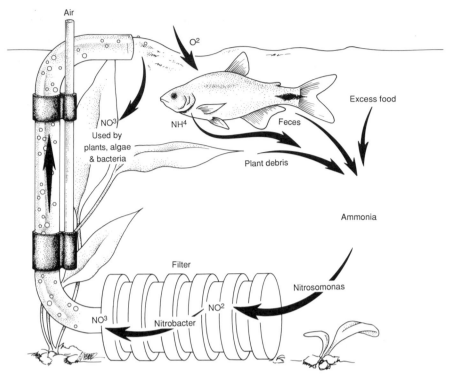

The nitrogen cycle in a freshwater aquarium. Ammonia from fish waste and from bacterial decomposition of protein-containing foods is converted to nitrites by *Nitrosomonas* bacteria. These nitrites are then converted to nitrates by other bacteria (*Nitrobacter*). Living organisms, including algae and a variety of bacteria, utilize nitrates as nutrients. Plants, in turn, provide oxygen to the environment and a supply of food to plant-eating fish. The conversion of ammonia to nitrites and then to nitrates is called nitrification.

the country, it may form a precipitate (which will result in cloudy water); this is harmless to fish and will settle out within a few days.

Water softeners: As mentioned earlier, the difference between hard and soft water lies in the amount of calcium and magnesium salts. Harder water almost always has higher alkalinity (a higher pH), more carbonates, bicarbonates, and hydroxides, and a good buffering capacity. Since this type of water is naturally buffered at a higher pH, lowering the pH will be difficult unless the water is softened using ion-exchange resins. Ion-exchange resins are available which will remove calcium and magnesium ions as well as carbonates.

The placement of peat in a filter also will soften water, as well as reduce pH levels, presumably by the release of humic acids. Ammonia adsorbers which have ion-exchange capabilities will not only adsorb ammonia but will soften water and stabilize pH at approximately 7.5.

The aquarist is always advised to measure hardness levels carefully and to monitor pH levels when using softeners, buffers, or pH adjusters. Overuse of softeners could deplete essential minerals required by the fish and could cause radical lowering of pH by reducing alkalinity.

Ammonia removers: Ammonia adsorbers sold in aquarium supply stores are naturally occurring clays (zeolites) which have ion-exchange properties. They are efficient in reducing ammonia during the run-in period, but nitrite production is not significantly reduced. Zeolites incorporated into a filtering system will tend to stabilize pH and soften water. They can be easily regenerated by immersion in a 1 percent salt solution. Liquid ammonia removers are also commercially available.

Nitrification starters: A variety of products are sold to reduce the elevations of ammonia and nitrites during the initial conditioning period of a new aquarium system. Some of these products consist of freeze-dried bacteria—presumably species of *Nitrosomonas* and *Nitrobacter,* which oxidize ammonia to nitrite and nitrites to nitrates, respectively. Laboratory tests using a wide variety of such products

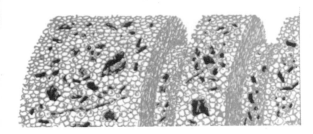

Filtration based on a continuous nitrogen cycle is referred to as biological filtration. Waste products are broken down biologically into a relatively harmless substance, nitrate. Mechanical filtration is based on the removal of impurities from the water through filters (above). Proper filters, containing activated carbon or charcoal, allow an equal flow of oxygen through the filter cartridge (below); this ensures colonization of nitrifying bacteria and a continually functioning cycle.
Source: Tetra Archives.

have failed to demonstrate that they significantly lessen the conditioning period.

Problems During the First Weeks After Setup

Understanding nitrification: After fish are added to a new aquarium, the water chemistry of the aquarium gradually changes as a result of the excretion of fish wastes and the presence of uneaten food scraps. Unless initially seeded with a source of nitrifying bacteria, any new closed aquatic system will pass through a period characterized by elevated levels of ammonia and nitrites. This run-in or conditioning period ends when nitrites disappear from the aquarium. This period is variable and can only be determined by periodic water testing.

At different times during the conditioning period, water testing for ammonia, nitrites, and nitrates will give varying results. A test done a few days after the fish are introduced into the aquarium may result in a positive ammonia test only. After a few more days, a test of the water may be positive for both ammonia and nitrites. Toward the end of the conditioning period, nitrites will gradually disappear. Subsequent testing will reveal the presence of nitrates only, which signals the completion of the conditioning period, and additional fish may be introduced. The entire conditioning period may last from four to twelve weeks.

How to minimize the run-in or conditioning period: Although some run-in period is inevitable, whether this initial period of elevated ammonia and nitrates is seriously stressful or relatively mild depends upon the aquarist's actions.

Prior to the addition of fish, condition the aquarium by seeding it with bacteria and a suitable nutrient for the bacteria. Salts of ammonia can be used, as can urea (10 ppm). This system can be accelerated by seeding the tank with some gravel from a conditioned tank, or if such is not available, adding a cup of organic soil (such as from a compost pile) to provide nitrifying bacteria. If organic soil is used, it is a good idea to mix the soil with a quart (about 1 liter) of water, shake briskly for a minute or two, and then filter the mixture through a few layers of cheesecloth prior to adding it to the aquarium.

With any of these methods, water should be checked for ammonia and nitrites periodically. In the event that water test kits are not available, frequent (twice a week) water changes of 50 percent or more will solve many problems. Massive daily water changes for five or six days may be needed to keep nitrite levels below a toxic level.

For immediate conditioning, add 20 percent of used or biologically active gravel from a conditioned aquarium, or place a conditioned foam filter in the new aquarium. In some cases, addition of conditioned gravel or foam filters may greatly reduce the levels of ammonia and nitrites as well as shorten the conditioning period. Failure to eliminate the conditioning period completely most likely results from not adding enough gravel or gravel with active bacteria.

Start by adding a very few hardy fish for the first month or two. Then add additional fish over time until the capacity of the aquarium is reached.

Toxicities associated with the conditioning period: Ammonia can be present in two forms, as ammonia (NH_3) which is toxic to fish and as an

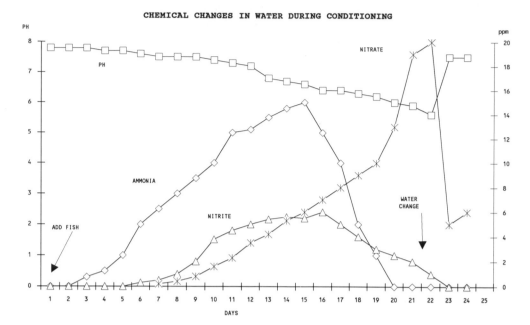

CHEMICAL CHANGES IN WATER DURING CONDITIONING

Ammonia, nitrate, and nitrite levels during conditioning when the water is not given the recommended changes. Conditioning ends when nitrites and ammonia are absent. This requires variable lengths of time. In the example shown above, it occurred after about twenty-three days. In an established conditioned aquarium, ammonia and nitrites ordinarily should be undetectable. Nitrates, on the other hand, are normal and indicate that the biological filtration system is operating properly. When water was finally changed, nitrate levels were reduced and pH was readjusted.

ammonium ion (NH_4^+) which is nontoxic. The percentage of these forms depends on the pH. The higher the pH, the more ammonia will be present. For this reason, the pH values of freshwater aquaria are best kept close to neutral (pH 7).

Ammonia toxicity is more of a problem with saltwater fish than with freshwater fish for two reasons. One is that saltwater aquaria are kept at a pH between 7.8 and 8.3, so any ammonia present has a higher proportion in the toxic form. The other is that saltwater fish swallow water continuously, a behavior which results in the absorption of more ammonia than freshwater fish, which do not drink. Consequently, a positive ammonia test is more serious in saltwater aquaria than in freshwater aquaria.

Ammonia can result from lack of biological filtration, which may occur during the conditioning period, from overloading the capacity of the biological filter by the addition of too many fish, or from overfeeding, which overwhelms the capacity of the filter to oxidize the excess ammonia resulting from degradation of protein.

The toxic effects of ammonia can be acute or chronic. Very high levels of ammonia may kill fish in a short period of time by decreasing the oxygen-carrying capacity of blood and interfering with neural function and with osmoregulation.

The chronic effects of ammonia poisoning are related to hyperplasia and hypertrophy, or thickening, of gill epithelium. These result in decreased gas exchange and decreased excretion of ammonia, which in turn lead to increases in blood pH and osmoregulation problems, including the inhibition of the transport of monovalent cations. The toxicity of ammonia is intensified with increasing temperature and low oxygen levels.

How to solve ammonia problems: When ammonia appears in the conditioning period, it may be present alone or in combination with nitrite. If the ammonia accumulation is not accompanied by nitrite elevations, the problem can be approached in one of three ways.

1. Water changes are the best way to immediately solve ammonia problems. Water changes, along with the introduction of a conditioned foam filter or conditioned gravel, are a good idea if the aquarium has not passed through the condition-

ing period. The more conditioned gravel added, the faster the response will be.

2. If the pH of the water is in the 7.5 to 8.4 range, decreasing the pH to neutrality will decrease the toxicity by converting ammonia to nontoxic ammonium.

3. Ammonia adsorbers (zeolites) can be used to remove ammonia. However, if they are used during the conditioning period, the development of nitrites will not be inhibited and may still cause problems.

4. Zeolites will not absorb ammonia from salt water. Ammonia problems in saltwater aquaria must be solved by increasing biofiltration, avoiding overstocking and overfeeding, and instituting a program of water changes.

After taking remedial action by any of the above methods, ammonia levels should be monitored frequently to determine whether the problem has been solved. Additionally, fish should be observed closely. They should eat better and be more active in response to correction of ammonia problems.

How to solve nitrite problems: Nitrite is generally toxic in both freshwater and marine aquaria. When nitrites are absorbed by fish, nitrite ions combine with hemoglobin to form methemoglobin, which cannot transport oxygen, resulting in oxygen deprivation and death of the fish. Nitrite toxicity is diagnosed by positive nitrite tests of water and by detection of brown blood on postmortem examination of fish.

Nitrites are usually present during the run-in period or whenever the biological activity of the filter is destroyed. However, some freshwater and saltwater fish are resistant to the effects of nitrites, probably because these fish do not adsorb nitrites or because they have the ability to metabolize or excrete nitrites quickly. For example, channel catfish are very susceptible to nitrites and will concentrate nitrite ions far beyond those levels found in water. Goldfish are much less susceptible to nitrite toxicity than are channel catfish, and various species of tetras appear to be completely resistant. Consequently, in a mixed community tank during the conditioning period, some species will die while others will survive the effects of nitrites.

Nitrite problems can be solved in a number of ways.

1. The quickest way to rid an aquarium of nitrites is to change the water. In a home aquarium or even a large central system, nitrites will accumulate during the conditioning period until *Nitrobacter* bacteria have proliferated sufficiently on filter materials to a point where nitrites are cleared. Water may have to be changed daily for four to seven days before the nitrite levels drop to safe (0.1 ppm) levels. Massive amounts of water need to be changed to dilute nitrites to safe levels. In some cases the gravel also may have to be flushed to remove nitrite ions from it.

2. Moving fish to a "hospital" or holding aquarium will stop the adsorption of nitrites immediately. Fish can be returned to the main aquarium after water tests are negative for nitrites. Water quality in the hospital aquarium need not be a problem, since the fish should stay in it no longer than four to seven days. The hospital aquarium can be as simple as a large plastic pail. Water quality can be maintained by water changes, but aeration and mechanical filtration are required. A small corner-box filter is suitable for such uses, especially if loaded with ammonia adsorbers.

3. If you had added gravel or a foam filter from a conditioned aquarium when the new aquarium was initially set up, it would have either eliminated ammonia and nitrite problems or greatly reduced the length of the run-in period and the amounts of offending toxins produced therein. When a nitrite problem is encountered after the aquarium is established, the addition of a small amount of conditioned gravel will not reduce nitrite levels as appreciably or quickly as a conditioned foam filter will. There is more water movement through the sponge, which has more surface area with nitrifying bacteria.

Various products are available which claim either to shorten or to eliminate the conditioning period. Some of the products are advertised as containing nitrifying bacteria. However, in the face of a nitrite problem, the addition of a relatively few active bacteria would not appreciably reduce nitrite levels quickly enough to avoid severe stress or death of fish.

4. Raising the concentration of table salt (NaCl) in aquarium water to 100 ppm will prevent the uptake of nitrites by some fish. Approximately 38 grams (1.16 ounces), or about 7 teaspoonsful, of salt added to 10 gallons (38 liters) of water will attain this level. Many characins and cyprinids, as well as some types of ornamental catfish (*Corydoras* species), will not tolerate such salt concentrations, however.

5. Methylene blue has been used to treat methemoglobinemia in humans and domestic animals. However, its addition to aquarium water containing nitrites does not effect a cure, probably because it is not readily absorbed by fish. Furthermore, methylene blue has been shown to kill nitrifying bacteria in aquaria. Its use is not indicated to treat nitrite toxicities in the aquarium.

The Established Aquarium

When an aquarium has an efficient nitrification system, regular water changes with simultaneous cleaning of the gravel should keep water conditions optimal. A conditioned aquarium will have no detectable levels of ammonia or nitrites, and will have a pH between approximately 6.5 and 7.8 if freshwater or 7.6 to 8.4 if saltwater.

If water changes are not done on a regular basis, a conditioned aquarium may undergo chemical changes as a direct result of the process of nitrification and accumulation of waste products, collectively referred to as dissolved organics.

Trouble-Shooting Problems

In aquaria where water is low in alkalinity and unbuffered, hydrogen ions accumulate and pH drops. Severe drops, usually to pH lower than 5.5,

An example of typical chemical changes in an unbuffered established aquarium in which water is low in alkalinity. Nitrification and accumulation of waste organics can cause a sudden severe acidity, called a pH crash.

THE ESTABLISHED AQUARIUM

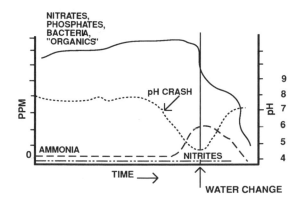

can lead to an inhibition of nitrification and the accumulation of ammonia related to the inhibition of *Nitrosomonas*. The accompanying figures illustrate changes in an established aquarium which has gone through such a pH crash.

Ammonia/ammonium problems: Ammonia levels should remain undetectable in an established aquarium unless the system is overloaded with fish, or decomposing excess food results in ammonia levels which surpass the capacity of the biological filtration system. A positive ammonia test after overfeeding is common. The ammonia spikes from one overfeeding incident will disappear within twenty-four hours. A dead fish will also add to the ammonia load in the aquarium. Occasionally, a cadaver will remain hidden by plants and go unremoved, leading to such a problem.

Transitory pulses of ammonia can also result from the use of medications such as antibiotics and some parasiticides. Removal of the medicant by a water change will usually restore nitrification and eliminate ammonia. Note also that the presence of some medications, such as formaldehyde, in the water will give a false test for ammonia.

Nitrite problems: In an established aquarium, nitrites should be undetectable. While ammonia levels may increase due to pH drops, nitrites usually are not observed. Nitrites can appear after adding some medications to an aquarium, but as in the case of ammonia, nitrite levels will drop after the bacteria-inhibiting medication is removed by a water change. Some parasiticides such as methylene blue have been shown to destroy nitrifying bacteria, resulting in nitrite elevations.

pH problems: Fluctuations of pH in an aquarium will depend on several factors, including the amount of fish, level of organics, nitrification, and the buffering capacity (alkalinity) of the water.

The relative acidity or alkalinity of water is measured by pH. During the process of nitrification, hydrogen ions are given off by the oxidation of ammonia to nitrites by *Nitrosomonas*. The greater the amount of biological activity (nitrification), the more hydrogen ions are released. Organic materials in the aquarium also release hydrogen ions as they are decomposed by nitrification. Overstocking and overfeeding of fish thus can lead to pH problems, especially if the water is soft and poorly buffered. Finally, the natural alkalinity of the water (i.e., the levels of carbonates, bicarbonates, and hydroxides) determines the extent to which the water is buffered against pH drops. In some areas of the country where alkalinity levels in the water are very low, the pH of an aquarium must be watched carefully and buffers may need to be added.

Correcting low pH: The following methods may be used to correct low pH.

1. A water change will replenish the natural buffers in the water supply, but if these are low, pH may revert to low levels within a matter of days.

2. If low pH is a recurring problem, the water can be buffered using commercially available buffers preset to various pH values, usually between pH 6.5 and 7.5. If such buffers are used, they must be used in sufficient amounts to hold the pH at the desired level until the next water change. The amount of buffer to add can be determined by trial and error. Adding more buffer does not significantly change the pH, but only extends the time that the pH of the water will be held at the desired level. Generally, in soft-water areas where acid rain is a problem, buffers should be added with every water change.

3. Dolomitic limestone, coral gravel, or oyster shell can be incorporated into an outside filter or an inside corner filter. Ammonia adsorbers also buffer freshwater aquaria to approximately pH 7.5. The amount to use must be established by trial and error. For each 10 gallons (38 liters) of water, 100 grams (about 3 ounces) of any of the above substrates should be adequate for pH adjustment. With time, the natural carbonates elaborated from these natural elements will become exhausted, and fresh materials may be required. Another disadvantage is that dolomitic limestone may result in a pH which is too high, unlike commercially available buffers which are set to adjust the pH to a specific level.

4. Sodium bicarbonate is a pH adjuster rather than a buffer. If added in excess to an aquarium, the pH can be elevated to unacceptably high levels. A 10 percent solution of baking soda can be safely used to raise the pH of an aquarium. Gradually add small amounts, with frequent testing of the pH. Unless extreme care is taken during this process, the pH can quickly jump to very high levels. Also, since sodium bicarbonate by itself is not a buffer, the desired pH may not hold for very long.

Correcting high pH: High-pH water is usually hard, high in alkalinity, and well buffered. Consequently, lowering the pH of this water often requires removing some of the natural hardness and alkalinity. Mixing softened with unsoftened water may result in water with a desirable pH. Determining the proper proportions must be done by trial and error.

1. By softening the water with a mixed resin (anionic and cationic exchanger), the natural buffering capacity of the water will be reduced and the pH in the aquarium will most likely be lowered. One may use softeners sold for residential use, large canisters, or small units sold exclusively for aquarium use. All contain ion-exchange resins. Distilled water (or water treated by reverse-osmosis processes which remove all minerals) can be used if some unsoftened water is added to the softened water. Consider 4 parts of reverse-osmosis water to 1 part of tap water; some experimentation with proportions may be required. Commercial water softeners remove calcium and magnesium ions by an exchange process with sodium ions.

In addition to commercially available ion-exchange resins, water can be softened by ammonia-adsorbing clays which are in fact natural ion exchangers. The softening ability of ammonia adsorbers can be renewed by soaking the chips in a strong salt solution (3 percent salt) for a few hours.

2. Monobasic sodium phosphate (NaH_2PO_4) may be added slowly, with frequent pH testing. In very hard water, a precipitate may develop, causing cloudy water. This causes no harm to the fish and will settle out in time.

3. Dilute solutions of acids such as phosphoric or hydrochloric acids have been used to reduce pH. In addition to the obvious dangers of handling strong acids, acids are adjusters and unless added slowly with frequent monitoring, they could cause pH levels to drop below optimal levels. Frequently, such acids are used to adjust pH in commercial establishments with central filtration systems.

4. Commercially available buffers are highly effective in soft-water areas, but are not effective for decreasing pH in very hard water. However, after the water is softened, buffers can be added to adjust pH.

5. Placement of some types of peat moss in the filter will soften water and lower pH, but water will take on a brown color from the tannins present. This is not harmful to fish and can be removed by filtering water through activated carbon.

A distended-end siphon tube allows easy removal of accumulated wastes from the aquarium's gravel bed.

Nitrate problems: Nitrates are the end product of nitrification and are essentially nontoxic for freshwater fish. In the aquarium, the appearance of nitrates suggests that the biological filtration system is operating. Generally, nitrates will increase in an aquarium, but levels will be reduced by the plants, including algae, and by certain nitrate-utilizing bacteria such as *Pseudomonas* and *Aeromonas,* which may be pathogenic for fish.

Plants should not be introduced into an aquarium until the conditioning period is complete and nitrates are present. Normally, regular water changes will keep nitrate levels between 5 and 25 ppm, depending on the frequency of change.

Phosphates, which also stimulate plant and algal growth, also increase in an aquarium over time. Under normal aquarium conditions, where

Water plants don't always receive the attention they deserve. Regular water changes, fertilizer, elimination of old or brown leaves, and proper illumination help maintain a healthy aquarium as seen at right. *Source:* Tetra Archives.

water is partially replaced every two to three weeks, phosphorous compounds pose no problem to the health of fish. Some city water supplies may have high concentrations of phosphates.

Organics: The term "organics" covers a wide variety of substances and can include products from any living creature within an aquarium system. In addition to the obvious fish and plants, aquarium water contains a variety of bacteria and organic molecules resulting from the metaboic processes of plants, fish, bacteria, and all of the phytoplanktonic and zooplanktonic forms found in an aquarium.

Pheromones may accumulate in aquaria and act as growth inhibitors or even inhibitors of the immune system of fish. Despite a paucity of knowledge in this area, such putative inhibitors are removed by regular water changes and, possibly, through the regular use of activated carbon in the filter system.

Maintaining a Healthy Aquarium

Avoiding problems is always preferable to solving them. Simple preventative measures will increase your chances of maintaining a trouble-free aquarium.

The importance of water changes: Fresh water

dilutes accumulated waste products, including ammonia, nitrites, and nitrates; corrects pH problems; and reduces the numbers of pathogenic bacteria and parasites which may be present during a disease.

The amount of water to change should be proportional to the number, size, and type of fish in the aquarium. As a rule of thumb, many aquarists change 20 to 30 percent of the water every seven to fourteen days. In special cases where an aquarium may be overloaded with fish, changes of up to 80 to 90 percent may be required. In such cases, it is important to avoid sudden temperature and pH shifts.

Planted aquaria require some periodic water changes, but because of the plants' ability to use nitrates, excessive water changes may reduce the vitality of the plants. On the other hand, some plants do not prosper under autotrophic water conditions and actually relish the reduction of nitrates that follows partial water changes. In the author's experience, changes of 10 to 20 percent of the water every two weeks did not alter the vitality of plant life.

Water changes should be done so that accumulated wastes are removed from the gravel bed by use of a distended-end siphon tube. Gravel should be cleaned with every water change. By inserting the end of the siphon tube deep into the gravel, detritus is removed which otherwise would clog the gravel bed, depriving nitrifying bacteria of oxygen and ammonia and/or nitrites. Such clogged areas would develop into anaerobic pockets where nitrates and sulfates could convert to nitrites and hydrogen sulfide, both of which are toxic to fish. The cleaning of gravel in this manner will not dislodge nitrifying bacteria from the surface of the gravel particles.

The benefit of plants in the aquarium: Plants in the aquarium provide cover, hiding places, territorial limits, and protection for very young fish. More important, plants utilize nitrates and phosphates, and consequently assist in maintaining water quality in the aquarium. Planted aquaria have been referred to as "natural" or "balanced" aquaria. Strictly speaking, a balanced aquarium is one in which the production of fish wastes is utilized completely by plants. Plants provide oxygen for the fish while consuming carbon dioxide, nitrates, and phosphates.

Keeping fish healthy: For a healthy, thriving aquarium, remember these points.

1. Initially add only a few fish to avoid rapid buildup of ammonia and nitrites. Only add additional fish after thirty to forty-five days, when a good biological system has been established.
2. During the initial conditioning period, test the water every day for ammonia, nitrites, and pH. If ammonia and/or nitrites are present, make a water change.
3. For tropical fish, maintain the water at a temperature no lower than 70 degrees F (21 degrees C) and preferably at 75 degrees F (24 degrees C). Goldfish and other cold-water fish tolerate lower temperatures.
4. Feed fish a high-quality food in amounts which they will consume in three to five minutes. Although most aquarists feed their fish once or twice a day, several feedings of smaller amounts of food are desirable if time permits. Avoid overfeeding, for this can lead to water-quality problems. Remove excess uneaten food in case of accidental overfeeding.
5. Periodically change the water and clean the gravel. A distended-end siphon tube will remove fine silt from the gravel without removing gravel. The amount of water to change depends on the number of fish. Many aquarists change 20 to 30 percent of the water every seven to fourteen days.
6. Quarantine new fish prior to adding them to your aquarium.
7. At the first sign of a problem, check water for pH, ammonia, and nitrites.

Selected References

Baensch, U., and Baensch, H. A. 1975. *Beginners Aquarium Digest.* Tetra Press.

Moe, M. A., Jr. 1982. *The Marine Aquarium Handbook: Beginner to Breeder.* Marathon, Fla.: Norns Publ. Co.

Hawkins, A. D., ed. 1981. *Aquarium Systems.* New York: Academic Press.

Spotte, S. 1979. *Fish and Invertebrate Culture: Water Management in Closed Systems.* 2nd ed. New York: Wiley-Interscience.

———. 1979. *Seawater Aquariums: The Captive Environment.* New York: Wiley-Interscience.

Ward, B. 1985. *The Aquarium Fish Survival Manual.* New York: Barrons.

Physiological Mechanisms of Fish Disease

Richard E. Wolke

Pathological physiology appears a contradiction in terms—the abnormal normal. However, it is a well-recognized field of study in which the scientist seeks to understand the development and mechanisms of disease processes. It concerns itself with upsets in the dynamic biophysical and biochemical pathways which are necessary for life rather than with the static gross and histopathological findings reported in all autopsy protocols. For this reason, pathophysiology allows one to explain and to understand why an animal dies. It is the kind of information needed to bridge the gap between a prosecutor's report, which might read "chronic hepatitis" or "granulomatous hepatitis," and an appreciation of what killed the animal. This knowledge, coupled with clinical diagnostic skills and the principles of treatment, can help a breeder or culturist to prevent further losses and to recognize signs of illness should they arise again.

That is not to say that the term "chronic hepatitis" is without information. Rather, these terms presuppose that the reader has a pathophysiological knowledge of the liver and knows what will go awry under these circumstances and how this might be incompatible with life. To have such an understanding, one must know the functions of the major organs and how disease may alter those functions. In addition, one should be aware that some groups of animals have different organs than other groups of animals and that these organs may solve the same problem in a different fashion. Fish are such a group.

Fish are basically the same physiologically as higher vertebrates, but there are some surprising differences. For instance, fish are cold-blooded (poikilothermic), that is, they reflect the temperature of their environment. Most possess an air bladder for buoyancy and gills for respiration. They lack bone marrow and parathyroid glands. They possess baroceptors such as the lateral line and they have a corpuscle of Stannius, which functions in calcium metabolism. These kinds of differences cause the pathophysiology of fish to be unique and require its understanding to explain how piscine diseases result in death.

In order to determine the cause of death, the pathologist conducts a postmortem examination. This examination observes and records deviations from the normal using both the unaided eye and the microscope. The morphological deviations are referred to as lesions.

Lesions occur before death, and may reflect degeneration or cell death (necrosis), inflammation, healing, increases in cell number (hyperplasia) and increases in cell size (hypertrophy).

New growth (neoplasia), that is outside the body's regulatory controls (autonomous) is part of the cancer complex. All of these lesions occur in fish, and in this respect, fish differ little from homeothermic (warm-blooded) vertebrates. All of these changes are morphological, are seen as static, and represent an instant in time. Their development, however, reflects changes at the molecular level brought about and often maintained by disease-causing agents. Disease is an ongoing process, which, if allowed to continue unabated, results first in cell injury at the biochemical level, then loss of function which may progress from the cell to the organ and then to the organism, and finally, cell death. Cell death and advanced degeneration are the lesions apparent microscopically. The disease agents, therefore, affect cellular function and result in morphologic changes. If sufficient cells are altered, then the tissue or organ function is altered. Altered organ function may result in the organism's death or may cause malfunctioning of other organs, with the same outcome. It cannot be overemphasized that the body is highly integrated and organs are interdependent, so that separation of functions is an academic exercise which allows isolation for ease of understanding and classification. *In vivo,* this concept is absurd.

Disease agents responsible for cell and organ injury in fish are the same as those in higher vertebrates. They include microbiological agents (viruses, bacteria, fungi, protozoa, and helminths), chemical agents (heavy metals, pesticides, drugs, etc.), physical agents (mechanical trauma, heat, cold, electromagnetic radiation, etc.), nutritional imbalances, and possibly hypersensitivity reactions (allergy).

In order for the cell to live and reproduce, certain conditions must be maintained. These conditions are interrelated, and variations in one may cause variations in another. The organism will attempt to maintain the status quo (homeostasis) through autoregulation. If it is unsuccessful, the cell will be unsuccessful in living and reproducing.

The environmental conditions necessary for cell life include: maintenance of the cell membrane (wall integrity); availability of oxygen at suitable arterial partial pressure; availability of carbohydrates, proteins, and lipids for energy, structural purposes, and enzyme production; maintenance of blood pH between 7.23 and 7.5; maintenance of an appropriate blood osmotic concentration; and removal of waste products (urea and ammonia). In addition, the ultrastructural organelles of the cell must function so that energy may be produced (in the mitochondria), electrolyte and water exchange may occur with the intercellular compartment (the plasmalemma), enzymes may be produced (in the endoplasmic reticulum), cellular products packaged (in the Golgi apparatus), foreign substances and effete cellular products destroyed (by the lysosomes), and reproduction allowed (in the nucleus). If any of these environmental conditions are upset or if the organelles are injured, it is probable that the cell will begin to degenerate and eventually die.

To understand how a disease causes death, it is necessary to understand the major functions of the affected organs and how alterations of these functions may destroy the environmental conditions necessary for cell life. Of course, it is not the loss of the organ per se which is of major import, but rather the effect of that loss on the whole organism which causes somatic death.

Respiratory System

The gill of all fishes is a highly vascular organ which is in direct contact with the aqueous environment. It presents the blood to that environment, separating the two by a single or at best double epithelial cell layer, basement membrane, and an endothelium. By its very nature, it is subject to environmental abuse. Its only immediate responses for protection are to produce excessive mucus, for which it has specialized cells, or to increase its epithelial layer.

The functions of the gill are fourfold and are absolutely essential to maintain life: 1) respiration (exchange of oxygen and carbon dioxide); 2) excretion of ammonia; 3) acid-base balance; and 4) monovalent ion exchanges. Note that all are included in the list of environmental conditions necessary for cell life.

Respiration occurs because the red blood cell (RBC) carries the pigment/protein hemoglobin (Hb), which has an affinity for the oxygen molecule. The anatomical arrangement of the gill is lamellar, so that many vessels are exposed to the oxygen in the water. The partial pressure of oxygen in water is higher than in the RBC, which has given up its oxygen to body cells, and an exchange occurs by simple diffusion. The exchange works

Normal gill with 5 primary lamellae and many secondary lamellae at right angles to them. 25x, hemotoxylin and eosin (H&E) stain.

because the flows of water and blood are opposite to one another, that is, countercurrent. This allows the most oxygenated water to oppose the least oxygenated blood. The exchanges are further dependent upon the partial pressure of CO_2 in the blood. That in water is less than that of oxygen, and this may be a limiting factor in the respiratory exchange. The pH may alter CO_2 concentration—the more basic the pH, the less available is the CO_2.

The ability to oxygenate tissue cells may vary from fish to fish, which explains the ease with which catfish or goldfish withstand poorly oxygenated situations, for instance, warm, stagnant aquaria or ponds. This ability is dependent on the affinity for, and capacity of, the Hb molecule for oxygen. If the percentage of Hb oxygen saturation is plotted against the partial pressure of oxygen, a typical sigmoid curve results. Fish with a high affinity for oxygen at a low partial pressure of this gas will have a curve to the left (catfish, goldfish, carp). Moving the curve to the right indicates a lesser affinity but a quicker release to tissue. This phenomenon would be present in highly active animals (mackerel, trout, salmon). Such a shift to the right will also occur if the partial pressure of arterial CO_2 or pH is increased (Bohr effect). These observations are important in regard to gill dis-

ease, in that fish with a higher affinity for oxygen may better adapt to and cope with chronic gill injury.

The second function of the gill is ammonia excretion. (Unlike higher vertebrates, the primary site for ammonia excretion in the fish is not the kidney.) Ammonia is excreted by both active and passive transport mechanisms. Active transport is dependent upon the exchange of Na^+/H^+ (sodium/hydrogen ions) for NH_4^+ (ammonium ion) and a transport enzyme. Ammonia (NH_3) buildup in the environment can be toxic because the fish is unable to pump enough of the product out of its body. The exact mechanism by which the ammonia is toxic is uncertain, but if water levels of the un-ionized form (NH_3) exceed 0.02 parts per million (ppm), death may occur.

Acid-base balance of the blood is also controlled by the gill. An increase in blood CO_2 will lead to an increase in blood carbonic acid and a drop in blood pH. This in turn is offset (buffered) by bicarbonate ions, which can be exchanged for water, Cl^- (chloride) ions, via specialized cells known as chloride cells. Hence, the two substances (carbonic acid and bicarbonate) playing a large role in maintenance of blood pH are in turn dependent upon the partial pressure of CO_2 and the activity of chloride cells.

A fourth gill function, monovalent ion (Na^+, K^+, and Cl^-) balance, varies with the fish's environment (salt or fresh water) and works in conjunction with the gut and kidney. In fact, of the three organs, the gill plays the smallest role but is responsible for Cl^- excretion via chloride cells and Na^+ via Na^+/K^+ ATPase in fresh and salt water. Since saltwater fish swallow seawater and since over 70 percent of the water is absorbed by the gut, marine fish must excrete these excess monovalent ions to maintain proper osmotic balance. Examination of gills from marine teleosts reveals more chloride cells and a different distribution of these cells than those present in freshwater animals.

It can now be understood how lesions of the gill may alter environmental conditions compatible with life. Gill lesions may be of two types: necrosis of the epithelial cells lining the lamellae, or hyperplasia (increase in number) of these same cells. In the first instance, the cells no longer present a semipermeable membrane, the integrity of the cell membrane is compromised, fluids flow back and forth, and bacteria, water, and

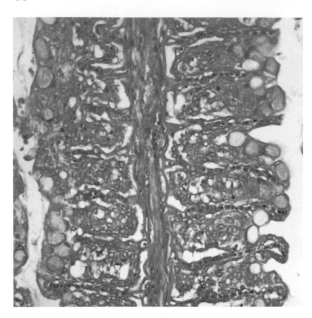

Gill with secondary lamellar epithelial and mucous cell hypertrophy and hyperplasia. 63x H&E.

debris are made available to the blood vessels. Similarly, in saltwater environments, fluid may rush outward from the vessels. Massive upsets in osmotic forces take place and infection occurs. These phenomena would be associated with a diagnosis of "acute necrotic branchitis."

If the causative agent is an irritant that does not immediately result in necrosis, the inflammatory response may be a protective overgrowth of cells (hyperplasia and hypertrophy). In this case, the problem is not that of breaching a cell membrane but rather that of having too many cell membranes. These present an essentially impermeable barrier to normal respiratory exchange, ion exchange, and NH_4^+ excretion. A histopathological diagnosis of "chronic hyperplastic branchitis with lamellar fusion" would be made in this instance.

Organisms and toxicants responsible for the necrosis of gills include myxobacteria (*Flexibacter columnaris* and *F. psychrophilia*), fungi such as *Saprolegnia,* protozoa (*Ichthyobodo*), and heavy metals (copper, zinc, and chromium). Organisms responsible for the proliferation of epithelial or inflammatory cells include *Cytophaga* (bacterial gill disease), *Mycobacterium* (tuberculosis), *Ichthyophthirius* (white spot disease or ich) and its marine counterpart, *Cryptocaryon,* as well as *Exophiala* and *Dermocystidium* (fungi). Poor water quality (combinations of NH_3, sediment, and low oxygen levels) and toxicants such as crude oil, benzene, and other hydrocarbons produce similar lesions.

A third lesion of the gill is infarction. This is a localized area of necrosis secondary to a slowed or absent blood flow (ischemia) resulting in a lack of oxygen (anoxia). While relatively uncommon, it may be the result of the fungus *Branchiomyces* growing within a lamellar blood vessel.

It can now be appreciated that destruction or overproduction of functioning gill cells may lead to oxygen deprivation, upset osmotic forces, upset acid-base balance, and retention of toxic waste products, all of which are incompatible with life.

The pseudobranch (false gill) is a structure arising embryologically from the first visceral arch. It lies on the under surface of the operculum and is easily seen as a reddish structure resembling gill tissue. Histologically, it also resembles the gill but it does not function in gas exchange; in fact, it receives oxygenated blood and shunts this blood directly to the choroid gland, which in turn oxygenates the retina. It is hypothesized that the pseudobranch may also function in controlling gases within the air bladder. The organ is seldom involved in pathological processes, but bacterial infections such as furunculosis, *Renibacterium,* and exposure to the constituents of oil spills may result in swelling, degeneration, and necrosis of its cells.

Circulatory System

The circulatory system of fishes is similar to that of higher vertebrates, although some genera contain auxiliary hearts in the caudal peduncle that assist with the pumping of blood. Arteries and veins are also similar in structure to those of higher vertebrates, with the exception that some arteries may contain valves. Both are lined by an endothelium which, on the surface of the atrium and ventricle, is multifunctional. That is to say, when stimulated by particulate foreign material in the blood and probable chemical mediators, these cells may become phagocytic. Stimulated cells are seen to swell, ingest foreign material, and eventually "bud off" to become free within the atrial lumen, hence they are called atrial macrophages.

The heart has been variously described as two-

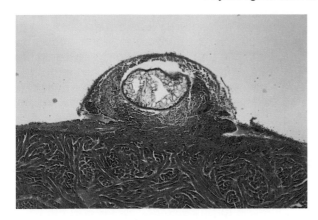

Heart with normal myocardial fibers overlaid by
thickened pericardium, within which lies a
parasite surrounded by inflammatory cells.
25x, H&E.

and four-chambered. There is an atrium and a
ventricle. Just before the atrium is a sinus venosus
and just after the ventricle, a bulbus (conus) arte-
riosus. The latter is composed almost solely of
elastic fibers and helps maintain arterial blood
pressure.

After leaving the heart, the blood passes via the
ventral aorta to the gill and from the gill posteriorly
by way of the dorsal aorta. Blood is returned
through the caudal vein, cardinal veins, and sinus
venosus.

Histologically, the myocardium is quite loose or
spongiform in its architecture. One notes a compact outer cortical area and a spongy inner area.
This loose arrangement allows blood to bathe the
myocardial fibers, and blood cells are freely inter-
mixed in the cardiac musculature. The ventricle
and atrium are covered by a pericardial sac which
appears closely adherent.

Diseases specific to the circulatory system are
few. Arteriosclerosis has been reported in isolated
populations of trout. Sanguinocoliasis, caused by
an intravascular digenetic trematode and the piscine counterpart to schistosomiasis in humans,
is not uncommon in salmonids. Most lesions
present in the circulatory system are, however,
secondary to other infections. Parasitic pericardi-
tis due to metacercariae is common, as is bacterial myocarditis due to *Aeromonas.* Protozoa
(micro- and myxosporidia) may also be found in
the heart. Fungi such as *Exophiala* and *Branchiomyces* may infect arteries and veins. The
latter is specific to blood vessels, apparently only
able to grow in areas of high oxygen tension.

The effects of circulatory diseases are profound
and cause damage because they result in anoxia.
If the major pump is affected even slightly, anoxia
of the brain may result, synapse or permanent
neuronal damage ensue, and the animal may die.
Vasculitis usually has more localized effects (infarction), with blockage of blood flow causing
death of tissues that lie beyond the point of damage. Myocardial infarction (heart attack) is as yet
unknown.

Alimentary Glands

Liver: The liver is the largest organ of the body.
Commensurate with its size, it has multiple functions which cover a broad range of metabolic
activities. The organ has, in addition, two capabilities which allow it to withstand extensive damage before the host shows serious signs of illness.
These capabilities are regeneration and a large
reserve of tissue that can be called upon when
disease strikes.

Because of the liver's many functions, the
signs of disease in affected animals are also
multiple. They can be far more easily evaluated in
warm-blooded terrestrial animals than in fish,
both by physical examination and by clinical
chemistry. However, liver destruction in the fish is
no less incompatible with life than it is in mammals.

The basic structural unit of the mammalian liver
is the lobule, which is composed of radially arranged cords (plates) of liver cells, the hepatocytes. They are arranged about a centrally located

Liver of this killifish (*Fundulus*) shows normal
hepatocyte arrangement, but vacuolated areas
contain spores of the coccidian parasite, *Emeria.*
100x, H&E.

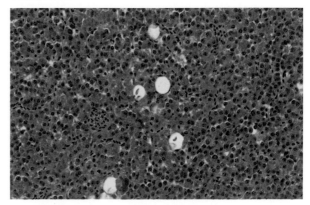

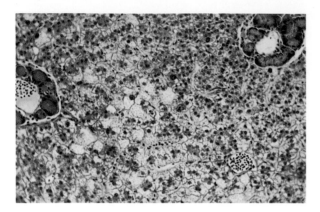

Hepatocytes of this killifish (*Fundulus*) liver are filled with fat. Vessels are surrounded by exocrine pancreas. 100x, H&E.

blood vessel known as the central vein. Blood enters the lobule from peripherally located portal triads. The triads are composed of the hepatic artery, portal vein, and the bile duct. Hence, the liver has two sources of blood: oxygenated blood from the hepatic artery, and blood carrying nutrients from the intestine via the portal system. This blood courses about the cords and empties via the central vein. The bile ductules carry bile from the hepatocytes through an ever-enlarging series of ducts to the gallbladder and eventually to the anterior intestine. The fish liver, however, is not so highly organized as that of the mammal. It lacks lobules and portal triads, and its hepatocytes are conical and arranged radially in double rows. The liver can be envisioned as a highly active organ metabolizing and detoxifying substances presented to it by the blood. Because of its anatomical arrangement, it can come in contact with disease agents or toxins by at least three routes: through the portal system, with source of origin the intestine; similarly through the bile system; and from hepatic blood in cases of bacteremias and toxemias. It is therefore evident that this organ frequently is involved when fish are exposed to aqueous toxins or suffer from generalized bacterial and viral infections.

A better appreciation of the tendency for the liver to be involved in disease processes can be acquired when one understands its physiological functions. The organ functions in three primary areas: 1) the metabolism of nutrients; 2) the detoxification of endogenous and exogenous toxicants; and 3) vitamin storage and the formation of plasma proteins and clotting factors.

The liver is responsible for the metabolism of lipids (from fats), carbohydrates (from sugars and starches), and proteins (from amino acids). In the first instance, it is bile which emulsifies fats in the gut, allowing their absorption. They are then carried via the portal system to the liver for breakdown and use. Fats are necessary for the production of cell membranes and as a source of energy. If the bile system is blocked or if bile cannot be formed properly, the lipids will not be absorbed for utilization. In instances in which aqueous toxicants are present, the ability of the hepatocyte to process fat may fail and the cells will fill with fats, leading to so-called fatty change or fatty metamorphosis. This is a nonspecific change which alerts the pathologist to the fact that something is amiss. Similarly, fatty change may occur in high-fat diets or with other upsets in nutrition, which are reflected by an increased hepatocyte lipid content. This is not an unusual finding in captive fish and reflects our rather primitive knowledge regarding fish nutrition. A deficiency of utilizable lipids, for whatever reason, is not compatible with cell life, especially as regards membrane integrity. Death of the organism may result, following a prolonged illness.

Carbohydrates are also metabolized within the liver. These sources of energy are used in the Krebs cycle and are stored as glycogen within the liver, which may store them as lipids when they are in excess. The liver plays a major role in maintaining blood sugars by manufacturing glucose from glycogen and from other sources (gluconeogenesis) such as amino acids. In cases of liver damage, these functions cannot occur. This results in a nonavailability of carbohydrates for energy sources, a condition inimical for cell life.

It is in the metabolism of proteins that fish differ most remarkably from homeotherms. Fish are ammonotelic rather than ureotelic. That is to say, they excrete ammonium ions (NH_4^+) as ammonia rather than as urea, which they also produce in smaller amounts. Higher vertebrates are ureotelic and uricotelic. Nonetheless, the source of NH_4^+ in each instance is the deamination of amino acids, and in the case of carnivorous fish, primarily the deamination of arginine. This deamination produces ATP from ADP and thereby energy. In other respects, however, the fish liver appears similar to homeotherms in its nitrogen metabolism. It is responsible for formation of new amino acids and for the synthesis of protein.

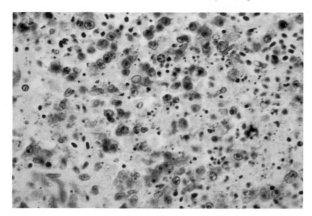

Exposure to high levels of dimethylnitrosamine resulted in necrotic, nonfunctional hepatocytes in this fish liver. 100x, H&E.

Labile proteins in carnivorous fish frequently are used for energy, even before lipid utilization. Hence, destruction of liver tissue prevents transamination and synthesis of proteins, and in carnivorous fish, results in loss of an important energy source. If amino acids are not available to viable cells, then reproduction and production of structural elements and enzymes cannot occur.

The liver is also responsible for detoxification of endogenous and exogenous toxicants. Endogenous means substances produced by the body which, in excess or in the wrong place, may be toxic. An example is bilirubin, an important constituent of bile. Bilirubin is a breakdown product of hemoglobin, the oxygen-carrying pigment of the red blood cell. In its initial stages of formation (hemobilirubin), it is toxic in excessive amounts. It is detoxified by conjugation with glucuronic acid. The conjugation takes place in the liver and results in cholebilirubin, a water-soluble, relatively innocuous substance. Similarly, exogenous toxicants such as benzo[a] pyrene also may be detoxified, in some instances also with glucuronic acid. It is important to note that the liver may produce toxicants inadvertently. When metabolized by the liver, some substances such as polycyclic aromatic hydrocarbons (PAH) are changed to a form which is highly toxic or carcinogenic. The organ does not always function in the best interest of the host. It can be appreciated, however, that because of its high metabolic activity, its wide range of biochemical reactions, and its ability to break down substances, the liver is of great interest to the pathologist and toxicologist studying aquatic pollution.

A third area of liver function is the metabolism and storage of vitamins and the production of plasma proteins and clotting factors. Of primary interest are vitamin A, which is stored in the liver and supplied to other organs on demand, and vitamin K, needed for the intrahepatic production of the clotting factor, prothrombin. Both are fat-soluble vitamins and cannot be absorbed from the gut if the liver is not producing or supplying a sufficiency of bile.

The liver also functions in the production of fibrinogen, a blood protein. This protein is the precursor of fibrin, which forms the meshwork of blood clots. Liver destruction may lead to generalized hemorrhaging, with decreases of blood oxygen at the necessary partial pressure, and cell death.

Another plasma protein, albumin, is also produced within hepatocytes. This protein is the major substance responsible for the maintenance of a normal blood osmotic concentration. In its absence, fluid tends to run into the interstitial spaces, resulting in the condition known as edema, the collection of a normal fluid in an abnormal place. The most common example of this in fish is the swollen abdomen or "water belly" which is technically known as ascites. It is a condition which is seen in a number of piscine diseases and may be due to liver destruction.

Massive destruction of piscine liver tissue may occur due to such diseases as mycobacteriosis (fish tuberculosis), systemic fungal infections such as that caused by *Exophiala,* water-borne toxicants (dimethylnitrosamines), and coccidiosis. Many helminth parasites also spend some portion of their life cycles within the liver. Most cause only local lesions as space-occupying organisms, but when their encapsulating cysts break down, severe inflammation (granulomata) may ensue and in heavy infestations, considerable tissue may be destroyed. Vitamin E deficiency may lead to excessive lipid peroxidation and fatty metamorphosis, indicated by hepatocyte lipid overloading. Such degenerations may be precursors of more serious cellular problems and eventually lead to necrosis.

Pancreas: The fish's exocrine pancreas, unlike that of warm-blooded animals, is diffusely distributed throughout the interpyloric mesenteric fat. In some species (*Morone saxatilis, Fundulus*), the exocrine pancreas is found in the anterior liver surrounding bile ducts.

The function of the exocrine pancreas is to supply digestive enzymes to the foregut. The enzymes are produced within the acinar cells (zymogen granules) and dumped into a series of pancreatic ducts which culminate at the anterior intestine close to the bile duct. The enzymes responsible for the breakdown of fats are lipases, for starches are amylases, and for proteins are proteases. Digestion is therefore dependent on the proper functioning of the pancreas, with protein and energy sources seriously depleted in its malfunctioning.

Enzymes contained in the pancreatic cells are potentially toxic to the surrounding tissue. If the pancreatic cell membranes are destroyed and the various enzymes are freed, they may digest this tissue. The mesentery contains large amounts of fat which is broken down by the freed lipases. This condition results in steatitis, or the inflammation of fat, and is referred to as acute pancreatitis.

The agent most commonly responsible for pancreatic destruction is the virus of infectious pancreatic necrosis (IPN). It is responsible for mass mortalities of young cultured salmonids and is known to affect warm-water species experimentally. A similar virus has been reported in marine fish. It is not unusual to find pancreatic necrosis microscopically in aquarium fish. The cause of this necrosis is uncertain but may be viral in origin.

Pancreatitis is also secondary to systemic bacterial diseases such as those caused by *Mycobacterium, Nocardia,* and *Renibacterium,* as well as protozoan infections (such as those caused by microsporidia) and helminths (resulting in sanguinicoliasis and metacercariae). There appear to be no specific clinical signs associated with pancreatitis, though "corkscrewing" (spinning about the longitudinal axis) has been reported as a diagnostic sign of IPN in trout.

Gas bladder: The gas bladder does not function in respiration and is embryologically an outpocketing of the alimentary tract (esophagus). It is an elongate, distensible organ which lies in the upper peritoneal cavity just below the dorsal aorta and kidney. The organ is variable in shape, according to species. The carp bladder is constricted in its middle, resulting in two compartments, while some members of the fish family Gadidae have bladders which appear corrugated about their lateral edges.

The bladder may connect with the outside

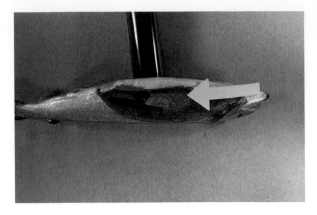

Salmonid pyloric caecae (arrow) superficially resemble worms.

through a duct to the dorsal esophagus. Fish with this arrangement are known as physostomous and include the salmonids. They can empty their gas bladders rapidly and therefore can move vertically in the water column with ease. In most instances, however, the duct is absent (physoclistous) and gases are secreted and resorbed by a gas gland and a resorptive oval, respectively.

The function of the gas bladder is to aid the fish in maintaining neutral buoyancy so that muscular energy need not be expended to keep the animal at any level in the water column. Malfunctions of the gaseous exchange within the bladder may lead to an inability of the fish to dive or to excessive energy expenditure in attempting to reach the surface. In either instance, the animal would feed inefficiently and be subject to predation. Fish with gas bladder problems are often seen floating on or near the surface with distended abdomens. When disturbed, even major efforts will not allow the animal to dive. Similarly, a gas bladder unable to be filled may cause the fish to struggle to maintain a position in midwater or near the top. When fin movement is stopped, the fish will sink. While not immediately life-threatening, such malfunctions can lead to starvation and an inability to reproduce.

A number of organisms have been found to affect the gas bladder. Among carp, *Rhabdovirus carpio* and the secondary bacterial invader *Aeromonas hydrophila* result in a thickening of the bladder wall and a filling of its lumen with a tenacious material. Myxosporidia, trematodes, and the nematode *Philometra* have also been found within the gas bladder, often resulting in an inflammation. Two fungi have been incriminated in gas bladder disease, *Phoma* and *Philaphora*.

Digestive system: The piscine digestive system includes the oral cavity, esophagus, stomach, and intestine. However, some groups of fish (Poeciliidae, Cyprinidae) lack a stomach. All have a far less complex intestinal tract than homeotherms—that of fish may be designated simply as fore- and hindgut. Since the gastrointestinal portion may be rather short, special blind-ended outpocketings may be present to increase the absorptive surface. These structures often arise near the pylorus and are referred to as pyloric caecae. To the uninitiated eye, the caecae may be mistaken for small white parasitic worms (nematodes).

The function of the digestive tract is absorption of the three major classes of nutrients and water. The food is masticated to a small extent by the teeth, although in fish it would appear that the teeth help primarily to hold prey while swallowing. Like higher vertebrates, fish have stomachs which produce hydrochloric acid and digestive enzymes. In the foregut near the pylorus, bile and pancreatic enzymes (lipases, amylases, trypsin) are released which emulsify and reduce fats to smaller fatty acids, polysaccharides to simple sugars, and proteins to amino acids, all of which can then be absorbed across the intestinal mucosa. In addition, the pyloric caecae and the intestine also produce digestive enzymes.

The gut is composed of five layers; from within outward, these are the columnar epithelium and its basement membrane (mucosa), the submucosa, the muscularis interna (longitudinal smooth

Gut of goldfish (central tubular structure). Gut wall is greatly thickened in response to a coccidian, preventing proper absorption of nutrients. 25x, H&E.

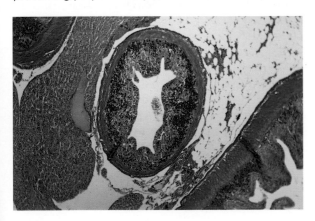

muscle), the muscularis externa (circular smooth muscle), and the serosa. Of primary interest is the mucosa, which gives rise to villi and may be further thrown into folds that increase the absorptive surface. The mucosa is a semipermeable barrier necessary for life. Since the lumen of the gut is essentially outside the animal, the barrier prevents lumenal bacteria from entering the bloodstream to cause disease. Further, it prevents a loss of fluid from within the body which would cause dehydration and death and manifests itself clinically as diarrhea. Damage to the gastrointestinal tract will therefore upset two of the environmental conditions necessary for cell life — availability of nutrients and blood osmotic balance. Compromise of the mucosal barrier allowing penetration of potentially pathogenic bacteria and production of toxins may cause death of exposed cells elsewhere in the body. Signs of gastrointestinal upsets in fish are difficult to observe. One cannot evaluate fecal changes as in higher animals; at best, chronic conditions manifest themselves in weight loss. At necropsy, gastrointestinal changes are similar to those observed in homeotherms.

Diseases affecting the digestive system are numerous. They include viral and bacterial infections such as infectious pancreatic necrosis, *Aeromonas hydrophila,* and *A. salmonicida.* In these cases the problem is usually acute and vascular. The submucosa may become congested, edematous, and even hemorrhagic. In severe infections, necrosis of the epithelium may lead to sloughing, dehydration, and death. At the necropsy table, early infections may be diagnosed by an empty gut with a catarrhal exudate. Later the gut will appear red, wet, and thickened in cross section.

Protozoa cause lesions of the gastrointestinal tract. Coccidiosis (*Eimeria*) may be an important problem in goldfish and carp. Nodular thickening of the gut may be followed by ulcerations. Scrapings of affected areas will yield oocysts. Similarly, tropical aquarium fish may be infected with the flagellates *Spironucleus* and *Hexamita* (formerly called *Octomitus*), which are generally included as the disease agents of hexamitiasis. Affected animals lose weight and have a tucked-up abdomen. The gastrointestinal tract is often empty, and small (1- to 2-millimeter or about 0.06-inch) ulcerations are present. Chronic intestinal infections also may occur, such as that caused by the

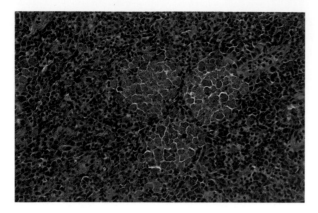

Normal clownfish head kidney with lymphoid and hematopoietic elements. The triad of brown circles is 3 macrophage aggregates. 100x, H&E.

microsporidian *Glugea,* which appears as raised nodular white masses randomly involving the intestine. Impression smears of the cut surface allow rapid identification of the organism.

Fungal infections occur as well but are less frequent. Of interest to the aquarist are helminth (worm) infections. Most adult helminths occupy the gastrointestinal tract, and it is rare that a wild fish has no parasite burden. In most instances these parasites live in balance with their host; it certainly is not to their advantage to be highly pathogenic. Nonetheless, heavy infestations with cestodes (tapeworms) or acanthocephalans (thorny-headed worms) may result in weight loss and even death. Diagnosis is difficult unless fecal material can be observed and eggs identified.

Hematopoietic System

The piscine hematopoietic system includes those organs producing blood cells, both the red (erythrocytes) and white (leukocytes). These organs are the spleen, the kidney interstitium, the anterior (head) kidney, and the thymus. The red blood cells (RBC) function to transport oxygen, while the white blood cells (WBC) function to protect the organism against disease. Piscine white blood cells are similar to those of other vertebrates in that they may be subdivided into two major groups: those which have granules in their cytoplasm (granulocytes) and those which do not (agranulocytes). The latter group includes monocytes and lymphocytes,

cells of the lymphoid system.

The fish lacks bone marrow and produces its red blood cells and granulocytes primarily in the interstitium (surrounding tissue) of the tubular kidney, head kidney, and the spleen. The RBC are oval, nucleated, and approximately 12 micrometers in length. They carry the pigment heme, which, in conjunction with the protein globin, forms the oxygen transport mechanism. The number of red blood cells varies as to fish type, an approximate mean number for bony fishes being 2×10^6 per cubic millimeter (3.3×10^{10} per cubic inch). It is of interest that the RBC count and hematocrit may be quite variable, necessitating larger experimental groups for controllable standard error. However, RBC counts in individual animals have clinical and diagnostic significance.

Diseases leading to RBC destruction or lack of production cause death due to failure to oxygenate tissue. This anoxia (nonavailability of oxygen at a sufficient arterial partial pressure) leads to cell death, especially of the brain and heart.

Diseases decrease numbers of circulating RBC, resulting in a decrease of hemoglobin and the clinical condition known as anemia. Anemia is a common problem in fish. It may result from destruction of circulating cells (primary anemia) or from a failure to produce RBC (secondary anemia). In secondary anemia, diseases which destroy the hematopoietic tissue prevent RBC production. Examples of such conditions include viral infections such as infectious pancreatic necrosis and infectious hematopoietic necrosis. *Renibacterium salmoninarum* and mycobacteriosis may also destroy kidney and splenic tissue, resulting in poor RBC production. *Aeromonas* and especially *Vibrio* cause severe hemolysis and acute (72-hour) anemia. Clinically, the infected animals are lethargic, mortality is high, and at immediate postmortem examination one observes very pale pink to white gill tissue.

These same diseases may be responsible for a decrease in granulocytic cells, a condition called leukopenia. The granulocytic cells of some fish include cells which correspond to the neutrophils, eosinophils, and basophils of higher vertebrates. The first of these cells in many fish is not morphologically a true neutrophil, for its cytoplasmic granules are gray with Rominoswsky stains and it is often mononuclear. It functions in much the same way, however, being weakly phagocytic and found in early infections. Its job is to engulf and kill invading organisms. *Aeromonas salmonicida* (which causes furunculosis and ulcer disease of goldfish) is known to produce a toxin which destroys white blood cells, thus paving the way for the invading bacteria. Total counts of WBC are approximately 15 to 17×10^3 per cubic millimeter (2.5 to 2.8×10^8 per cubic inch) but may range greatly, depending on species. Of these cells, about 30 percent are granulocytic, 70 percent agranulocytic.

Seen with great frequency in most fish is the coarse eosinophilic granulocytic cell (EGC). This cell has bright red, large granules and is produced and found in the submucosa of the stomach. It is seldom seen in the peripheral blood but is commonly seen in inflammations caused by helminths. Its function is uncertain, but it may be related to the mammalian eosinophil.

Fish lack a true lymphatic system and lymph nodes. However, they do have lymphocytes, both large and small. There is mounting evidence that these cells may be divided into T and B subsets. The cells are responsible for antibody production and are produced in the thymus, spleen, and kidney. Their destruction results in immune repression, allowing disease to occur. In addition to lymphocytes, large (12 to 15 micrometers) monocytes are also produced. Monocytes are present in the circulation and migrate to sites of inflammation. There is debate as to whether some phagocytic (ingesting organisms and debris) cells arise from endothelium (blood vessel lining) and are fixed in position or migrate there from hematopoietic sites. In the first instance, one would have a functional reticuloendothelial system (RES) and in the second, the more modern concept of a mononuclear phagocyte system. It is academic, but there is argument for the RES when one considers the atrial macrophages of fish and the pleuripotential epithelial cells of the gill. All these cells have a phagocytic function and are present in more chronic infections such as mycoses, mycobacteriosis, *Renibacterium,* and verminous infestations. Again, destruction of such cells allows bacteria and fungi to gain the upper hand and eventually to kill the host. Diseases affecting hematopoietic tissue affect these cells as well.

An interesting structure in all fish is the macrophage aggregate (MA). It has been variously named, most recently being termed "melanomacrophage center." This name, however, is a

A heavily infected fish with gross dermal and opercular ulcerations.

misnomer since not all aggregates contain melanin. The MA is thought to be a precursor of the germinal centers of higher vertebrates, and it functions in the collection and breakdown of organisms and foreign substances. Increases in number and size of the MA indicate disease, starvation, and/or stress, suggesting that the structures may be of value in monitoring fish health. These groups of macrophages contain three pigments: hemosiderin, lipofuchsin, and melanin. The aggregates are commonly found in the spleen, kidney, and liver.

Integumentary System

Fish skin, well adapted to its environment, differs structurally in a number of ways from that of

Epidermis covering a scale highlights an encysted metacercaria (central bluish structure). The black pigment on either side gives rise to name "black spot disease." 25x, H&E.

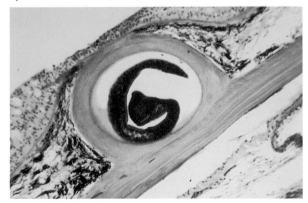

warm-blooded terrestrial vertebrates. The epidermis (outer skin) is composed, from within going outward, of a basal layer of germinal cells (stratum germantivum), a layer of squamous cells (stratum lucidum), and an outer circle. The cells formed in the basal layer move upward and outward until they are lost (exfoliated). Mitotic activity (cell division) is present in all layers. In addition, a number of special cells and structures may be present which are not present in homeotherms. These include: mucous cells which produce the thin mucous covering found on the surface of all fish; alarm cells, also known as club cells, which free a water-soluble substance that will alert other fish of danger; neuromast cells, which are multicellular organs of sense (tactile, odor, taste); chloride cells, which function in blood electrolyte exchange; pigment cells; white blood cells which serve a protective function; and scales.

The epidermis lies on a basement membrane which is above the dermis. The dermis is composed of a loose layer and a compact layer of connective tissue which also contain pigment cells (chromatophores).

The skin covers all surfaces, protects the fish from the outside environment, including microorganisms, and prevents upsets in fluid balance. It is, therefore, essentially impermeable and, in addition, its mucous covering contains antibodies (14S IgM) and lysozymes, which are antibacterial and/or antiprotozoal.

Because of its intimate relationship with the environment, the skin reflects many insults and is of clinical and diagnostic importance. For instance, when a fish becomes ill, one of the first signs is a change in color. Most frequently the fish becomes darker dorsally, and the diagnostician can see this change easily by looking down through the surface of the water. The darkening reflects changes mediated through the nervous system which cause the melanin-bearing cells to expand. (Lack of color may occur as well, but less frequently and later.) Similarly, increases in mucus production may occur in protozoal infections and in instances in which an irritant is present in the water. Commonly one may observe ulcerations of the skin. These ulcerations are often red in the center, white on their edge, and black on the periphery. The red center indicates hemorrhage; the white edge, dying (sometimes regenerating) epithelium; and the black periphery, an influx of melanophores. These ulcers may become cov-

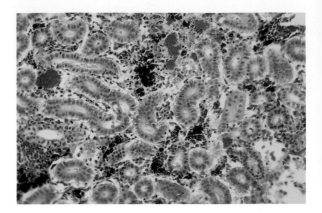

Salmonid kidney. Blue homogeneous areas to right and upper center are masses of *Aeromonas salmonicida* (furunculosis) bacteria. Black pigment is normal melanin accumulation. 100x, H&E.

ered with a white to brown cottonlike growth in fresh water which reflects secondary fungal involvement (saprolegniasis). These fungi, in the vast majority of cases, are saprophytes. The skin may reflect proliferative changes also. Reports of papillomas among saltwater fish are not unusual. Hyperplasia and hypertrophy secondary to protozoan infections are not unusual and appear as small to large white areas. Other neoplasms have been reported.

A common lesion of the skin in wild fish appears as small white or black spots (1 to 5 millimeters, or 0.04 to 0.2 inches) which are randomly distributed. These spots are the metacercariae, or encysted larvae, of various digenetic trematodes which may or may not attract melanophores to their outer cyst walls. Except in very heavy infestations, or infections of internal organs, they cause little damage.

The underlying cause of death in fish with extensive lesions of the skin is undoubtedly upsets in the electrolyte and osmotic balances of the blood. Hemorrhage also plays a role if ulcerations are extensive and acute, such as occurs in vibriosis.

Urogenital System

The urogenital system of the fish arises developmentally from a pronephros and the coelomic epithelium (gonads). The nephron (the functional excretory portion of the kidney) is not as specialized as is that of higher vertebrates but has a glomerulus, proximal and distal convoluted tubules, and in some instances, a collecting tubule, all of which dump into an archinephric duct. The latter carries waste products to the noncloacal bladder and, eventually, to a urogenital papilla. Products of the gonads (sperm and ova) also travel to the outside via the archinephric duct.

Although the fish is capable of producing urea, the primary function of the kidney is not the excretion of ammonia but rather the excretion or preservation of divalent cations (such as the ionic forms of calcium and magnesium). These cations are used to maintain proper electrolyte balance and therefore function in maintaining proper fluid distribution. Calcium is also needed for neuromuscular excitability and blood coagulation.

Fish regularly migrating from salt to fresh water (anadromous) or vice versa (catadromous) must have properly functioning kidneys to deal with the changes of the salts in the external environment. Destruction of the kidney will lead to upsets in interstitial and blood osmotic concentration, cellular hydration or dehydration, and upsets in blood pH.

The functions of the reproductive organs are self-evident. Destruction of these organs is not life threatening; in fact, sterile fish may grow more rapidly and result in a greater economic return to the culturist.

The urogenital system, especially the tubular kidney, is frequently involved in disease problems. A number of pathogenic bacteria may take up residence within the kidney and, in the process of reproduction, cause severe necrosis. Of interest to the hobbyist is *Mycobacterium,* which causes fish tuberculosis, and to the culturist, *Renibacterium salmoninarum,* which causes bacterial kidney disease. Both are chronic infections which result in slow, constant mortalities preceded by weight loss and/or poor growth. The latter is related to water hardness and the presence of divalent cations in the diet. It is reported that the harder the water, the lower the incidence and severity of the infection. *Aeromonas* may also strike the kidney, but it is more acute in its manifestation.

Mycotic diseases such as those caused by species of *Exophiala, Onchocronis,* and *Ichthyophonus* may be found in kidney tissue. Of the three, exophialosis is most prevalent and of greatest importance to the culturist.

Protozoa are also kidney pathogens, especially the coccidians and the micro- and myxosporidians. As these organisms reproduce and sporulate, they cause necrosis by expansion and pressure and may result in a severe granulomatous reaction. On occasion, external protozoa (*Trichodina* complex) may be found in the bladder and archinephric ducts. A disease of protozoan (myxozoan) cause, known as proliferative kidney disease (PKD), has become a major problem of the salmonid industry in recent years.

Diseases of the gonads are primarily of parasitic origin. Coccidiosis affects the testicles of both salt- and freshwater fish. Microsporidians cause necrosis of the ovary, and cestode larvae frequently cause marked inflammation of the ovary in many species of fish. All may be responsible for sterility.

Central Nervous System and Organs of Special Sense

The specialized and well-organized piscine nervous system uniquely suits the fish in its environment. The piscine brain lacks a cerebrum and is composed of sensory lobes, a cerebellum, and a medulla oblongata. The sensory lobes are the optic, which are located in the mesencephalon or midbrain, and the olfactory, which are preceded by the olfactory bulbs of the telencephalon or forebrain. Their functions are coordination of movement (cerebellum), sensory and motor control (medulla), sight (optic), and smell (olfactory). The degree of development of each part is often dependent on the habits of the fish. For example, bottom-feeding fish in murky water will have a more highly developed olfactory area than those depending upon sight.

The brain is surrounded by a rather simple meninx; clear differentiation into layers is not possible. The brain is further surrounded by a cushioning layer of liquid fat. Unlike higher vertebrates, fish have eleven rather than ten cranial nerves. The extra nerve functions in spinal sensation. In other respects, the cranial nerves are similar.

The organs of special sense include the eye, ear, olfactory system, taste buds, and lateralis system. The eye is highly developed, resembling all vertebrate eyes. It has a specialized retina with rod and cone visual cells and a lens which is capable of changing shape.

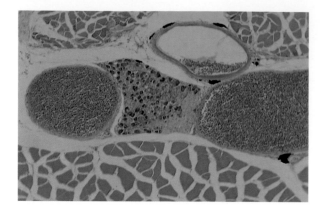

Section of a cranial nerve (center, dark and light blue) bounded on either side by spores (violet) of reproducing myxosporidia. 25x, H&E.

The ear is also highly developed, but lacks an external and middle division. Its inner portion contains semicircular canals and three chambers with otoliths. The organ functions in balance, with reception of sound waves. It is innervated by the eighth cranial (statoacoustic) nerve. The ear's innervation also includes the seventh cranial (facial) nerve, which in turn innervates the lateralis system of the head. This has led to conjecture about the function of the lateral line system, which may have some ability to sense sound waves.

The lateralis system or lateral line system is a baroceptor; that is, it is capable of sensing changes in water pressure. This allows the fish to sense prey or predators to the side or rear which it might not see. The system is composed of two canals which run the length of the body midlaterally and give rise to the so-called lateral line. In addition, there are cranial bifurcations of this system. The canals have pores to the outside and groups of sensory cells regularly spaced along their medial aspects. These cell groups are known as neuromast cells. The primary innervation to this system is the vagus (tenth cranial) nerve, but the facial nerve also plays a role.

The olfactory system is highly developed. Anteriorly the fish has two nasal openings on each side of its maxilla. These openings are in line, water passing through anterioposteriorly. Often the anterior nares have a flap of skin which may be extended to capture water or used to close the opening. The nasal chamber often contains folds lined by sensory epithelium. The anatomic arrangement of the sensory area varies greatly among families of fish. The sensory messages pass from the epithelium to the olfactory bulbs via the first cranial nerve and then are processed in the olfactory lobes.

Fish also have a highly developed sense of taste. Taste buds are plentiful on the tongue and throughout the oral mucosa. In addition, such sensory cells may be found in the skin of some species.

The consequences of a damaged central nervous system or sense organ are obvious. If the most primitive areas are involved, respiration or cardiac function will cease immediately and anoxia will result in cell death. Higher center damage will conflict with ability to feed or reproduce. In most instances, affected animals will become easy prey.

Few diseases of the brain have been reported in fish, and histopathological examination of brain sections rarely uncovers lesions. Vibriosis has been observed in association with severe granulocytic meningitis, as has an infectious pancreatic necrosislike virus. Recently, *Edwardsiella tarda* has been found in the brain of young catfish, resulting in marked encephalitis. Occasionally microsporidia may be present in brain tissue and cranial ganglia, as are metacercariae.

Lesions of the eye are more numerous. The most common clinical problem is exophthalmus, or protrusion of the eye from the orbit. This is a lesion often associated with viral and bacterial diseases. The protrusion may be due to postorbital granulomata or edema. Bacterial infections of the eye also occur, often due to corneal ulceration. The cornea may become damaged when captive fish in circular tanks touch the tank sides. Cataracts are a common problem and appear to be related to zinc or methionine deficiency. Similarly, vitamin E and vitamin A deficiencies have been associated with retinal degeneration and blindness in captive clownfish (*Amphiprion ocellaris*). A major parasite problem is *Diplostomum spathaceum* (eye fluke), a digenetic trematode which lives in the eye and causes blindness in salmonids.

Myxosoma cerebralis is a myxosporidian parasite of salmonids that occupies cartilage of the developing skull. It frequently affects the tissue surrounding the inner ear and damages the statoacoustic apparatus. Such damage is seen clinically as an inability to swim straight ahead. Affected animals appear to "chase their tails" or circle, similar to higher vertebrates with otitis. The disease is known as whirling disease and is a very serious condition which often requires slaughter of all fish in the affected hatchery.

Infections and necrosis of the lateralis system are diagnosed histopathologically. Few infectious processes have been reported. *Ichthyobodo necatrix* (causing costiasis) has been found in the head canal system. Heavy metals (cadmium, silver, zinc, copper) are known to cause a mononuclear inflammation of the supporting epithelial cells, but neuromast necrosis is rare.

It would appear that a sensory epithelium constantly exposed to the environment, such as that of the lateralis system and olfactory region, would serve to reflect water-borne toxicants quickly and perhaps diagnostically. However, this does not appear to be the case. The nasal epithelium, like the lateral line, undergoes inflammatory changes when exposed to heavy metals. It is interesting to note that salmon are capable of sensing and showing an aversion reaction to copper levels as low as 0.05 ppm. Seldom, however, are the sensory cells damaged in a fashion that can be diagnosed by the light microscope. A lesion of unknown origin sometimes present in the nares is the influx of tissue eosinophilic granulocytic cells coupled with vacuolar degeneration and necrosis of the sensory epithelium.

Endocrine System

Endocrine glands are ductless glands which vary greatly in their functions and control a wide range of activities. Among these are growth, metabolic rate, electrolyte levels, and immune response.

The piscine endocrine system is unique because it contains organs not found in the homeotherms and lacks a parathyroid gland. Endocrine glands present in the fish include the pituitary, thyroid, interrenal (adrenal cortex), chromaffin tissue (adrenal medulla), pancreatic islet cell, ultimobranchial, corpuscle of Stannius, and the urophysis spinalis or caudal neurosecretory system. The functions of the pituitary, thyroid, ultimobranchial, pancreatic islet cells, interrenal, and chromaffin tissue are similar to those in higher vertebrates.

The corpuscle of Stannius is found in the tubular kidney and grossly is present as random round white areas just below the ventral capsule. The gland may be mistaken for a lesion. It functions in calcium metabolism, causing hypocalcemia, and perhaps regulates sodium and potassium balance. The urophysis is a ventral extension of the caudal spinal cord. Its functions are multiple, including blood pressure regulation and osmoregulation.

Glands capable of such widespread effects may be subject to diseases that result in metabolic malfunctions and death in numerous ways. Examination of the literature regarding the pathophysiology of endocrine organs will reveal a dearth of information. This reflects the very few clinicopathological studies which have been done on metabolic diseases of the fish. Diabetes has been reported in Japanese carp secondary to the feeding of silkworm pupae (Sekoke disease).

Inflammatory reactions having multiple causes (for instance, IPN virus, furunculosis, mycobacteriosis, and exophialosis) may incidentally involve any of the endocrine organs. In addition, neoplastic processes have been found to affect the thyroid gland with some frequency, and goiter of uncertain cause is reported in many species of fish.

Selected References

Groman, D. B. 1982. Histology of the striped bass. *Amer. Fish. Soc.* Monograph no. 3.

Hoar, W. S., and Randall, D. J. 1969. *Fish Physiology,* Vol. 1. New York: Academic Press.

Hoffman, G. L. 1967. *Parasites of North American Freshwater Fishes.* Los Angeles: University of California Press.

Neish, G. A., and Hughes, G. C. 1980. Fungal diseases of fishes. In *Diseases of Fishes,* Vol. 6, eds. S. F. Snieszko and H. R. Axelrod, 1–159. Neptune City, N.J.: T.F.H. Publications.

Roberts, R. J. 1989. *Fish Pathology,* 2nd ed. London: Bailliere Tindal.

———. 1982. *Microbial Diseases of Fish.* New York: Academic Press.

Infectious Diseases and Parasites of Freshwater Ornamental Fish

John B. Gratzek, Emmett B. Shotts, Jr., and Donald L. Dawe

As do all animals, fish live in an environment that is full of disease-causing organisms and parasites. Parasites are organisms that derive their living from another organism, the host, and provide no benefit to the host. They are a diverse group ranging in complexity from viruses to arthropods.

In the interaction between host and parasite, the objective of a parasite is to invade the host, develop, and reproduce. The objective of the host, however, is to prevent the parasite from invading and reproducing. Thus, in this interaction parasites have evolved various structures and activities (virulence factors) which allow them to invade and survive in the host. Hosts have developed various structures and activities (defense factors) which act to prevent the invasion and development of the parasite. Several conclusions are possible in the interaction between virulence and host factors. The parasite may invade and be very active, leading to disease and possibly death of the host, an undesirable result for both host and parasite. The parasite may invade the host but be very mild in its activity, so that the host reacts mildly and both the host and parasite survive for a long time; this is desirable for the parasite and acceptable for the host. A third possible outcome is that when the parasite invades, the host's defense reaction overwhelms the parasite and eliminates it. This is the optimal result from the host's point of view.

Fish possess a highly developed and efficient system of external and internal defenses against disease, which allows them to survive and prosper in an environment that contains large numbers of disease-causing organisms. With time and continued better understanding of the nature of this system, it should become increasingly possible to manipulate these defenses and responses to prevent infection. Prevention is much more effective and cost-efficient than treatment of disease.

Fish Immunology and Defense Factors

For convenience, the defense factors of a fish can be divided into two systems, innate and acquired. Innate factors are constant no matter what parasite the host encounters or how many times the fish has previously encountered the parasite. The innate system is composed of physical barriers such as skin and scales, secretions such as mucus, phagocytic cells such as macrophages, and proteins in the blood such as the complement system. The acquired factors are the components of the immune system of the fish that have the ability to react specifically with parasites, develop, and "remember" the interaction. Thus, in the fish immune system, the reaction to a parasite increases after an initial encounter with it. The components of the immune system are certain white blood cells, lymphocytes, serum proteins, and globulins. A great many specialized terms are involved in descriptions of this system and its workings (see accompanying glossary).

Before a parasite can develop and reproduce, it must enter the fish. The first host defense is, therefore, an epithelial membrane, either the epithelium of gills and digestive tract, or the skin or scales. In addition to being physical barriers that are difficult to penetrate, epithelial membranes are also covered with a moving layer of mucus which the parasite must penetrate before it can attach to the membrane. In the digestive tract, peristaltic actions move the mucus along. On the surface of the fish, mucus moves from the head to the tail, where it is shed into the water. Often, parasites become trapped in the mucus and are moved out of or off of the fish before they have a chance to attach to epithelial cells. In response to a surface irritant such as the attachment of a number of parasites, fish often increase their production of mucus. In some cases of heavy parasite invasion, one can observe strands of mucus stringing out from the fins and tail of the fish.

If a parasite manages to attach to a surface membrane and penetrates into the tissues of the fish, it encounters another component of the host's innate defenses, the phagocytic cells (from the Greek *phagos,* "to eat"). These cells are found in the circulatory system, wan-

Terms Commonly Used in Fish Immunology

Anamnestic immune response: Specific immune response to a second or later encounter with the same antigen. Also called secondary immune response. Based on the presence of memory cells and generally more rapid and intense than the primary immune response.

Antibody: A specific serum protein called an immunoglobulin (Ig) which is produced by an animal in response to the presence of an antigen and which reacts specifically with the antigen *in vivo* and *in vitro*.

Antigen: A substance which can evoke a specific humoral or cell-mediated immune response when present in an animal and which reacts specifically with the induced antibody or activated cell.

B-Cells: Lymphocytes whose development is not directly influenced by the thymus. Develop into antibody-producing plasma cells after contact with an antigen.

Cellular or Cell-mediated immunity: Immunity mediated by specifically activated cells (T-cells).

Host: A plant or animal that harbors parasites.

Humoral immunity: Immunity mediated by the presence of specific antibody.

Immunity (immune): State of being protected from infection or injury by virtue of being able to resist and/or overcome harmful agents. May either be acquired during life (generally as a result of lymphoid cell action) or be innate (native or constitutive for a species and requiring no previous experience with external agents).

Lymphocyte: Mature cell of the lymphoid tissue, also found in circulation. Major functional cell of the acquired immune system. Divided into several major functional classes of cells, including B-cells, T-cells, and memory cells.

Macrophage: A phagocytic cell found in circulation, lining blood sinuses, and wandering in the tissues. These cells present antigens to the lymphocytes to initiate an antibody response.

Memory cells: Resting lymphocytes (T- or B-cells) that have been primed by exposure to an antigen. These cells react rapidly on second exposure to the antigen and are responsible for the anamnestic response.

Opsonin: A substance that coats a particle and thereby promotes its uptake by a phagocytic cell.

Phagocytic cells: Cells capable of engulfing particles.

T-cells: Lymphocytes whose development is influenced directly by the thymus. Made up of subpopulations such as T-helper cells, T-cytotoxic cells, and T-suppressor cells.

T-cytotoxic cells: T-cells that react with antigens on cell surfaces and kill antigen-bearing cells. Major effector cell in the cell-mediated immune response.

T-helper cells: T-cells that interact with the antigen and produce soluble factors that help B-cells and other T-cytotoxic cells mature.

T-suppressor cells: T-cells that react with antigen and release soluble factors that suppress the activity of B-cells and other T-cells.

dering in the tissues, and lining vessels in organs such as the spleen and liver. Phagocytic cells engulf and break down damaged host cells. These cells are the "cleanup crew" for the fish, the method by which foreign material and damaged cells are removed from tissues. Phagocytic cells engulf parasites by extending arms of protoplasm around the parasite. When the arms meet, a vesicle forms in the cytoplasm containing the parasite. This vesicle is then joined by a lysosome, which is a package of enzymes in the cytoplasm of the cell. The joining of the lysosome and the vesicle releases the enzymes, which break down the parasite. Phagocytic cells also have metabolic activities that directly kill engulfed parasites.

The fish immune system: Once a parasite gets into the tissues of the fish, it also encounters the host's immune system. The active cells of the immune system are small lymphocytes which arise from a common stem cell source in the anterior kidney, but develop into two functional populations of cells. One population of small lymphocytes, referred to as T-cells, is influenced by the thymus. This population of cells contains three subsets: T-helper cells that aid B-cells in antibody production, T-cytotoxic cells which kill parasite-infected cells, and T-suppressor cells which act to regulate the immune response. The development of the other population, referred to as B-cells, is not influenced by the thymus. After contact with antigens, these cells develop into antibody-producing cells. Antigens are substances that stimulate the immune system to produce antibodies or specifically sensitized cells and react specifically with them. Antibodies are serum proteins—immunoglobulins—which are produced by the immune system in response to the presence of an antigen and which react specifically with it. After the phagocytes break down the parasite, they display some parasite components on their cell membrane. This is antigenic material, and the T-cells and B-cells of the fish will interact with this material to produce an antibody response. In the development of T-cells and B-cells, individual cells develop specific antigen receptors. Each cell can react with only one antigen, but within the population of T-cells and B-cells are cells that can react with all possible antigens. The phagocytic cell presents the antigen to T-helper cells and B-cells. These cells react through their antigen-specific receptors. The T-helper cells then release soluble factors that stimulate the B-cells, and the B-cells develop into antibody-producing plasma cells.

Antibodies are active against parasites and parasite products that are in the circulatory system or the tissue fluids. In these cases, antibodies can react specifically with an antigen to neutralize it, to kill the parasite, or to render the invader more vulnerable to phagocytic destruction. Parasites that develop intracellularly are not affected by antibodies. In this situation the T-helper cells stimulate the development of another population of T-cells, the T-cytotoxic cells. The T-cytotoxic cells recognize antigens on the surface of infected cells and kill the infected cells. The cell debris and parasites are then taken up by phagocytic cells and processed. This is a cell-mediated immune response, in contrast to the previously described antibody-mediated response. Cell-mediated responses are the major defense against intracellular parasites such as viruses.

In both the antibody response and cell-mediated response, the specifically reactive cells multiply after contact with the antigen. Some of the multiplying cells continue in their development to become mature plasma cells or T-cytotoxic cells. Others (memory cells) persist in an intermediate developmental stage in the fish for long periods of time. When the fish encounters the parasite for the second time, these cells mature rapidly, so the secondary (anamnestic) immune response is faster and more vigorous than the first response was. Thus, fish that survive an initial encounter with a parasite are more likely to survive a second encounter with the same parasite; they are immune.

Protecting fish by immunization: The anamnestic response in the immune system is the basis for protection of animals by immunization. To immunize an animal, one exposes it to the antigen and induces an immune response. This response generates a population of T and B memory cells. When this animal encounters the parasite in the environment, it will exhibit a secondary immune response. As a result, it will be more likely to overwhelm the parasite and recover from the infection.

Fish can be immunized against various parasites, but there are two major problems in developing immunizing agents for fish diseases. First, how does one get the antigen into the fish? The simplest method is to inject the antigen, as is done with mammals and birds. While this method will induce good immune responses in fish, it is impractical for large populations. Alternatively, fish can be fed antigens, and good immune responses will develop. Because this generally requires that the fish be fed the antigen over long periods, instability of the antigen in the food can be a problem. The most efficient immunization method is to immerse fish in an antigen suspension or spray antigen on them. In both of these procedures the antigen appears to be taken up through the cells of the gills. Both methods are practical for the immunization of large groups of fish.

A second major problem in immunization of fish involves the preparation of the antigen to be used. Because fish parasites have been studied less extensively than the parasites of mammals and birds, selecting the best preparation of the parasite to use as an immunizing agent is often difficult. Furthermore, in many cases different parasite strains have different antigens, and use of one strain as an immunizing agent will not induce protection against other strains.

Factors influencing immunological responses: How well a fish responds to an antigen can be influenced by a variety of external and internal factors. Since fish are poikilothermic (cold-blooded) animals, their metabolism varies with the water temperature. Changes in water temperature also influence the immune response of fish. Different fish species have different optimum temperatures, and fish exposed to antigens when they are in water below their optimum temperature respond very slowly to antigens. Thus, trout produce good immune responses at water temperatures where catfish produce very slow and poor immune responses. It appears that temperature changes influence the activity of the T-cell population more than the B-cell population. This temperature effect on the immune response of fish is thought to be one of the reasons why disease outbreaks occur in fish during times when the water temperature in ponds is changing.

Other water quality factors also influence the immune response of fish. It has been shown that the presence of heavy metal ions such as zinc, copper, and cadmium can depress the ability of fish to respond to antigenic stimulation. Recent reports also indicate that certain antibiotics such as oxytetracycline can depress the immune response of fish.

A major internal condition that influences the immune response of fish is stress. In the stress reaction of fish, the adrenal glands are stimulated to release adrenal corticosteroids. These hormones act to depress the activity of cells of the immune system. Thus, any activity that induces a stress reaction in a fish will reduce the ability of that fish to mount an immune response. Shipping, handling, crowding, introduction of new fish, and changes in water quality all will tend to reduce the ability of fish to resist infection. This is a major factor that must be considered when developing methods to immunize fish, since the immunization process itself is likely to induce a stress reaction.

Protozoan, Metazoan, and Crustacean Parasites of Ornamental Fish

Before turning our attention to specific examples of protozoan, metazoan, and crustacean parasites, it is important to remind ourselves of some general principles that can affect the degree to which such parasites will be a problem.

First, in nature it is rare to find a fish which is parasite-free. Fish often carry a parasite (or a population of them in the case of a few classes of parasites) without apparent signs of disease. The carrier fish may, in fact, have developed a degree of immunity to a particular parasite. Many carriers are mature fish. When introduced into a group of uninfected fish, they will initiate an epizootic (a disease affecting many animals at the same time) within the aquarium without showing any signs of disease themselves. For this reason, quarantine is a valuable procedure.

Second, many parasites that infect fish can be transmitted by direct extension through the water. Crowding of fish will increase the chances of contact between parasite and potential host. Additionally, crowding of fish will lead to changes in the organic load of the water, promoting parasitism. Third, many fish parasites require an intermediate host. For example, nematode eggs passed from fish are eaten by free-living invertebrates such as *Daphnia* and *Cyclops,* which are in turn eaten by other fish. If such intermediates are not found in the aquarium, transmission is impossible. For digenetic trematodes, a variety of wild-caught or pond-raised ornamental fish serve as the secondary intermediate host. In effect, such fish are dead-end hosts when in an aquarium.

Finally, since fish will eat dead fish in an aquarium, failure to remove dead fish from an aquarium may enhance the spread of the disease, especially in the case of sporozoan parasites. Mycobacterial infections are also transmitted in this manner.

The first steps toward a diagnosis: In any fish disease situation, one must begin with the history of the fish in question. Also, before establishing a diagnosis of parasitism, one initially must exclude other problems by reviewing basic aquariology practices such as water quality management, nutrition, and the possibility of noninfectious disease problems. Determine the source of the fish and how long they have been in their current situation. Fish taken from a pond will almost certainly have some parasites, many of which will be lost when the fish is transferred to new water. Wild-caught fish and some pond-raised fish also invariably will be infected with roundworms or flatworms. Fish which have been residing in an aquarium for several months to several years would not be expected to be infected with a parasite unless it were introduced with a new fish. Specifically determine whether fish have been treated and/or quarantined prior to the onset of the problem. Lack of quarantine is a common method of introducing parasites into an otherwise well-functioning aquarium. It is helpful to establish the history of previous disease problems and their treatment. Fish which have been treated with effective drugs in correct dosages would not be expected to have parasites which are amenable to treatment.

The next step should be to observe the fish closely. Although many sick fish react similarly to a variety of parasites, close observation of the behavior and external appearance of the fish is sometimes very helpful in arriving at a tentative diagnosis. In some cases, the parasite may be large enough to be seen with the naked eye, or the signs of the disease are so characteristic that a microscopic examination may not be required. Often, protozoan, metazoan, and crustacean parasites can readily be identified. In other cases, diagnosis of a parasitic problem can be very specific, involving dissection of the fish and microscopic examination of the tissues. A diagnosis reached by a necropsy and examination of tissues will provide the most accurate information on the particular parasite and provide a basis for the treatment required.

Clinical signs of parasitic disease: Many parasites of fish induce similar lesions and/or behaviors. Skin and fin lesions can include excessive mucus (best seen with overhead incident light), ulcerations, pinpoint hemorrhages, white spots, or whitish discolored areas which may be restricted to fins or to various areas of the body.

Behavior changes in severe cases of gill parasitism generally include depression—fish lie motionless at the bottom of the aquarium. Opercula (gill covers) may be flared and opercular movements may be increased, indicating respiratory distress. In less severe cases, fish may appear to swim in twisting motions while scraping gills on solid objects. This behavior, which appears to be an attempt to rid gills of an irritant, is called "flashing." When fish are parasitized, feeding behavior is usually reduced or absent.

Submitting samples for laboratory examination: Fish, like other animals, cannot be examined over the telephone. A clinical evaluation can best be made while fish are in an aquarium, during which time routine water-quality tests can be done. If a site or home visit is not possible, the owner may need to bring fish and aquarium water to the laboratory for examination. A small pail containing aquarium water is adequate for transporting the fish. The diseased fish should be brought while it is still alive. Fish which have recently died can be submitted by wrapping them in wet paper or towels surrounded by ice. Dead fish decompose rapidly, becoming useless for diagnostic purposes. For pH, ammonia, and nitrite testing, bring a water sample from the aquarium in a separate container. Some state veterinary diagnostic laboratories also provide testing for various heavy metals.

Biopsy procedures: In the laboratory, the fish may be biopsied. A biopsy is the microscopic examination of a wet mount of tissue which has been taken from a live fish. Tissues examined usually are snips of gills, skin scrapings, or small pieces of fins. In most instances involving sick aquarium fish, a fish owner will not allow a fish to be killed, but may not realize that biopsies can be done. Although there is always a chance that any laboratory manipulation of fish might result in death, the procedure is relatively straightforward when performed by a trained individual. An experienced diagnostician trained in biopsy recovery and microscopic examination of wet mounts for parasites or other pathological conditions can provide valuable information to help one determine which medicament should be used and what could be done to avoid future problems.

During the biopsy procedure, the fish is held in a wet hand or in a wet towel. Obviously, the procedure must be done quickly. It normally takes no more than a few seconds to recover both a fin scraping and gill snip. Doing the biopsy over an aquarium ensures that the fish will fall into water in the event that it is not properly restrained.

The procedure for obtaining samples differs slightly with the sample type. Often a diagnostician finds it helpful to position the tail fin of a small fish on a glass slide to facilitate removing scrapings from the fish. Just enough material is removed to allow for examination of the specimen without undue injury to the fish. A skin biopsy is directed toward removing a sample from an obviously affected area. A routine biopsy to check for external parasites is best done by making a light scraping of the tip of the tail fin.

Wet mounts of tissues for microscopic examination are made as soon as possible after the sample is obtained. A drop of tap water is added to the specimen, and a glass coverslip is placed over it to flatten the field of observation. Wet mounts of specimens from the skin or gill of salt-water fish use salt water or a 2.5 percent salt solution.

Anesthetizing fish: The decision whether or not to anesthetize a fish prior to taking a biopsy is based on the health, size, and activity level of the fish. For example, anesthesia may be unnecessary for a fin scraping, but if a gill snip is to be taken and the fish is active, anesthesia may be necessary. To minimize the chances of additional stress, anesthetization should be done in the water in which the fish was transported or in fresh water with the pH and temperature adjusted to

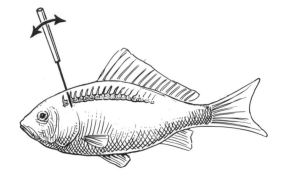

Fish can be pithed with a dissecting needle, which is inserted into the spinal canal and moved laterally, as illustrated here, or by severing the spinal cord with scissors.

that of the transport water. Water should be well aerated. Several anesthetic agents can be used (see table below), but their availability may be limited.

As a general rule, fish should be anesthetized for as short a period as possible, then removed immediately to fresh water for recovery. They should not be placed in a populated aquarium during recovery, since other fish may attack them and inflict injury.

Necropsy procedure: If enough fish are available, a microscopic examination of wet-mount preparations of gills, fins, and internal organs of a killed fish may be undertaken at the diagnostic laboratory. Select moribund fish for examination rather than dead ones; decaying fish usually teem with an array of saprophytic protozoans which were not associated with the initial problem. If there is a delay between the time of death and examination, the fish should be wrapped in a wet towel packed in ice. Even when this precaution is taken, some parasites will be impossible to observe after a period of hours. If fish happen to be preserved in formalin for histopathological evaluation, external parasites are likely to be found in the formalin. The parasites can be concentrated by centrifugation and a drop of the sediment can be examined as a wet mount.

Selected Anesthetics Which Have Been Used for Fish				
Anesthetic	Dose range per liter	Induction time (min.)	Recovery time (min.)	Source of chemical
Alka-Seltzer ®	1 tablet	1 – 2	5 – 10	Retail outlets
Quinaldine sulfate (2-Methylquinoline sulfate)	20 – 65 mg	1 – 3	5 – 20	Sigma Chemical
Benzocaine (ethyl p-amino benzoate)	25 – 100 mg	1 – 3	3 – 15	Veterinary supply outlets
Isoflurane	0.8 – 3.0 ml	3 – 8	3 – 10	Anaquest veterinary supply outlets

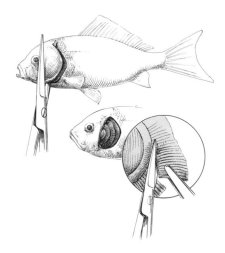

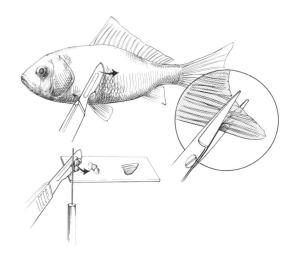

To make a gill lamellae preparation, remove the operculum. Cut out a section of the lamellae, avoiding the gill arch. Immediately place the section in water on a slide and tease the lamellae apart for microscopic examination.

Procedure for wet-mount microscopic examination of scales and fins. Use very small pieces of tissue, add plenty of water, and top with a glass coverslip. Apply gentle pressure on the coverslip to flatten the field.

Fish can be killed by pithing, that is, by severing the spinal cord with a sharp instrument. An overdose with an anesthetic agent is an alternative way of killing a fish. For this purpose, two tablets of Alka-Seltzer® in 500 to 1,000 millimeters (17 to 34 fluid ounces) of water will initially anesthetize and eventually kill the fish.

Examination of wet mounts of gills and skin should be done without delay after the fish is killed. To examine gills, remove the operculum and cut out a very small portion of the gill lamellae, avoiding the cartilaginous gill arch. Transfer the tissue to a glass slide, add a few drops of water, and use two needles to tease apart the gill lamellae. Top with a coverslip, and add enough water to fill the space beneath it completely. A slight pressure on the coverslip will serve to flatten the viewing field.

Scrapings of skin should be done from head to tail fin and should be deep enough to remove some scales. The tail fin should always be examined because parasites tend to accumulate there —perhaps from hydrodynamic effects or because these areas are devoid of scales. Take scrapings from any areas which do not look normal.

The examination of internal organs is an important part of the necropsy procedure. When the abdominal cavity is opened initially, bacterial cultures of kidneys and liver can be taken. Examination of wet-mount preparations of small pieces of

organs can reveal the presence of a variety of protozoan and metazoan parasites, granulomas, and bacteria. Staining of impression smears of internal organs such as the liver and spleen can provide a basis for the diagnosis of systemic bacterial infection. Sections of intestines of small fish can be mounted between two slides and examined for metazoan parasites by means of an inverted ocular microscope.

Factors influencing clinical illness: Young fish are more susceptible to parasites than are mature

To expose abdominal organs, three incisions are required. The first two produce a flap (A), which is then removed (B).To expose the brain, cut as shown (C) with a sharp scalpel or scissors.

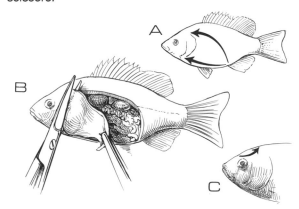

fish, partly because a smaller number of parasites is required to inflict damage to a host with a small versus a large body mass. Alternatively or additionally, mature fish may have developed specific immunity by response to previous subclinical infections or by exposure to antigens of non-pathogenic commensal organisms encountered in an aquatic system.

Environmental factors may enhance the clinical severity of parasitism, especially by those species involving the gills. Any water-quality change which can affect the efficiency of gills (pH, ammonia, nitrites, insufficient aeration) can exacerbate a parasitic infestation. Various parasites appear to be temperature-dependent. The common ciliated protozoan, *Ichthyophthirius multifiliis,* is predominantly associated with colder seasons. Coccidiosis of goldfish is a problem primarily during the winter season. Various types of monogenetic trematodes are affected by seasonal variations.

Immunity plays an important role in the relative resistance of fish to parasites. For example, fish have been shown to be resistant to *Ichthyophthirius multifiliis* after having survived an infection, and there is good evidence that fish will develop resistance to monogenetic trematodes.

Nutritional problems have long been associated with parasitism in mammals, and the same holds true for fish. For example, deficiencies in vitamin E appear to reduce macrophage activity in trout. From clinical experience it is apparent that fish fed a high-quality diet and kept in good water are less likely to develop a clinically apparent illness from parasites.

The presence of other parasites also has an effect. Mixed infestations are common and may influence the severity of the clinical disease. For example, fish debilitated with a massive infestation of metacercariae or nematodes are frequently the first to die in an epizootic caused by common external protozoans such as *Chilodonella cyprini.*

The pathogenesis of parasitic diseases: The eventual outcome of a parasitic infestation is variable. Parasites which kill fish can do so in many ways. Broadly speaking, these effects may be internal or external.

Internal parasites include those embedded in the skin as well as those which are located in specific organs of the body (muscles, intestines, liver, eyes, etc.) or within the peritoneal cavity. The types of parasites are diverse and include proto-zoan ciliates and flagellates, sporozoans, nematodes, trematodes, and tapeworms.

Massive infestations of gills and skin can result in death due to damage to gill epithelium, which leads in turn to failure of respiration, osmoregulation, and excretion. Heavy infestations by intestinal protozoans such as *Hexamita* apparently interfere with proper nutrition, possibly due to competition for essential nutrients and/or damage to intestinal epithelium.

External parasites often provide routes of entry for pathogenic bacteria which kill the fish. Heavy infestations of migrating nematodes or metacercariae of digenetic trematodes may be tolerated if vital organs are not involved. (However, in many cases, vital organs are involved, resulting in unthrifty and disease-prone fish.) Sporozoan parasites such as *Mitraspora* in goldfish may lodge specifically in kidney tubules, causing bloat and

Ichthyophthirius, the causative organism of "white spot," is apparent on a goldfish (below). Microscopic examination (bottom) shows round to oval organisms from 30 to 1,000 microns in size which move by means of surrounding cilia. Found on gills and skin, the organisms are common in aquarium fish.

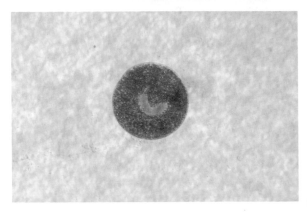

eventual kidney failure. Some parasites, such as species of *Oodinium,* may elaborate a toxin while infecting the fish.

External Protozoan Parasites

Ichthyophthirius multifiliis

This protozoan is the cause of white spot disease, commonly referred to as "ich." Distributed worldwide, it affects all freshwater fish and under aquarium conditions is very virulent. (The disease's counterpart in saltwater fish is caused by *Cryptocaryon irritans.*) These parasites are unique in that they have a complex life cycle which includes stages on the host as well as in the environment.

Ich is readily identified by most aquarists, who generally observe the disease several days after introducing new fish to the aquarium. Predominant signs include small white spots over the body. In some cases, infestation is limited to gills. Each white spot, called a theront, is the encysted feeding stage of a protozoan. Eventually, the theront enlarges, breaks through the epithelium, and drops to the bottom of the aquarium, where it attaches to objects such as gravel or tubing. At this point, the organism is referred to as a trophozoite (sometimes called trophont). The attached trophozoite then begins to undergo mitosis, producing numerous young individuals or tomites. Within the period of eighteen to twenty-one hours (at 23 to 25 degrees C or about 73 to 77 degrees F), hundreds of ciliated tomites are produced, which are released into the water. They actively penetrate skin and gill epithelium and enlarge until they are visible as white spots.

A diagnosis of ich can be confirmed by microscopic examination of skin or gills. Trophozoites may appear round or oval; occasionally a U-shaped nucleus is formed. Individual organisms vary in diameter from 30 microns to 1 millimeter. The organism moves slowly by means of cilia, which are observable with a high-power objective. *Ichthyophthirius* is one of the few fish parasites with cilia surrounding the entire organism.

Since medicaments cannot penetrate encysted theronts, all treatment is directed toward preventing reinfection of fish by free-swimming tomites. Malachite green, formalin, and malachite green–formalin mixtures have been used for treatment of freshwater fish. Copper sulfate has been used for saltwater fish.

In addition to chemotherapeutics, a few man-

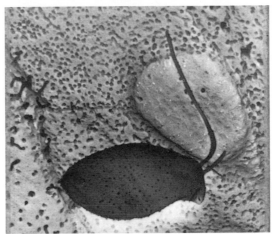

Ichthyobodo, or *Costia,* frequently affects aquarium fish. It is associated with respiratory distress and causes excess slime on the fish skin, which is noticeable as a white sheen (top). An electron micrograph (above) shows the small (less than 10 microns) flagellate that attaches to fish gills and skin.

agement procedures will serve to control infestation. Elevating the water temperatures to 26 degrees C (78.8 degrees F), several degrees over normal aquarium temperatures, for several days will tend to limit the infection by adversely affecting the heat-sensitive theronts as well as by enhancing the immune response of the host. This usually allows a cure in seven to ten days, but attention must be paid to temperature and pH regulation to avoid unduly stressing fish.

Heavy filtration with diatomaceous earth filters will tend to reduce the number of tomites. Transferring fish to a series of clean "hospital" aquaria once a day for seven days will limit the infection by keeping one step ahead of theront reinfestation. In practice, this can be done using one hospital aquarium and making daily water changes, and cleaning of the inside glass surface to remove trophozoites.

Some aquarists prefer not to medicate aquarium water because of the presence of plants and, especially in the case of marine aquaria, invertebrates. If fish are moved for treatment to a separate aquarium equipped with a heater and filter, parasites in the main aquarium will eventually die for lack of a host. To be absolutely sure that theronts are eliminated, make at least one complete water change along with removing debris from the gravel, and elevate the temperature several degrees over normal temperatures. In saltwater aquaria, it has been shown that aquaria devoid of fish for thirty days were still infective. With cleaning of gravel, water changes, and elevated temperatures, this period should be considerably reduced.

Ichthyobodo necatrix

This flagellated organism was previously named *Costia necatrix* and the name "costia" is frequently used as a common name for the parasite. A wide variety of fish can be infected, including trout, channel catfish, goldfish, and most common ornamental varieties. There is no known counterpart in saltwater aquarium fish, but similar organisms have been found on haddock off the coast of Nova Scotia.

Ichthyobodo infestations are seen more frequently in fish which have recently been shipped from a primary producer such as a goldfish producer or a tropical fish farmer. They are relatively rare in home aquaria since infestations normally affect fish at the wholesale or retail level, making them unsuitable for sale. The organism affects fish year-round, but the disease is more serious in warmer water.

Feeding directly on epithelial cells by penetration by the flagella, the parasite destroys gill and skin epithelium. Excess mucus production is frequently observed, which appears as a whitish film on the surface of the body. Respiratory distress is common, and fish appear depressed and refuse to eat. Some fish may die without visible external signs.

Diagnosis is confirmed by microscopic examination of wet mounts of skin and gills. Organisms are actively motile, small (7 microns), somewhat comma-shaped, and may be free-swimming or attached to cells by flagella. When attached,

Chilodonella has slow motility, and shortly after wet-mount preparation (top), it is apt to die. An electronmicrograph (above) shows a flat organism that tends to be heart-shaped, with apical cilia and longitudinal striations.

parasites move in a circular fashion. Treatments with common antiparasite drugs are effective.

Chilodonella cyprini

There is no common name for infestations with this parasite. A saltwater counterpart, *Brooklynella horridus,* is occasionally seen. Freshwater fish infections are common in cultured food-fish species, goldfish, and a variety of freshwater tropical species. As with *Ichthyobodo necatrix* infestations, *Chilodonella* infestations are infrequent in home aquaria, since the infestation would initially be encountered by wholesalers and retailers.

Respiratory distress, clamped fins, and depression are the principal signs of infection. Excessive mucus production is commonly observed. In a few clinical cases we have observed fish with *Chilodonella* die suddenly without apparent signs of disease.

Diagnosis is confirmed by examination of wet mounts of gills and skin. Organisms appear oval and flattened with a suggestion of being heart-shaped. Cilia appear in rows. Size is approximately 50 to 70 microns. Organisms move slowly, oftentimes in a characteristically slow circular fashion. In a matter of minutes after wet mounts are made, the organisms begin to die. Dead organisms appear round, with a granular interior. The parasite is susceptible to common parasiticides. Salt at 0.3 percent (3 grams/liter) is an effective treatment.

Oodinium

Infections with *Oodinium* are commonly called "velvet," "gold dust disease," "rust disease," and "coral fish disease." Three or four species have been associated with freshwater, brackish, and marine fish. In pet shops where the organism has been established and perpetuated by contaminated nets, many species of fish can become infected. Some, such as the danios and their relatives, may show more severe clinical disease than others.

A dinoflagellate, *Oodinium* can vary in size from 40 to 100 microns. It is found on the skin and gills of fish and contains chlorophyll, which imparts color to the organism. The principal sign of the infestation is the presence of the organism on the fish skin, which gives the skin a fine dusty appearance. Observation can be enhanced by directing the beam of a flashlight on the dorsal aspect of the fish in a darkened room. On microscopic examination of wet mounts of skin and gills, pear-shaped cysts attached to the underlying tissues can be observed.

Contained within the cysts are the maturing

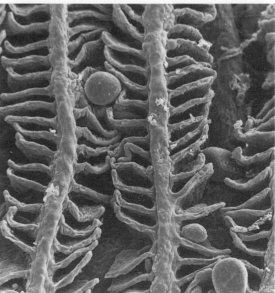

Oodinium is common in marine and freshwater aquaria. On the gills and skin of fish (below), it causes a yellow color. As is evident in both photomicrographs (top right) and electron micrographs (below right), the individual parasites are pear-shaped, anchor to tissues, and contain developing spores.

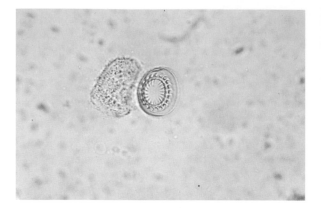

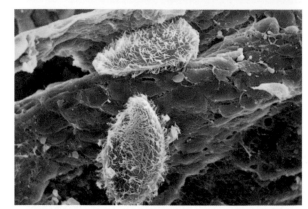

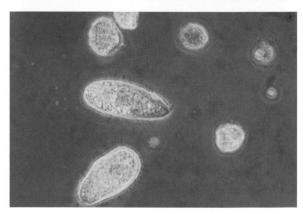

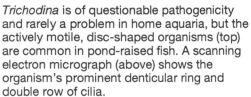

Trichodina is of questionable pathogenicity and rarely a problem in home aquaria, but the actively motile, disc-shaped organisms (top) are common in pond-raised fish. A scanning electron micrograph (above) shows the organism's prominent denticular ring and double row of cilia.

Tetrahymena is actively motile and frequently invasive on aquarium fish (top). An electronmicrograph (middle) shows organisms on the surface of a fish eye, and a stained preparation (above) outlines pear-shaped, ciliated organisms with vacuoles.

dinospores, which are released at some time after the cysts drop off the fish. The dinospores have flagella and are motile. Treatment of both freshwater and saltwater species involves maintaining a level of 0.1 to 0.2 parts per million (ppm) of copper in the aquarium for a period of ten days. Reinfection is a common problem and may be associated with the parasite's ability to colonize the intestine.

Trichodinids

Trichodinids are ciliated, circular, and flattened, and have denticular rings. They measure approxi-

mately 40 to 60 nanometers in diameter. Three common genera include *Trichodina*, *Trichodinella*, and *Tripartiella*. Species of the latter two genera are smaller than *Trichodina* and have incomplete rings of cilia. They also appear to inflict more injury to gills of fish, since they attach firmly to gill tissue. A marine counterpart similar to *Trichodinella* has been associated with gills.

Parasites in this group are common on the skin and gills of pond-reared fish, especially if the water has a high organic load. All cultivated fish are susceptible, including pond-reared tropical fish, goldfish, channel catfish, and trout. Heavy infestations can cause respiratory problems in fry reared in ponds. Skin lesions have been observed, and some parasite species have been reported to infect the urinary bladder and oviducts.

Trichodinids are rarely a problem in the home aquaria, since water changes associated with shipping and transportation usually cure infected fish. It is not uncommon to observe *Trichodina* infestations on goldfish in wholesale or retail establishments; infestations are generally very light and apparently do not affect the host fish. Infected pond fish are easily treated with common antiprotozoan drugs. Removal of fish to fresh water often is also effective.

Tetrahymena

The ciliated protozoan *Tetrahymena pyriformis* is usually found as a free-living infusorian, but occasionally will become parasitic. It can be found in decaying food in any aquarium and is frequently a secondary (or tertiary) invader of lesions initiated by other parasites and/or bacteria. It is possible that various strains of *Tetrahymena* have a potential for being more virulent, especially with immunologically weakened fish in water with high organic content. Unfortunately, the term "guppy killer" has been used for the disease. Although many species of live-bearing fish can become infected, the parasite has been associated with a variety of ornamental fish, including cichlids and various tetra species.

On the body of affected fish, whitish areas surrounded by hemorrhage may occur. Foci of parasites have been found in many internal tissues, including muscles and brain, and in tissues surrounding the eye. A diagnosis is confirmed by wet-mount preparations, which will reveal hundreds of actively motile, pear-shaped, ciliated parasites approximately 60 by 100 microns.

A marine counterpart, *Uronema miamiensis*, is frequently seen on marine ornamental fish. Large areas of skin are discolored and may be hemorrhagic. Scrapings reveal many pear-shaped ciliates. The lesions appear to be complicated by

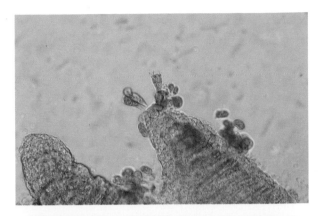

Epistylis, stalked organisms considered epiphytes, are common in aquarium fish and may mimic true fungi. Here, *Epistylis* is attached to the gill lamellae (top). Colonizing fish in highly organic water where epiphytes normally flourish, these organisms appear as white tufted areas such as these colonies (above) on the pectoral and anal fins of an ornamental catfish (*Corydoras julii*).

invasion of *Pseudomonas*, which may be responsible for the death of the fish.

Prospects for the treatment of the disease are discouraging. Improvement of water quality to reduce infusorial growth will help to avoid the problem. Baths in external parasiticides (formaldehyde, etc.) may reduce external parasites but will not affect internal parasites. Maintaining good water quality and good nutrition should assist in preventing attack by this opportunistic parasite.

Epistylis

This and related species such as *Vorticella* are stalked, ciliated protozoans which are generally found attached to vegetation or crustaceans. In aquaria or ponds high in organic matter, they proliferate and attach to fish or eggs. *Epistylis* can be found on any fish coming from any source of organically enriched water. The organism is frequently seen to affect goldfish and many species of bottom-dwelling fish such as ornamental catfish. The problem appears to be limited to freshwater fish. Frequently the parasite will be seen as a white area or white tuft on the surface of the fish body or fins. It has been found in ulcerated areas from which the bacteria *Aeromonas hydrophila* has been isolated, but which organism initiated the problem is unknown. Fish eggs may become infested, resulting in low hatchability. Diagnosis is confirmed by making wet-mount preparations of affected areas. Bell-shaped ciliated organisms on stalks are characteristic. Apical cilia are present. The body of the organism will be seen to contract periodically from an elongated form to ball-shaped. The stalk tends to coil during the contraction phase.

In aquaria, *Epistylis* problems are best avoided by regular cleaning of gravel and careful feeding to minimize the organic substrates on which the organisms multiply. Treatment can be accomplished by swabbing the affected area with tincture of iodine. Formaldehyde at 25 ppm would also be a good approach for treatment of fish. Among ornamental fish, eggs affected with the organism can be dipped (for thirty seconds) in 66 ppm of malachite green or in solutions of iodophores.

Another epistylid, *Heteropolaria colisarum,* has been associated with a variety of North American fishes, causing a problem called "red sore" disease. The same species was isolated from the skin of giant gouramis. A single treatment in a 1.5 percent salt bath for three hours or until the fish is stressed has controlled this species.

Glossatella and *Scyphidia*

Like epistylids, these organisms are considered to be free-living and problematic to fish only in water high in organic content, where they also can be found on vegetation and inanimate objects. Both of these genera are rarely found on fish in home aquaria, but may occasionally parasitize fish in production ponds. Both have a vaselike morphology with one or two rows of cilia. Heavy infestations on the body and gills of small fish can cause respiratory problems and death. These organisms are associated with pond-raised goldfish, channel catfish, and ornamental fish varieties. No marine counterpart is known. They apparently are removed from the fish when exposed to fresh water and consequently are rarely

Scyphidia is a vase-shaped organism found attached to skin and gills. It is common in pond-reared ornamental fish, goldfish, and channel catfish, but is rarely a problem in ornamental fish.

seen in commercial or domestic aquaria. Treatment in ponds can be accomplished by a variety of external parasiticides, including formaldehyde, potassium permanganate, malachite green, or copper sulfate.

Glossatella, a protozoan inhabitant of ponds high in organic matter, is characterized by a single row of cilia and a pear-shaped form. Although it can be found on the skin and gills of pond-reared fish, it is rarely a problem in home aquaria.

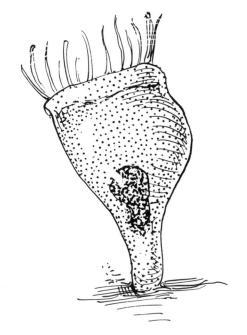

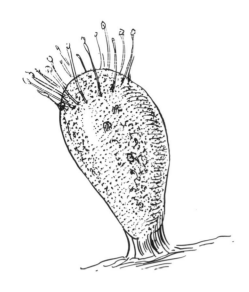

Trichophrya is a suctorian parasite common on the gills of pond-raised fish, and can be associated with respiratory distress. However, it is rare in ornamental fish in home aquaria.

Trichophrya

Suctorian parasites associated with fishes reared in ponds, *Trichophrya* frequently are found in channel catfish and may reach a level of infestation at which respiration is impaired. They have not been a problem in ornamental fishes, but it is

Cryptobia frequently affects the gills of pond-raised fish, especially goldfish.

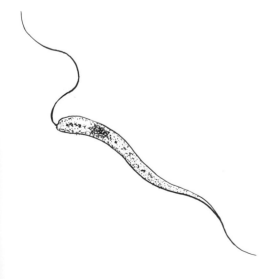

likely that infestations occasionally do occur in pond-reared tropical fish. These parasites are usually found on the gills and are identified by their characteristic pin-cushion appearance.

Cryptobia

Cryptobia are found on gills of goldfish and could be confused with *Ichthyobodo necatrix*. The parasites are flagellated and are approximately 10 microns long. By microscopic examination, the parasites appear to be attached to gill tissues by the flagella and have a wavelike movement when compared to *Ichthyobodo.* The organisms apparently are quite common but do not appear to cause disease.

External Worms

Monogenetic trematodes

Flatworms are common parasites of freshwater and marine fishes. Most species are associated with the skin and gills of fish. A few species can infect the stomach of fish, and some have been found in the urinary bladder. Monogenetic trematodes of ornamental fish can be broadly classified into two families, the Dactylogyridae and the Gyrodactylidae.

Dactylogyridae may be recognized by a four-pointed anterior end, a sucker near the anterior end, and four anterior eyespots. At the caudal end of the worm, a fixation apparatus (haptor) consists of one or two large hooks surrounded by up to sixteen smaller hooklets. Mature worms are approximately 200 microns in length. The worms have both testes and ovaries (a condition called hermaphroditism). Self-fertilization is followed by the release of eggs which develop off of the host. Eggs from some species hatch into ciliated forms in as few as sixty hours; hatching of other species may require four to five days. The ciliated larvae attack suitable hosts and lose their cilia.

Of the many genera, *Dactylogyrus* is the most important. Many species have been described. Dactylogyrids are usually associated with the gills, and for that reason are called gill flukes. If present in sufficient numbers, they can cause hyperplasia, destruction of gill epithelium, and clubbing of gill filaments, resulting in asphyxiation.

Gill flukes are common in aquarium fish and can infest species of all major groups. Pond-raised fish such as goldfish may be heavily infested. Infections often appear in imported and domestic tank-reared angelfish and discus. Clini-

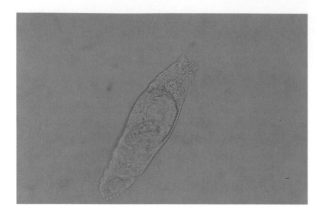

Gyrodactylus is a monogenetic trematode found on the skin and fins of fish; closely related forms are found on gills. It is common in both freshwater and marine ornamental fish. Note the embryo visible within the body of this hermaphrodite organism.

cal signs are rarely if ever associated with infestations of fish in the wild or in uncrowded ponds. However, such signs are common in aquaria and holding vats, where crowding greatly enhances the probability of transmission.

Clinical signs can include rapid respiratory movements, clamped fins, flashing or rubbing, inactive fish at the bottom of the aquarium, and death. Diagnosis can be confirmed by biopsies of gills; worms are readily apparent. Gill flukes can proliferate to numbers which can cause clinical disease in channel catfish (*Ictalurus punctatus*) held in 76-liter (20-gallon) aquaria. Under these conditions, we have determined that the parasite load per fish from a single aquarium can be quite variable—from hundreds of parasites in each of the four gill arches to none. Whether this variability is attributable to immunity or chance is not known.

A second genus of flatworms, *Gyrodactylus,* is commonly found on fish. Many species have been described. Although they occasionally may be found on the gills, these parasites are usually found on the skin.

The worms may be up to 0.8 millimeters in length, and have two points at the anterior end. An anterior sucker is present, but eyespots are absent. The worms are viviparous, and embryos with prominent hooks are commonly seen within the adult parasites. An attachment organ (haptor) with two large hooks surrounded by up to sixteen smaller hooklets is located at the caudal end.

The parasites move about the skin surface by grasping the host alternately with the anterior sucking disc and the haptor.

Inapparent *Gyrodactylus* infections are common. Parasites feed on blood and epithelium by scraping and sucking. When present, lesions can include localized hemorrhagic areas, excessive mucus, and localized ulcerations. Infected fish may have a ragged-appearing tail resulting from localized hyperplasia, necrosis of the tips of the fins, and loss of epithelial cells. Secondary infections with bacteria (*Aeromonas, Flexibacter*) are common. We have isolated *Aeromonas hydrophila* from gyrodactylids removed from goldfish, which suggests that the worms may actively transmit bacteria.

Specific treatments for monogenetic trematode infections include long-term exposure to 25 ppm of formaldehyde, short-term formaldehyde baths at concentrations from 50 to 250 ppm, 2.5 to 3 percent saltwater baths (for freshwater fish), or freshwater baths at pH 8.3 (for saltwater fish). Organophosphates have been used at 0.25 ppm for freshwater fish and 0.5 to 1.0 ppm for saltwater fish. However, it appears that with extended use of organophosphates, monogenetic trematodes have developed resistance. Experimentally, we have shown that praziquantel (Droncit™) will effectively remove monogenetic trematodes from gills and body surfaces in infected goldfish when added to aquaria at 2 ppm.

Turbellarians

Occasionally seen as free-living pests in an aquarium, these flatworms can be a source of concern for aquarists who observe small (5 to 7 millimeters, or 0.2 to 0.3 inches) white worms on the sides of the aquarium. On microscopic examination, two eyespots may be visible on some species, and living young may be seen developing within mature worms. Turbellarians may lodge on fish—especially on those which prefer the bottom of an aquarium. The worms generally have a greater effect on the aquarist than on the fish. Marine turbellarians are common.

Turbellarians develop where organic matter accumulates from overfeeding of fish and failure to clean gravel. The worms usually can be controlled by reducing feed, promptly removing excess food, and regularly cleaning gravel with a distended-end siphon hose. Formaldehyde treatments at 25 ppm for twelve to twenty-four hours followed by a water change and gravel cleaning will rid the aquarium of these pests.

Leeches

In home aquaria, leeches are occasional pests and are most frequently introduced with plants, stones, snails, and almost any other object taken from an infested pond. There are several genera, and leeches are found worldwide. They can be seen with the naked eye as small (5 millimeters to 1 centimeter, or 0.2 to 0.4 inches) wormlike organisms frequently found on the gravel or clinging to real or artificial plants. When disturbed by water motion, leeches will lengthen, and on contacting a fish (or human), immediate attachment results. Leeches will suck blood from their host, then eventually detach and drop to the bottom of the aquarium, where they multiply.

Leeches are a principal vector for *Trypanosoma,* a flagellated blood parasite. Damage to the fish during the sucking process creates an entry site for bacteria. There is a potential for leeches to transmit mycobacterial infections.

Leech contamination can be prevented by bleaching any inanimate objects (rock, gravel, pieces of wood) taken from ponds or rivers before using them for decorative purposes in the aquarium. Live plants frequently are a source of leeches and should be soaked in alum (1 tablespoon per gallon of water, or approximately 1.7 grams per liter of water) or rinsed under tepid tap water prior to addition to the aquarium. To rid an aquarium of leeches, treat it with an organophosphate at 0.25 ppm. In the authors' experience, 25 ppm of formaldehyde followed by a cleansing of the gravel twenty-four hours after treatment was successful in removal of leeches from fish and aquaria.

External Crustaceans

Parasitic copepods

Crustaceans belonging to the subclass Copepoda include the parasites *Lernaea* and *Ergasilus.* Like most other crustaceans, they lay eggs. The first larvae to hatch swim freely at first, then attach to the gills of a suitable host and enter a nonswimming phase in which they complete their maturation. After mating, the males cease being parasitic, but mated females reattach to or penetrate the fish and mature to forms which can be seen with the naked eye.

Commonly called the "anchor worm" because of the wormlike appearance of the females as

Lernaea, commonly called the "anchor worm," is a parasitic copepod. The anchor, actually its head, is embedded in the dermis of this goldfish. Eggs of *Lernaea* pass through several molts prior to parasitizing new hosts. Infected fish commonly enter commercial trade.

they cling on the fish's skin, *Lernaea* is an elongated copepod (up to 1 centimeter, or 0.2 inches). Several species have been described. A female anchors herself on the fish by burrowing into its body with her head. At its maximum length, the anchor worm takes on a characteristic V-shape from the two egg sacs protruding from the free end of the worm's body. Fish may be affected with many of these parasites, causing irritation and localized hemorrhagic reactions at the point of entry, which may become secondarily infected with bacteria.

The problem is generally seen in koi and goldfish production ponds, but any species of fish can be affected. In wholesale or retail establishments having central systems without adequate filtration or ultraviolet light sterilization, the infestation can spread throughout all aquaria. In individual aquaria within pet retail outlets, an introduced carrier fish can initiate an infection which will affect any species within the aquarium.

Since the parasite is easily recognized, continued treatment with organophosphates will control infections in large operations. Dipping freshwater fish into saltwater aquaria for five to ten minutes a day will result in death of the parasites. During this treatment, parasites will eventually turn a greenish color, wither, and be expelled from the fish. In situations where only a very few fish are affected, worms may be removed by extraction; use forceps and avoid breaking the worm. Local treatment can be done with cotton swabs perme-

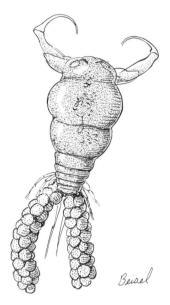

Ergasilus is a parasitic copepod found on the gills of wild-caught or pond-raised ornamental fish. It is rare in home aquaria.

ated with a suitable disinfectant (iodine, acriflavine, alcohol). Any treatment of fish should also include the removal of juvenile forms. This can be done by adding organophosphates (0.25 ppm) or by a simple successive series of water changes with gravel cleaning. Dimilin™ at 2 ppm is effective in controlling the parasite.

As a result of infection with anchor worms, many fish may not be marketable because of the external lesions. Antibiotic treatment of larger fish by intraperitoneal injection of chloramphenicol (1 milligram per 40-gram [1.4-ounce] fish) may accelerate healing of lesions. Where injection is not practical, antibiotics may be added to water to stem secondary bacterial problems. Consider using tetracyclices, kanamycin, or sulfa drugs at 12 ppm for three treatments on alternate days. Water changes between treatments are recommended. Remove activated carbon from filters and remove air stems from undergravel filters to avoid pulling medicaments through filter media. Continue aeration.

The parasitic copepod *Ergasilus* resembles the anchor worm. It is found firmly attached to the gills of fish by specialized prehensile hooks. It occasionally is found in ornamental fish production ponds, but rarely is a problem in commercial outlets or home aquaria. Under microscopic ex-

amination, the parasites appear to be multicolored. They are too small for mechanical removal. Treatment in production ponds is done with organophosphates at 0.25 to 1 ppm.

Argulus

The fish louse *Argulus* is a member of the subclass Branchiura. It is flat and has prominent eyes, sucking discs, and a stiletto. Transparent, it tends to take on the color of the fish which it parasitizes. Fish lice are easily seen with the naked eye, for they range from approximately 5 to 8 millimeters (0.2 to 0.3 inches) in length.

While sucking blood, fish lice inflict injury with the stiletto, the injection of which causes a focal hemorrhagic area. It is thought that toxic substances released by the parasite during feeding are responsible for the severe local reaction surrounding the area of the sting. Ulcerations often follow fish lice infestation; they probably are the result of secondarily invading bacteria such as *Aeromonas* and *Pseudomonas.* It has been suggested that argulids may carry these bacteria in addition to blood parasites such as trypanosomes. Wounds are frequently infected with fungi.

Fish lice can parasitize any fish but are most important in goldfish production ponds. Under pond conditions, argulids lay their eggs on plants and stones. Hatching occurs in four weeks, at which time they actively seek a host. Sexual maturity develops after lice have parasitized a fish for five to six weeks. Organophosphates at a concentration of 0.25 to 1 ppm are used to control fish lice in these situations.

Occasionally, fish lice appear on individual fish in wholesale and retail outlets. Individual para-

Argulus, the fish louse, is a parasitic branchiuran. It is common in ponds and at the wholesale level, but is rare in home aquaria.

sites can be removed with forceps. In cases involving many fish, lice can be removed by treating aquaria with organophosphates (0.25 to 1 ppm), dipping fish in potassium permanganate baths (50 to 70 ppm) for fifteen seconds, or bathing fish in formaldehyde baths (150 to 200 ppm) for fifteen to thirty minutes or until fish appear stressed.

Livoneca

Parasitic isopods (order Isopoda) are rare but spectacular when found on fish. The organisms are segmented, have several pairs of legs, and can be 1 to 2 centimeters (0.4 to 0.8 inches) in length. They generally burrow into the gill or buccal cavity, but may excavate and live in a cavity in the lateral musculature. One species, *Livoneca symmetrica,* has been described. Apparently parasites attack fish in the wild or in production ponds, and on some fish, well-concealed parasites may go unnoticed by wholesalers and retailers. *Livoneca symmetrica* can move about the fish and is readily recognized and easily removed.

Internal Protozoans

Hexamita

These flagellated protozoans are found in the gastrointestinal tracts of a variety of fish. *Octomitus* is an old term for the protozoan when the parasite was thought to have eight flagella. Similarly, the name "discus parasite" has been used because of its frequent infection of discus fish. A closely related parasite, *Spironucleus,* may be a distinct species from *Hexamita* and appears longer and possibly more sinuous. However, for practical purposes both appear to cause a similar clinical disease.

In many fishes, including trout, goldfish, and a variety of freshwater aquarium species, infections can be inapparent. However, in certain ornamental fishes such as angelfish, discus, and gouramis, the disease is characterized by poor condition, lack of appetite, unthriftiness, weight loss, and death. Clinically apparent disease most often is associated with young fish. It may be seen at the producer, wholesale, or retail level, and in home aquaria. Infestations in adult breeding angelfish can result in reduced levels of hatched eggs or in death of young fry after hatching.

The parasites are about the size of red blood cells and are very motile. Microscopic observation will show highly motile flagellates in feces, or if a fish is available for necropsy, massive

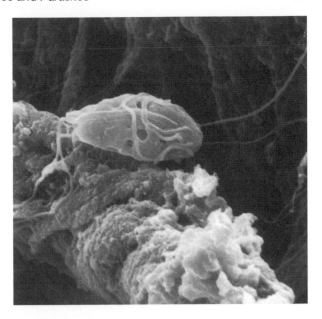

Hexamita is an important cause of mortalities in home aquaria. These actively motile flagellates are found in the intestines (and infrequently in the liver) of angelfish, goldfish, discus, and gouramis.

infestations in the intestines. In severe cases, the organisms can be found in the liver, gallbladder, and occasionally the kidney. Infections can be effectively treated by the addition of 5 ppm of metronidazole to aquarium water. Since *Hexamita* can be kept alive in laboratory media, we assume that it is an inhabitant of aquaria where organic material has been allowed to accumulate. Cleaning of gravel and filter materials will assist in treating this problem.

"Hole-in-the-head," a disease frequently seen in discus, angelfish, red oscars, and other cichlid fishes, has been associated with the presence of *Hexamita.* However, a direct causal relationship has not been established. Massive doses of metronidazole will not resolve the lesions seen along the lateral line system. In scanning electron micrographs, we have not been able to associate either bacteria or parasites with lesions. The "hole-in-the-head" condition has been variously attributed to *Hexamita,* bacterial infections, poor nutrition, dirty aquaria, and use of activated carbon. The latter observation comes from breeders of cichlids, who claim that the problem is avoided when they delete activated carbon from their filter systems. In any case, treatment should be directed toward therapy with antibiotics and metronidazole,

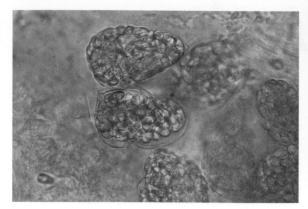

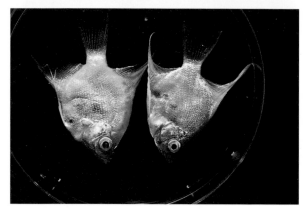

The microsporidian *Pleistophora hyphessobryconis* is the causative agent of neon tetra disease, a common affliction of aquarium fish associated with high mortalities. An affected neon tetra (top left) shows whitish area containing spores. Affected fish (below left) may have a lumpy appearance. A squash preparation (above) shows the spores typically found in wet mounts of muscles.

regular cleaning of aquarium gravel with water changes, and improved nutrition.

Sporozoans

Coccidiosis is one of the most familiar sporozoan diseases recognizable by veterinarians in mammals and birds. Coccidia are also common intestinal parasites of fish, where their life cycles are just as complicated as in mammals and birds, and the clinical signs can vary as widely.

Among ornamental fish, coccidiosis is most often observed in goldfish during the winter and spring, particularly under pond conditions when fish may not be fed and their immunological responsiveness may be decreased. *Eimeria* species are the culprits. The disease is also occasionally seen in home aquaria. Clinical signs include depression and emaciation with sunken eyes. A yellow-colored fluid can be expressed from the intestines. Diagnosis is made by identifying the oocysts in wet-mount preparations of intestinal scrapings or feces. Treatment, if required, may be attempted by inclusion of anticoccidials in food. Monensin™ at 100 ppm in food may be a good choice, or possibly Salinomycin™ at 10 ppm in food.

Other sporozoans belonging to the subphylum Cnidospora, classes Microsporidea and Myxosporidea, are frequent parasites of ornamental fish. Members of both classes have spindle-shaped polar capsules within their spores; microsporids have one, and myxosporids have two. Identification of genera of the Myxosporidea is based on position of the polar capsules.

A common microsporid is *Pleistophora hyphessobryconis.* Infection causes a disease whose signs include the appearance of whitened areas in the musculature and a resultant aberrant swimming motion. The name "neon disease" reflects the fact that this condition was originally found in neon tetras, but is misleading in that many other species of fish also are susceptible. We have diagnosed the disease in a variety of angelfish, barbs, rasboras, and tetras. In neon tetras, high mortality rates are common. In angelfish, we have noted that the parasite can cause muscle necrosis, which results in an uneven, undulating look to the body surface. In other cases involving white angelfish, a strong focalized melanophore response results in an appearance which the fish producer refers to as "black holes."

The course of the disease in groups of infected neon tetras is invariably fatal. It is not uncommon to see bloated fish, but bloating appears to be attributable to a variety of bacteria which are secondary invaders. Mycobacterial infections are also common in neon tetras, as are concomitant infections. In mature angelfish the disease has a chronic course, resulting only in deformities of the musculature.

Diagnosis of *Pleistophora* is confirmed by examining impression smears or wet mounts of muscles from the affected area in which pansporoblasts are observed, filled with spores containing one polar capsule. Treatment attempts have been discouraging. Claims of cures using either formaldehyde or naladixic acid have not been substantiated in controlled experiments. Our experience suggests that the mortality rate in a group of infected fish is initially high. The remaining fish appear healthy at first but will die off over a period of weeks, suggesting a gradual extension of the parasite within the body.

Within an aquarium system, the disease can be limited by removing dying fish before they are cannibalized. Periodic cleaning of gravel helps remove any spores which may have accumulated. In pond systems, control can be approached by draining and disinfecting ponds.In fish hatcheries in the Far East where many neon tetras are raised, the infection is probably spread by the feeding of live invertebrates such as tubifex worms, which may serve as intermediate hosts.

Many genera of Myxosporidea have been found in ornamental fish. Prominent among these are *Myxobolus, Henneguya, Myxidium,* and *Mitraspora. Myxobolus* can cause nodules on the skin and gills of various ornamental fish. Nodules may be few or numerous and from microscopic to several millimeters in size. Because of the whitish appearance of the infected areas, the

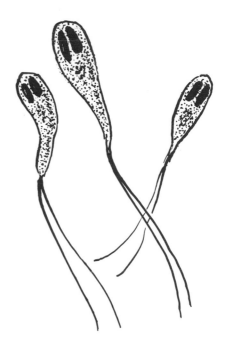

Henneguya sporoblasts appear as discrete white nodules on the fins and scales of some ornamental species. Hundreds of spores can be found in a sporoblast. The disease is not fatal.

disease has been given the common name "milk-scale disease." Infections with *Myxobolus* could be confused with other parasites, such as ich. Cysts do not appear to affect the fish in any way except in appearance; they are common and largely incidental findings in routine postmortem examinations of wild-caught fish. If cysts are objectionable, they can be lanced, followed by local application of antiseptics. Isolation of fish during recovery is suggested. Prevention of the disease in ornamental fish farms would be limited to ridding ponds of carrier fish, and liming and drying ponds between production runs.

Henneguya and *Myxidium* are also found as white cysts on the body surfaces and gills of a variety of wild-caught ornamental fish. *Henneguya* is frequently found on gills of wild-caught species of *Corydoras* and on dorsal fins of *Leporinus.* Again, these parasites cause no apparent harm except in appearance. Cysts associated with *Henneguya* infestations frequently disappear in time. Presumably, spores are released into the aquarium. Whether these infections are spread from infected to noninfected fish in aquaria is unknown, although from our observations, it ap-

Myxobolus produce a disfiguring disease but are not highly pathogenic. The spores produce white spots or nodules on the skin and gills of fish.

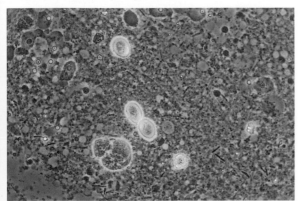

pears that some species of parasites may spread. On the other hand, *Henneguya* infections of *Leporinus* do not appear to spread to other fish species within an aquarium. It is possible that some species of these parasites require an intermediate host whereas others may spread directly.

In goldfish and koi, *Mitraspora cyprini,* commonly called "kidney bloater," causes massive kidney enlargement resembling a tumor. Fish become infected in ponds during the summer, but clinical signs are not seen until September or October. This disease is frequently observed in retail outlets and is common in goldfish kept in home aquaria. Apparently, asymptomatic fish are purchased in the summer and gradually bloat during the winter months. Though severely bloated, affected fish may live for months. The

Black spot disease on a silver-dollar fish is caused by larval forms of the digenetic trematode *Neascus*. The black spots may be mistaken for normal fish coloration.

Digenetic trematodes have a complex life cycle which includes both a ciliated stage that infests certain snails and a later form that attacks fish. The nodules on this live-bearer (below) contain digenetic trematodes. A histological preparation (bottom) shows trematodes in the gill cartilage of a golden barb.

disease is transmitted when spores are shed from urine in the spring. In a few case studies, it appears that the infection has spread to uninfected goldfish within the aquarium.

Drainage of the ascitic fluid is not recommended since fluid will reaccumulate almost immediately. Experimental injections of Lasix™ have not reduced the accumulation of fluids. Addition of 0.3 percent salt to the aquarium water may assist the fish in osmoregulation. Eventually, severely bloated fish will die. Chances of the infection spreading within an aquarium could be reduced by isolation of sick fish. Any treatment with anticoccidial drugs in food would be purely experimental and unpredictable. A diagnosis can be confirmed by wet-mount preparations of kidneys and identification of trophozoites or spores.

Cryptosporidia have been demonstrated in a marine ornamental fish, the naso tang (*Naso lituratus*). Signs include anorexia, regurgitation of food, and passage of feces containing undigested food. We have identified a cryptosporidia-like organism in intestinal sections of angelfish which had signs identical to those described for the naso tang. The condition appeared to be widespread in an angelfish hatchery. Fish were anorexic, lost condition, regurgitated food, and eventually died. The many unexplained deaths seen in angelfish may eventually prove to be infections with cryptosporidia or a closely related sporozoan.

Clinostomum "grubs" are actually larvae of digenetic trematodes. Here metacercariae are shown in the gill cavity of a pond-reared cichlid.

Internal Helminths

Digenetic trematodes

Digenetic trematodes in fish may occur as adult forms in the intestine of the fish or, more commonly, as intermediate stages encysted in tissues. It is rare to find tropical fish as final hosts with adult forms of the parasite within the intestine, but tropical fish frequently serve as the secondary intermediate host. In the majority of cases, the definitive host is a fish-eating bird which sheds parasite eggs into the water. These eggs eventually form ciliated miracidia which penetrate specific species of snails. After asexual development in snails, procercariae are released which penetrate fish. Here they develop into metacercariae enclosed in cysts.

Many genera of digenetic trematodes have been described, and many unidentified species exist. Since heavily infected fish are obvious to the exporter, the problem is relatively rare in retail outlets. However, some fish with inapparent signs may be shipped. Four groups of digenetic trematodes commonly seen are discussed below.

Larval forms of the genus *Neascus* are frequently seen in ornamental fish as round black spots (2 to 3 millimeters or about 0.08 to 0.12 inches) in the skin of fish. The black spots represent a melanophore reaction surrounding the encysted metacercariae. Silver-dollar fish are frequently infested. The black spots are not particularly offensive and are often mistaken for normal coloring or genetic variations!

The white to yellow larvae of species of *Clino-stomum* are commonly called grubs. Severely infected fish are not marketed, but cysts may occasionally be seen in retail stores. In such cases, the fish should not be sold until the parasite is removed by simple excision. In many cases, grubs are within the body cavity and deeply embedded in the musculature, and thus escape detection. Heavy infection with grubs results in fish which appear to be stunted. In one instance, we removed over 100 grubs from a fish 10 centimeters (4 inches) long.

In recent years, we have noted encysted metacercariae in gills of fish raised on some fish farms in Florida. These parasites belong to the family Heterophryidae. In some cases infestations have been massive, resulting in an extensive proliferation of gill cartilage and destruction of secondary lamellae. Severely infested fish may have protruding gills. Infested fish cannot be handled and will not survive standard shipping conditions. Cysts cannot be removed by chemicals. The infestation can be controlled in fish ponds by eliminating the snails (*Pleuracerca*) which serve as intermediate hosts.

Commonly called eye flukes, *Diplostomum* larvae can be found in the lens of a fish. The resulting opacity of the lens is noted as a "white eye." Fish are frequently blinded. A wide variety of birds may serve as final hosts for the mature parasite. The problem is rarely seen in retail outlets but could be a problem in fish farms. The disease can be controlled by snail control. Fish cannot be treated.

Tapeworms

While tapeworms are common in wild-caught fish, they are rarely found in ornamental fishes. When present, they are found within the intestines of fish, attached to the intestinal wall by means of a scolex, a headlike structure with four suckers. On some species of tapeworms, hooks may be present on the scolex. A common feature of many tapeworms is that they are segmented, with each segment (proglottid) having a complete set of reproductive organs. Tapeworms are disseminated by release of proglottids and eggs. These are eaten by some invertebrate, which is in turn eaten by the fish. The parasite develops into the adult form in the fish. Ornamental fish may serve as the secondary intermediate hosts for tapeworms of fish-eating waterfowl. In such cases, encysted larvae are embedded in internal organs of the fish or on the surfaces of internal organs. Larvae can be identified by the presence of a

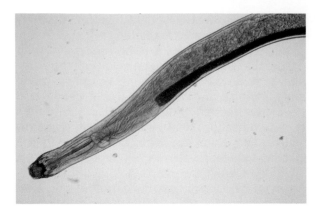

Intestinal nematodes are frequent parasites of live-bearing ornamental fish.

scolex with four suckers. Recent work suggests that praziquantel at 2 ppm in aquarium water will eliminate the parasites.

Nematodes

Often called roundworms in deference to their circular cross-section, nematodes are common in fish and can cause many problems. Worms are white to red in color, depending on species, and may range from a fraction of a centimeter to several centimeters in length. The external covering of the worm consists of a firm cuticle which maintains the circular shape of the parasite. Adult or larval nematodes can be found in ornamental fish within the lumen of the intestine, as free migratory forms in the peritoneal cavity, or encysted in internal organs or musculature. The life cycle is initiated when female worms in the intestine of infected fish shed eggs into the environment. An intermediate host such as an aquatic invertebrate (*Cyclops, Daphnia,* tubifex worms) may eat the eggs, which develop within it as larval parasites. When the invertebrate is eaten by a fish, larvae mature in the latter's intestine. At this point larvae may migrate to various organs or remain in the intestine. If this fish in turn is eaten by a larger fish, the predator also becomes infected. Details of the life cycles, required intermediate hosts, and migratory tendencies of larvae vary with the species of nematodes.

A number of nematode genera are associated with tropical fish, and it is generally believed by ornamental fish farmers that nematodes can be detrimental to fish. Larval forms of *Eustrongylides* are frequently found encysted in the muscles or peritoneum of fish. Most cause no harm and are found as red-colored worms on postmortem ex-

amination. Occasionally, cysts containing nematodes located close to the skin are confused with tumors. Nematodes found within the lumen of the intestine include *Capillaria* and *Camallanus*. *Capillaria* frequently are associated with ornamental fish, but their clinical significance is difficult to determine. They also are usually noted in routine postmortem examinations. Fish with heavy infestations should be treated (see below).

In clinical practice, infections with intestinal nematodes will initially be noticed as a red-colored worm protruding from the anus of a fish. The infestations appear to be seasonal and are frequently found in live-bearing fish such as guppies or swordtails. Treatment for *Camallanus* should be approached using common nematocides with food at the rate of 0.25 percent of food. Fenbendazol (Panacur™) would appear to be a good candidate for use with infected fish. We would suggest mixing it in commercial food enhanced with cod-liver oil and bound with gelatin. Since fish are quick to refuse food which has been medicated, withholding food for a few days prior to feeding medicated food may aid in acceptance.

Recent studies in which ivermectin has been added directly to aquarium water suggest that this drug may be useful in treating nematodes in fish. The dose used was 0.7 millimeters of a 1 percent injectable solution per 76 liters (20 gallons) of water. The dose was added over a period of four days (0.1, 0.2, 0.2, and 0.2 millimeters). At this writing, we suggest that any use of ivermectin for nematodes of fish be limited strictly to investigative purposes because of the high toxicity of the drug. Migratory forms of nematodes cannot be treated; one must avoid feeding fish with fresh-

Acanthocephalans are called "thorny-headed worms" for obvious reasons.

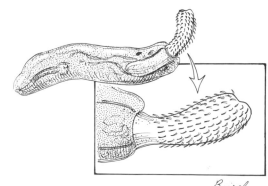

Beisel

water insect larvae or free-living copepods which may carry immature forms of the roundworms.

Acanthocephalans

Found in the intestinal tract of fish, acanthocephalans receive their common name, "thorny-headed worms," from small spicules which cover their heads and serve to anchor them to the intestinal lining. Acanthocephalans can be a problem in wild marine or freshwater fishes, but are not common in ornamental freshwater fish. In the few observed cases examined at the University of Georgia, the parasite load per fish was very low—generally, one or two parasites per fish. We observed no problems under these conditions. Worm infestations were detected during routine postmortem examinations. Wild-caught ornamental fish can serve as intermediate hosts when the final host is a bird or possibly a larger fish. The presence of the intermediate forms in low numbers does not appear to affect the fish.

Bacteria and Fish Disease

Bacteria are single-celled organisms characterized by a rigid cell wall and an indefinite-shaped nucleus. Thousands of species exist, functioning in roles as varied as nitrogen fixation, decomposition, fermentation, and disease production. Bacterial nutrition is very similar to that of higher animals, though on a simpler scale. Certain amino acids are essential for growth, and while some bacteria may utilize fat or protein, the nutrients of choice are carbohydrates. Because of a rigid cell wall, bacteria excrete enzymes into their environment which break down food into a form suitable for use. Similarly, the cell wall requires that food for bacterial use be soluble. Selective mechanisms in the bacterial cell wall control the type and quantity of nutrient needed for optimal bacterial growth. Growth is also controlled by the temperature and pH of the environment, since both of these factors exert a control over enzyme breakdown of food for bacterial use.

Bacteria vary greatly in average size, and range from 0.5 to 1.0 micron in width by 8 to 10 microns in length. They occur in a number of shapes and arrangements. Most commonly they are either rodlike (bacillus) or spherical (coccus) and occur either separately or in chains. A third, less common shape is spiral. All multiply by simple cell division.

Although bacterial shape and ability to use certain types of food separate species to a certain extent, classification of bacteria is complex. The most classic separation is by cell wall structure. A Danish physician in the late 1800s noted certain staining characteristics when using dyes. Those bacteria which stained blue and had little or no fat in the cell wall were termed gram-positive. Those with more fat in the cell wall were termed gram-negative. The majority of bacteria associated with fish and aquatic environments belong to the gram-negative group.

Pathogenicity: Two facts are fundamental, relative to bacteria in aquaria: (1) not all bacteria cause disease, and (2) in any aquarium or aquatic environment, a great number of different bacteria should be considered normal flora.

In an established aquarium containing fish, one would expect to find between one million and one billion bacteria within each one-half teaspoon (5 milliliters) of water, depending on the abundance of organic nutrients and the frequency of water changes. The largest proportion of these bacteria, the normal flora (normal inhabitants), live benignly in the environment, aiding in the establishment of the dynamic equilibrium of factors necessary to assure the survival of the ecosystem. This dominant group includes bacteria responsible for decomposition of waste products (nitrifying bacteria) as well as bacteria which can utilize nitrates under conditions of low oxygen.

A second group within this bacterial population could be considered opportunistic pathogens. Under a given set of conditions, these could cause disease, usually when some other factor in the aquatic environment weakens the fish enough for the bacteria to attack successfully. It is now understood that weakening of fish results in a compromised immune system which renders the fish susceptible to bacterial attack.

Only occasionally is a third and much smaller group of bacteria present: the primary pathogens. These organisms have the ability to cause disease in normal, healthy fish. Since primary pathogens are seldom encountered in fish culture, most bacterial disease control programs center upon controlling the opportunists and maintaining the inherent immunity of fish by careful attention to nutrition and water quality. Water quality, especially avoidance and control of excessive amounts of organic materials, becomes very important and provides the basis for good aquarium management practices. Bacteria require soluble nutrients for growth and multiplication, and these foods may be provided by increased organic matter.

Site of infection: Bacterial diseases in fish may be either external or internal, but in a sense this differentiation is somewhat artificial since all pathogenic bacteria of fish release toxins, which freely diffuse throughout the body of the fish. Generally, bacterial disease of fish involves what is termed the virulence of the bacteria, that is, its ability to break down the fish tissue through the secretion of extracellular enzymes (toxins or virulence factors). This breakdown of fish tissue increases the availability of food for the bacteria, thus stimulating bacterial growth, and leads to further deterioration of the fish, and ultimately, fish death.

Many pathogenic bacteria of fish are able to initiate infections in the internal organs of fish by way of the intestines or by penetration of blood vessels in the skin or gills. In some cases, parasites may carry the bacteria and infect the fish while feeding. Parasites may provide an entry for bacteria simply by disrupting the fish's first line of defense, the mucous layer and skin. This protective layer can also be disrupted as a result of handling, crowding, or netting fish.

Regardless of the manner in which bacteria enter into a fish, essentially all of the internal organs and their critical functions can be affected. Infections which are disseminated throughout the body are called systemic infections. If the result of the infection appears very rapidly, without obvious signs of bacterial disease, the infection is said to be acute. When the course of a bacterial infection extends over a period of time and typical lesions are seen on the fish, the infection is chronic. So-called internal infections most likely arise from a combination of reduced immunity and associated stress factors. Whether or not a particular infection has an acute or chronic course depends on the type of bacteria and the virulence factors released.

Signs associated with bacterial diseases: Unfortunately, the signs and behavior of fish with bacterial diseases are common to many different kinds of bacteria, some parasites, and some non-infectious problems. The most frequent behavioral change is simple weakness, in which fish are observed to remain motionless on the bottom of the aquarium. Generally, fish which lie on their sides are close to death. In some cases, fish will swim in circles. Others may lose their spatial orientation and continuously swim upside down. This latter problem is common in goldfish, and although a specific bacterium has not been identified, affected fish respond to antibiotic injections.

Among the physical signs of bacterial disease are hemorrhages, ulcerations, skin erosions, and ascites. Hemorrhages are particularly common. Their size may vary from pinpoint (petechial hemorrhages) to paintbrushlike reddened areas (echymotic hemorrhages). Ulcerations are distinct, often circumscribed areas of the skin where a central core of dead tissue is surrounded by a ring of reddened tissue. Pus is not associated with ulcers of fish.

Erosions of skin with scale loss are common with, but not limited to, infections with *Cytophaga columnaris.* A bacterial enzyme destroys tissues, which appear as white areas. Such areas have been termed "fin rot," "tail rot," "body rot," "mouth fungus," and "cloudy eye." Erosions can involve the loss of all tissues between fin rays or may result in total erosion of fins, including the fin rays. Frequently, muscle tissue is exposed.

Ascites, or bloat, is a fluid-filled distention of the abdomen of a fish. Frequently it is associated with exophthalmia ("popeye"), a condition in which one or both eyes protrude from the head. Ascites has been associated with chronic bacterial diseases such as those caused by species of *Mycobacterium.* The underlying cause of the fluid accumulation is destruction of kidney or possibly liver tissue.

Diagnosis of bacterial infections: In practice, the diagnosis of a bacterial infection can be done either by an educated guess or by isolation of the bacterium from the fish. The preferred term for the educated guess method is differential diagnosis, which implies that the diagnosis is certainly not definite but that a bacterial problem is a very good probability as the primary problem or as a complicating factor. (Even when the evidence points to a bacterial problem, a diagnosis is still tentative unless confirmed by isolation and identification.)

Among aquarists, retailers, and wholesalers, differential diagnosis is certainly more common than isolation and identification of the bacteria. This is largely due to the inavailability of bacteriological diagnostic services, costs, and relative worth of the fish. A tentative diagnosis of a bacterial problem can be made on the basis of observed signs and should always be preceded by attempts to identify any stress factor which may have weakened the fish. These may include extended length of transport time, poor water quality, inadequate cleaning, poor nutrition, or the presence of a concomitant parasitic infection. Such information will provide a rational basis for the avoidance of the problem, or for the simultaneous use of a parasiticide and an antimicrobial drug.

Isolation of the bacteria (etiologic diagnosis) should be left in the hands of individuals with experience in culturing fish for bacteria and interpreting results. However, for the fish producer, an etiologic diagnosis will allow records of prevalent bacteria encountered and their sensitivity or re-sistance to antibiotics available for treatment. Fish can be submitted to appropriate private or state-supported diagnostic laboratories that may provide the service. Veterinarians have access to such laboratories, and samples may have to be submitted by them.

The selection of representative sick fish is of paramount importance in establishing a diagnosis of a bacterial infection. The fish to be cultured must be still alive, since bacteria in the water invade a dead fish within thirty minutes of death. The external site from which a sample is taken should be selected in such a position on the fish that contamination due to handling may be avoided. Where possible, restraining the fish physically to obtain the culture is preferable to the use of anesthesia, which may be toxic to some bacteria. Before obtaining internal samples, care should be taken to sterilize the external surface of the fish so as to avoid contamination by external bacteria.

To provide an etiologic diagnosis, the fish microbiologist follows very specific procedures. Material from the diseased fish is streaked onto an appropriate growth medium so as to achieve a good separation of the sample on the agar plate. This may be done by flaming (sterilizing) between streaks to reduce the bacterial population or by punching the inoculating needle into the agar plate. The growth medium to use is a matter of some dispute. Some use a growth medium which will support the growth of most bacteria (nonselective). Others use a selective medium, in which additives prevent the growth of bacteria other than those desired.

Plates are incubated next. Most bacterial organisms associated with fish diseases and aquatic environments will grow at 20 to 37 degrees C (68 to 98.6 degrees F), with an optimum at approximately 25 to 30 degrees C (77 to 86 de-

Bacteria Associated with Disease in Freshwater Ornamental Fish		
Common	**Infrequent**	**Rare**
Gram-positive, aerobic to facultatively anaerobic species:		
Renibacterium salmoninarum	*Lactobacillus*	*Nocardia*
	Mycobacterium	
	Streptococcus	
Gram-positive, anaerobic species:		
Clostridium botulinum	*Eubacterium tarantellus*	
Gram-negative, aerobic to facultatively anaerobic species:		
Aeromonas hydrophila complex (eggs)	*Acinetobacter*	*Serratia liquefaciens*
Aeromonas salmonicida a) typical, b) atypical	*Edwardsiella tarda*	*Yersinia enterocolitica*
Cytophaga psychrophila	*Flavobacterium*	*Pseudomonas aeruginosa*
Edwardsiella ictaluri	*Pasteurella piscicida*	*Salmonella*
Cytophaga columnaris	*Pseudomonas putida*	*Proteus*
Myxobacter	*Pseudomonas fluorescens*	*Hafina alvei*
Yersinia ruckeri	*Pseudomonas*	*Escherichia coli*
Vibrio	*Plesiomonas shigelloides*	*Enterobacter*
Pseudomonas putrifaciens		
Citrobacter freundii		

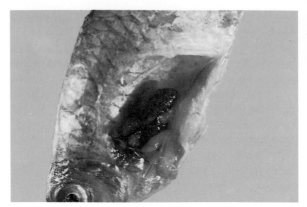

Mycobacterial infections cause a variety of gross lesions. Top left: A neon tetra shows wasting, "hollow belly," and evidence of secondary bacterial infection. Below left: An angelfish exhibits the chronic ulcers associated with systemic mycobacteriosis. Above: The white spots in the liver of this red-eyed tetra are granulomas.

eral classification of gram-positive rods and cocci, gram-negative nonpigmented rods (oxidase-positive and oxidase-negative), and gram-negative pigmented rods. The table on page 75 provides an overview.

Gram-Positive Rods

Most of the gram-positive rods which have been reported in fish are aerobic. Few anaerobic gram-positive rods have been linked with disease in fish, probably because they require anaerobic culture conditions for growth in the laboratory. It is clear that some gram-positive anaerobes are associated with fish problems, however, because isolates have been made from diseased fish.

Mycobacterium

Mycobacteriosis is a condition of both fresh- and saltwater fish. The disease is caused by a number of different bacterial species of the genus *Mycobacterium,* including *M. marinum, M. fortuitium, M. anabanti, M. chelonei, M. piscium, M. ranae, M. platypoecilus,* and *M. salmoniphilum.* Mycobacteriosis has been reported worldwide and has been reported in over 150 different species of fish. Mycobacteria cause a chronic progressive disease, which may be noted grossly in fish as emaciation, skin inflammation, exophthalmia, and ulceration or open lesions. On postmortem examination, gray to white nodules (granulomas) are present on internal or-

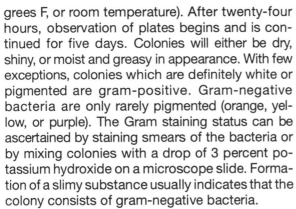

grees F, or room temperature). After twenty-four hours, observation of plates begins and is continued for five days. Colonies will either be dry, shiny, or moist and greasy in appearance. With few exceptions, colonies which are definitely white or pigmented are gram-positive. Gram-negative bacteria are only rarely pigmented (orange, yellow, or purple). The Gram staining status can be ascertained by staining smears of the bacteria or by mixing colonies with a drop of 3 percent potassium hydroxide on a microscope slide. Formation of a slimy substance usually indicates that the colony consists of gram-negative bacteria.

Further identification requires characterization utilizing biochemical reactions. The next steps in the procedure are to identify the bacterium as a fish pathogen and to determine its antimicrobial drug sensitivity. Investigative studies on bacteria associated with aquarium fish suggest no differentiation between bacteria attacking ornamental fish and those attacking food fish. Rather, the main difference appears to be between cold-water and warm-water species. The descriptions which follow center upon those bacteria associated with ornamental fishes, arranged into a gen-

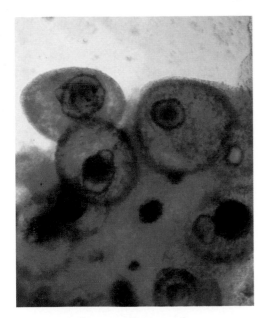

A wet-mount preparation reveals granulomas on a fish with mycobacteriosis.

gans such as the liver, kidney, and spleen. On small fish, these are best seen on wet mounts, where granulomas appear circular with a well-defined capsule.

In home aquaria, mycobacteriosis is characterized by a long course where affected fish refuse to eat, waste away, and eventually become so weak that they are unable to swim upright. Ascites (bloat) with exophthalmia is occasionally seen, indicating extensive damage to either kidneys or liver. On close observation, scales may be seen to jut out perpendicularly from the fish, indicating fluid accumulation under the scales. Older fish, long-term inhabitants of the aquarium, are frequently affected. Although many fish in an aquarium may be afflicted with mycobacteriosis, our experience suggests that only a few of these infections will be fatal.

Since it is well known that the organism is present in soil and is a normal inhabitant of the aquatic environment, the aquarist should assume that *Mycobacterium* is always present. Control by complete sterilization of the aquarium and gravel is unnecessary since reinfection is likely to occur. The disease is best controlled by a combination of strict cleaning of aquarium gravel, maintaining water quality through weekly changes, and assuring that fish are in peak nutritional condition through a balanced diet. Pay special attention to fish requirements for C, E, and B-complex vita-

mins, which may have become inactivated in dry food during storage.

Although little is known regarding how fish are initially infected, most probably the bacteria are taken in with food. It has been well substantiated that ornamental fish can become infected by eating fish food prepared from infected fish. Aquarists should be wary of feeding diets containing uncooked fish. Likewise, the feeding of sick or dying fish to large carnivorous species such as oscars is a bad practice, since fish which are doing poorly may be infected with mycobacteria.

Remove all obviously sick or dying fish prior to death since bacteria are easily spread by cannibalism. Moribund fish will die soon after removal from the aquarium or they can be humanely killed by an overdose of carbon dioxide using sodium bicarbonate or Alka-Seltzer®. Wrap fish in paper and dispose of by burial or removal in dry trash. Disposal by "flushing" always has the potential of spreading the disease to the environment.

The use of antibiotics for treatment is of questionable value since mycobacteria are surrounded by a granuloma which is relatively impervious to antibiotics. The use of antibiotics should be limited to situations where an active mycobacterial infection is suspected in a group of fish. The antibiotic should be incorporated into food and fed for at least three weeks. Compounds such as minocycline or rifampicin could be used at 0.3 percent in gelatinized diets fortified with C, E, and B-complex vitamins. The addition of antibiotics to water for treatment is controversial, since antibiotics may not be adsorbed to effective blood levels. Even when fish are fed antibiotics and seem to respond, it is a safe assumption that they are still infected.

Aquarists should be aware that mycobacterial infections can be transmitted from aquaria to humans, where the lesions appear as nodules on the fingers. Problems appear to be limited to situations where an aquarist with an open cut cleans an aquarium. Persons with cuts on fingers or hands either should avoid cleaning aquaria or should use protective gloves during cleaning.

Lactobacillus (Carnobacterium) piscicola

This is the bacterium responsible for pseudokidney or "big kidney" disease, which has been reported in salmonid fish from England, the United States, and Canada. It may be worldwide in scope and potentially could affect all freshwater and saltwater fish, since these lactobacillilike organisms are normal flora of fish. We have isolated them from ornamental species which showed no overt signs of bacterial disease.

In infected salmonid fish, the disease condition is most frequently noted in stressed fish one or more years old. Most commonly, mortality appears after spawning or as a result of handling. The disease signs vary, but usually include an ascitic abdomen and small blood-filled vesicles along the side of the fish. Internally, the liver, kidney, and spleen are involved, along with internal hemorrhaging and muscle abscesses. No control measures other than avoidance of stress have been recommended. The organism is sensitive to antibiotics, including ampicillin, tetracycline, and chloromycetin.

Nocardia

In both freshwater and saltwater fish, species of *Nocardia* (primarily *N. asteroides* and *N. kampachi*) may cause a disease that is very similar to mycobacteriosis on a clinical basis and which can be distinguished from it only by verification of staining characteristics. Signs of the disease include a long course and formation of granulomas. The organism is aerobic. Cultivated on bacteriological media, *Nocardia* organisms are longer and thinner than *Mycobacterium* and show filamentous branch formation. About 30 percent of *Nocardia* strains are acid-fast. Species of *Mycobacterium* are all acid-fast and are uniformly rod-shaped. The distribution of *Nocardia* is worldwide. From the limited data available, it appears that fish contract the disease in the natural environment. In cases of suspected nocardial infections, control measures appropriate for control of mycobacterial infections should be initiated.

Eubacterium tarantellus

This anaerobic organism has been isolated from fish in two situations in brackish water in the United States. Signs of the disease were neurological; affected fish twirled on a longitudinal axis until they died. In these outbreaks a number of estuarine species, but primarily mullet, were infected.

Clostridium

This anaerobe has been reported as a cause of a chronic disease of farmed trout in Denmark, England, and the United States. To the present time, only salmonid fish have been involved. Infected fish appear listless and have a sluggish and erratic swimming movement, alternately floating and sinking. Eventually death results. No characteristic external lesions have been noted. *Clostridium botulinum* is widespread in marine and freshwater environments, soil, and in the gastrointestinal tract of most animals, including fish. Starvation of fish has removed the organism from the gut of fish and aided in recovery. Since the organism can be part of normal gut flora, demonstration of circulating toxin aids in diagnosis. At present, this condition in salmonid fish has not been shown to present any hazards to human health.

African cichlid disease, also called "African bloat," is a disease of cichlids characterized by the development of ascites, exophthalmia, and in many cases, generalized hemorrhages. Common genera of fish involved are *Pseudotropheus zebra* and *Haplochromis moori.* Evidence points to the involvement of a *Clostridium* species as part of the African bloat problem. We have isolated a species of *Clostridium* and *Aeromonas hydrophila* from infected fish. On postmortem examination of affected fish, ascitic fluid is found and livers are yellow. Microscopic examination of liver sections or smears indicates a large amount of fat accumulation, suggesting poor nutrition.

We hypothesize that the disease onset is brought about by overfeeding, which results in the elaboration of toxins from resident *Clostridium* species. Toxins affect kidney function, resulting in bloat. Secondary bacterial invaders such as *Aeromonas hydrophila* then invade the weakened fish. Aquarists interested in African cichlids have noted that the avoidance of overfeeding (and possibly instituting a higher-fiber diet) will effectively prevent the occurrence of African bloat. This hypothesis is freely borrowed from the well-known disease in sheep which results from overeating and which is known as pulpy kidney disease. This sheep disease is induced by a toxin produced by *Clostridium perfringens* as a response to increased carbohydrates in the diet.

Control of bloat in African cichlids therefore should be directed to feeding high-quality complete diets in moderate amounts. Antibiotics are ineffective against toxins which destroy tissues. This may explain the lack of response of fish with bloat problems to common antibiotics added to aquarium water.

Large ulcers result from infection by several sorts of bacteria. Top: a gourami with ulcers. Above: a goldfish with an *Aeromonas* infection.

Gram-Positive Cocci

Staphylococcus

A species of *Staphylococcus* has been reported only in food fish from Japan and Argentina. The Japanese reports were associated with cultured yellowtail, whereas trout were affected in Argentina. The diseased fish were described as having typical signs of congestion, exophthalmia, and ulcerations of the tail. Identification of these isolates grouped them as *Staphylococcus epidermidis* and subsequent serological studies further showed these isolates to be different from human isolates of this same species. It was concluded that infection occurred from water rather than from human association, and it has been shown that this species is present in the aquatic environment. Studies in our laboratory have indicated that various species of staphylococci are common in shipping water. We have isolated staphylococci from neon tetras affected with *Pleisto-*

phora hyphessobryconis, the causative organism of neon tetra disease. We suggest that in this case, and possibly other cases, species of staphylococci may be secondary problems in fish.

Streptococcus

Species of *Streptococcus* have been shown to affect a large number of freshwater and marine fish in Japan, Norway, England, the United States, and South Africa. Fish affected include striped mullet, stingray, spot pinfish, silver trout, menhaden, sea catfish, golden shiner, Atlantic croaker, channel catfish, rainbow trout, eels, tilapia, yellowtail, danio, and ayu. External signs include exophthalmia, distended abdomen, erratic swimming, eye hemorrhage, blood-filled vesicles on the body, darkening of the skin, and vague neurological signs such as erratic twirling movements. When present, internal lesions include pale organs and accumulation of ascitic fluid. Some problems noted in Japan have been associated with Lancefield group D isolates, but the balance of disease has been attributed to a nonhemolytic Lancefield group B organism, regardless of the type of fish involved. Control of the condition rests with improved fish management.

In tropical fish farms, streptococcal infections have been a problem. A predominant sign noted by fish farmers is circling of the fish. On close examination, hemorrhages are apparent. The course of the infection is very rapid. Typically, fish still appear normal within twenty-four hours of death. Streptococci can be isolated from all organs of infected fish, including the brain. Many fish are potentially able to be infected, but most isolations have been from zebra danios and tiger barbs.

This case of fin rot resulted from infection by an atypical variant of *Aeromonas.*

We assume that stressed fish are infected by streptococcal species found in the environment. However, attempts to isolate the organisms from water, tadpoles, or fish food have been unsuccessful. A confirming diagnosis would depend on cultivation and isolation of the organism. The most effective of the antibiotics commonly used to control problems encountered on fish farms is erythromycin, which is particularly effective against gram-positive organisms.

Gram-Negative, Oxidase-Positive Rods

This group of bacteria includes some of the bacteria most frequently associated with aquarium fish. Many are found in the water and are associated with healthy fish.

Aeromonas

Since 1891, the *Aeromonas hydrophila* complex (*A. liquefaciens, A. formicans, A. punctata*) and *A.sobria* have been associated with a disease condition known as motile aeromonas septicemia (MAS), bacterial hemorrhagic septicemia (BHS), or hemorrhagic septicemia of fish. The disease has been reported worldwide in freshwater fish and from time to time from estuarine fishes. All freshwater species are susceptible.

The organism is common in the aquatic environment, and disease outbreaks usually follow a period of stress. In studies involving well-managed home aquaria, it is not uncommon to find 1,000 or more *Aeromonas hydrophila* per cubic centimeter of water. We have shown that the bacteria is associated with healthy fish. In freshwater aquarium fish, the disease strikes after some stress, such as recent shipment, lack of aeration, or poor water quality associated with nitrogenous wastes.

Aeromonas infections frequently follow infestations of parasites, which provide a route of entry for the bacteria. Monogenetic trematodes, fish lice, or a variety of external protozoan infections could be the initiating factors. All stresses, including specific vitamin deficiencies, may lead to a failure of the immune system to repel bacteria from disseminating throughout the body.

When external signs are present, they may include pinpoint or paintbrush hemorrhages in and around the gills and anal area. Large ulcers are common in advanced cases. Abdominal distention is frequently found and exophthalmia is common. On necropsy, hemorrhages may be found in all organs. Bloated fish contain ascitic fluid. Bacteria can generally be isolated from kidneys.

Control of this disease is by careful attention to minimization of stress. The disease is rare in well-managed home aquaria where fish are given a balanced diet. Unfortunately, it is most difficult to eliminate stressful conditions associated with long periods of shipping. Before shipping, attention should be given to pretreating fish with antibiotics, buffering pH, and minimizing ammonia accumulation. Importers should assume that fish are stressed and should initiate antibiotic treatments either before or at the first sign of problems. Good care of stressed fish would include water changes, a complete diet, water temperature of 75 to 80 degrees F (about 24 to 27 degrees C), shaded conditions, and antibiotic therapy. In addition to treating the aquarium water with antibiotics, larger fish with ulcerations can easily be injected with antibiotics intraperitoneally. (Antibiotics must be selected carefully and used with some care; see under "Antibiotics and Their Usage"). The effectiveness of experimental vaccines tried to date is questionable.

Aeromonas salmonicida has been reported as a disease of salmonid fish since 1894. All freshwater and marine fish are considered susceptible to this organism, which is known to exist worldwide either in the typical form or as an atypical variant. The typical disease in salmonid fish is of no particular interest to aquarists other than the fact that it is a principal disease of trout and salmon characterized by lethargy, bloodshot fins, hemorrhages of the muscles, and bloody discharges from gills and vent. Internal lesions include an enlarged spleen, kidney necrosis, and liver hemorrhage.

In nonsalmonid fish, atypical variants of *Aeromonas* can cause diseases characterized by gradually enlarging skin ulcers, with death occurring from other opportunistic bacteria. We have isolated such variants from swordtails with fin rot.

Ulcer disease in goldfish is initiated by such an atypical variant of *A. salmonicida*. A problem facing goldfish producers, it is occasionally seen at retail outlets. On goldfish farms, control measures are directed toward minimization of stress and incorporation of antibacterial drugs such as tetracycline, oxolinic acid, and potentiated sulfonamides in food. Some fish farmers claim that co-cultivation of goldfish with shiners will decrease the incidence of the disease. Others give fish bath treatments in oxolinic acid (an antibiotic) after handling. Despite active research for over forty years, no adequate and dependable vaccine is yet available.

At the retail or hobby level, ulcer disease may appear shortly after fish have been shipped. We have found that infected fish respond well to injections of antibiotics at dosages normally used for mammals. In our hands, intraperitoneal injections of chloramphenicol at levels as high as 25 milligrams per 100-gram (3.5-ounce) goldfish effected a cure. Other injected drugs such as gentamycin or tetracyclines might also be used. One injection of chloramphenicol given intraperitoneally usually gives satisfactory results; in some cases, a second injection after a week may be required. The site of injection is off-center anterior to the anal area (about 2 centimeters, or 0.8 inches). Fish can be restrained by netting. Lesions will ultimately heal. Frequent water changes, elevated water temperatures (to 75 to 80 degrees F, or about 24 to 27 degrees C), and addition of 0.2 to 0.3 percent salt to aquaria may enhance healing.

Pseudomonas

A dominant part of the aquatic bacterial population, *Pseudomonas fluorescens* for many years has been associated with a disease problem referred to as *Pseudomonas* septicemia. Isolates have been reported worldwide from diseased fish from both freshwater and marine sources. Currently, it is thought that all species of aquarium fish are potentially susceptible to this organism, which is a normal inhabitant of both freshwater and marine aquaria. Signs of the disease may be identical to those associated with a number of other bacteria. They range from fin and body ulcers and erosions to a systemic disease involving internal organs. Large ulcers on freshwater or marine fish may be caused by species of *Pseudomonas.* In all cases, infections are thought to be stress-related. Under pond conditions, they occur most commonly during cold weather.

Treatment is difficult, since several *Pseudomonas* strains are resistant to a number of antimicrobial drugs. Chemotherapeutics include tetracycline, gentamycin, or in some cases, sulfa. With larger fish we suggest intraperitoneal injections using gentamycin.

Pseudomonas anguilliseptica causes red spot disease, which has been described primarily in eels cultivated for food. It is likely that it or a related strain induces similar diseases in ornamental eels. Lesions include petechial hemorrhages in the skin of the mouth region, on the ventral aspect of the body, and on the gill opercula. Internal lesions include pale organs and generalized hemorrhages. Suggested therapy includes elevation of water temperature and antibiotic therapy using nalidixic or oxolinic acid.

Vibrio

Vibrios are commonly found in the marine environment and many species, including *V. anguillarum, V. ordelli, V. alginolyticus,* and *V. vulnificus,* are capable of causing disease. As with bacterial problems associated with freshwater species, many produce disease in fish under stress.

Red pest, caused by *V. anguillarum,* was first described in 1718 from eels in Italy. Since that time it has also been called saltwater furunculosis, boil disease, Hitra disease, and ulcer disease. Typical external disease signs are skin discolorations and red necrotic lesions of the abdomen; bloody infection at the base of fins, in the mouth, and in the vent; exophthalmia; and distention of the gut. Internally, there is a bacteremia with swelling of the kidney, liver, and spleen, and a clear viscous fluid in the gut. *V. anguillarum* has been divided into three subspecies, one of which (type B) has been given the name *V. ordelli.* The latter represents a major disease problem in the United States.

Vibrios have a worldwide distribution, and all freshwater and saltwater species are considered susceptible. Several control measures are available. An effective vaccine is used for food-producing species. Antibiotics placed in the fish food have also been used. Presently, only tetracyclines and sulfa drugs are legal for use in food-producing fish.

A number of other vibrios have been recovered from disease outbreaks from time to time. They are mentioned here because they may represent emerging fish-disease problems or may constitute a potential public health hazard. The generalized disease caused by these bacterial species is similar to that described for *V. anguillarum.* *V. alginolyticus* has been reported to cause disease in sea bream. However, this may represent environmental contamination rather than disease, since this species of bacteria is a very common organism in the marine environment. *V. carchariae* has been isolated with regularity from diseased sharks in the past five years and is an established pathogen for sharks. It has been noted as a disease problem in compromised rather than healthy fish. *V. damsela* has been reported to cause ulcers in a number of marine species. The organism is very cytotoxic, is common in the marine environment, and has been reported in human disease. *V. vulnificus* has been isolated from eels in Japan and England. The organism is common in the marine environment and has been isolated from humans.

In marine aquaria, *Vibrio* infections occur in fish which have experienced severe stress, such as recent shipping. Signs may include extensive hemorrhages, ulcerations, fin and body erosions, and involvement of internal organs. Fish may bloat from the accumulation of ascitic fluid. In well-managed saltwater systems where fish are kept in good nutrition and in good water, lesions attributable to these bacteria are rarely a problem. Seawater collected for routine water changes can be a source of *Vibrio*. We suggest sterilization of such water using 5 ppm of free chlorine followed by dechlorination.

It is important to stress that *Vibrio* infections may be indistinguishable from lesions resulting from *Pseudomonas* species and possibly from mycobacterial infections. The latter two types of bacterial infections are more difficult to treat due to the protective granulomas in the case of *Mycobacterium* and the high percentage of antibiotic-resistant strains in the case of *Pseudomonas* infections. Treatment of bacterial infections in marine fish can be approached either by injecting fish with antibiotics or by adding antibiotics to water. Normally, fish with ulcerations will respond better to injections. We suggest intraperitoneal injections of either chloromycetin or gentamycin. The dose for chloromycetin is 25 milligrams per kilogram of body weight; for gentamycin, 0.5 to 1 milligram per kilogram of body weight. A fish 4 to 5 inches (about 10 to 13 centimeters) long weighs approximately 70 to 100 milligrams. We have found that excessive treatment with chloromycetin does not result in toxicity, but since gentamycin is toxic for kidneys of fish, its dosages should be calculated carefully. Fish can be weighed by first weighing the aquarium with water but minus fish on a scale, then weighing it with fish, and subtracting the former weight from the latter.

Plesiomonas shigelloides
Over the past eight to ten years, this bacterium has been recovered from a variety of aquarium

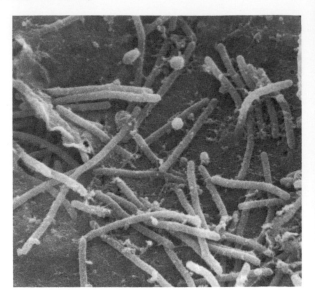

The bacteria that cause columnaris disease are evident in this electronmicrograph.

fish as well as from channel catfish. As with most bacterial infections of fish, signs of the disease include hemorrhages on the body, muscles, and internal organs, and accumulation of ascitic fluid resulting in bloat. In our laboratories we have used tetracycline, chloromycetin, and naladixic acid with success.

Gram-Negative, Oxidase-Negative Rods

Yersinia ruckeri
This member of the enteric group of bacteria was first reported from fish in the mid-1950s. Associated with a disease referred to as enteric red mouth (ERM), Hagerman red mouth, or red mouth, it has been implicated in disease problems in the United States, Denmark, Canada, Germany, England, Italy, Norway, Australia, and France. The disease characteristically affects salmonid fish, but it has been reported from various nonsalmonid fish, including goldfish, carp, lake herring, and emerald dace. External lesions include subcutaneous hemorrhaging of the mouth and throat, hemorrhage at the base of the fins, sluggishness, exophthalmia, darkening of the skin, and in some instances, erosion of the jaw and palate. Internally, there may be massive petechial hemorrhaging of the muscles, enlargement of the kidney and spleen, and a characteristic yellow fluid in the intestines.

Yersinia ruckeri is part of the common flora of

the freshwater environment and is not an obligate pathogen. Stress and water quality seem to influence the occurrence of disease. Control measures include a very effective vaccine (used in the trout industry) and an array of antibiotics and chemotherapeutics, including sulfa, tetracycline, Romet®, and oxolinic acid. Within the aquarium-fish industry, this problem appears to be limited to goldfish producers and wholesalers. The management practice of keeping water as cool as feasible will tend to limit the disease in goldfish, as will the use of antibiotics in feed.

Edwardsiella ictaluri

Another enteric bacterium, *Edwardsiella ictaluri* was first reported to infect fish in 1976, producing a disease in channel catfish which was characterized by inflammation of the intestines. A chronic version of this bacterium in channel catfish has been called "hole-in-the-head" disease, but this organism is not associated with the "hole-in-the-head" disease frequently seen in a variety of cichlids such as angelfish, oscars, and discus.

The organism also has been shown to be associated with aquarium fish. In danios, the principal sign of infection was circling of the fish; bacteria were isolated from internal organs and from the brain. The organism also has been isolated from a black ghost knife fish with neurological symptoms and from walking catfish from Thailand.

E. ictaluri should always be considered as a potential problem on fish farms and included as a possibility when neurological signs are seen in fish. When diagnosed, active infections can be treated with antibiotics given with food or in water.

Gram-Negative Pigmented Rods

Cytophaga

Since the first report of this genus in 1922, its members have appeared in the literature under a variety of names, including *Chorndococcus, Cytophaga, Flexibacter, Myxobacterium,* and at one time, *Flavobacterium.* The most common species is *columnaris,* named for the characteristic columns or stacks of organisms noted in diseased tissues.

Recent phenotypic studies of this group of yellow-pigmented bacteria, often referred to as YPB, indicate that *Cytophaga* may be separated from other YPB based upon its gliding motility, resistance to neomycin, production of the pigment flexirubin, and growth on special media. This group has been further subdivided into five subgroups. The first two have type species; the other three are undefined. The first subgroup, represented by *Cytophaga columnaris,* produces the enzyme chronditinase and is capable of initiating disease in healthy fish. The second subgroup usually causes disease at lower temperatures but lacks chronditinase and attacks fish which are stressed. The three remaining subgroups are associated only with stressed or compromised hosts.

Since taxonomic problems exist and the growth characteristics of *Cytophaga* are similar in disease situations, all infections are considered as a single etiology. The disease is commonly called columnaris disease. The bacterium is found worldwide, and all fish species are susceptible. All marine fish species are susceptible to the less well-defined marine counterparts of this group of bacteria.

A tentative diagnosis may be made from characteristic external lesions. These vary greatly from gill involvement to necrosis of fins and the development of large necrotic areas on the fish. These signs are often referred to as fin rot or body rot. A common form of the disease is the development of a necrotic area over the area of the dorsal fin; this particular lesion sometimes is referred to as "saddle back." Very few if any gross lesions are noted internally, but from the high percentages of isolations from blood and kidneys, it appears that bacteremias are common. Other types of bacteria, such as *Aeromonas,* may also infect fish concurrently.

Columnaris organisms are considered to be a part of the environment and have been observed growing on uneaten fish food. Most likely, the bacteria feed on organic wastes, and numbers of bacteria per volume of water increase with the amount of organic material present. These bacteria can be found on healthy fish. Development of disease is related to a stress-related decrease in disease resistance. In aquarium fish, the disease is frequently seen immediately after shipping. In well-managed home aquaria the disease condition is not common, although bacteria are present.

Columnaris may be controlled by reduction of environmental bacteria through minimization of organic substances by regular water changes with cleaning of gravel beds. When fish are showing lesions, antibacterial drugs and antibiotics must be used. Chemicals such as formaldehyde, quaternary ammonium compounds, and copper sulfate can have an antibacterial effect on *Cytophaga columnaris.* These chemicals have been used successfully in pond culture. Treatment of *Cytophaga* infections in aquarium fish should be initiated as soon as lesions are seen. In the aquarium trade, exporters attempt to reduce the incidence of this disease by pretreatment of fish with antibiotics before shipping. Wholesalers importing fish treat known problem-fish species automatically upon arrival. Antibiotics used have included sulfa drugs, tetracyclines, nitrofurans, and naladixic acid.

Flavobacterium

Another prominent member of the yellow-pigmented bacteria is the genus *Flavobacterium.* The classification of this group is in confusion at this time. For years, its primary characteristics were that its members were gram-negative, pigmented, and nonmotile. As a general rule, *Flavobacterium* may be separated from *Cytophaga* in that the former have nondiffusing pigment, are nonmotile, and do not require a special medium for growth. These organisms are found worldwide in both freshwater and marine (estuarine) environments, and all fish species are susceptible. As with *Cytophaga,* infections are more frequently associated with stressed fish. Lesions are similar to those caused by *Cytophaga,* and recommended control measures currently are the same. Under practical conditions, diseases caused by *Cytophaga* and *Flavobacterium* can be differentiated only by culture and identification of the organism.

Antibiotics and Their Usage

Antibiotics are compounds which are antagonistic to the growth of bacteria. These compounds act in a variety of ways, depending upon the type or "family" of antimicrobial drugs to which they belong. In general, their action on the bacterium is rather specific and is directed against some vital part of the bacterium.

Antibiotics in the beta lactam group, which includes penicillins and cephalosporins, interfere with formation of the bacterial cell wall. Their use in treatment of aquarium fish is limited to treatment of conditions caused by gram-positive bacteria. Polypeptides (polymyxins) interfere with the development of the cytoplasmic membrane. Aminoglycosides (gentamycin, kanamycin, tobramycin, streptomycin) interfere with protein synthesis at the 30 S ribosome level. Gentamycin and kanamycin have been used for treatment of ornamental fish, but both can be toxic to kidneys. Macrolides (erythromycin) interfere with protein synthesis at the 50 S ribosome level. Quinolines (naladixic acid, oxolinic acid) interfere with DNA metabolism. Sulfa drugs and potentiated sulfa drugs (Tribrissen®, Romet®) affect folic acid metabolism.

Mechanism of killing bacteria: Antimicrobial action upon bacteria is considered to be either "static" or "cidal." The antimicrobial drug either prevents further bacterial multiplication, allowing the host body defenses to eliminate them (static), or kills the bacteria directly (cidal).

Dosage of antibiotics: The concentration of antimicrobial drugs used to treat a bacterial disease is determined by a number of criteria. Of primary concern is the relative toxicity of the agent on the host animal. Some antibiotics tend to accumulate in a particular organ, and overdosage may kill fish. Because of species differences regarding adsorption, one should be aware of potential dangers if using antibiotics on which toxicology studies have not been done.

The effectiveness of an antibiotic will depend on the level of activity it attains, both in the water and in the fish. These effective concentrations are expressed as the minimal inhibitory concentration (MIC), which is the smallest amount of agent which will inhibit growth of the bacteria being tested, and the minimal bactericidal concentration (MBC), which is the lowest concentration which will kill the bacteria. The MBC is usually measurably higher than the MIC in the case of static agents, but will be close to the MIC in the case of cidal agents.

Since a portion of the antimicrobial drug will be broken down by body organs and/or bound to proteins in the animal tissue, only that portion which remains is available for antimicrobial drug action. For this reason, dosing must allow for some excess, usually from four to fifty times the MIC, depending upon the route, the drug, and the conditions under which the compound is being administered.

Antibiotic suitability: The suitability of an antibiotic to retard a specific bacterium may be assessed in several ways. The most common laboratory assay is a complex method referred to as the Kirby-Baur (KB) test. Results of this essay are reported as S (sensitive), I (intermediate), or R (resistant).

An alternative is the "shotgun" approach, in which treatment is empirically determined and evidence of clinical response represents success. This is the approach most used by the tropical fish industry and often by hobbyists as well. In many instances, bacterial disease strikes, and antibiotics are blindly added to the water with the hopes that they will stem the infection. In many cases, the addition of an antibiotic to aquarium water will result in a cure; in other cases, there may be no obvious amelioration of the disease. Perhaps the antibiotic was not suitable for the bacteria causing the problem. An example would be the use of penicillin for the treatment of an infection caused by a gram-negative bacterium such as *Aeromonas*. Or perhaps the bacteria were antibiotic-resistant.

Bacteria may evolve resistance to not just one, but many, antibiotics. The mechanism by which resistant strains develop is complex. Usually a basic mutation in the DNA codes for a new substance elaborated by the bacteria which makes it insensitive to the antibiotic. Another way in which bacteria become resistant is by the transfer of resistance factors. When the bacteria conjugate, a small circular fragment of DNA containing information for antibiotic resistance is passed from resistant to sensitive bacteria. The transferred fragment, or plasmid, divides along with the cell and makes subsequent generations resistant. Since the DNA associated with the plasmid is not a part of the DNA of the bacterium, this method of acquired antibiotic resistance is referred to as extrachromosomal or plasmid-mediated resistance.

In everyday practice, antibiotic-resistant strains often emerge when antibiotics are continually used in treatment. As susceptible strains are killed by the antibiotic, resistant strains come to predominate. Plasmid-mediated resistance, in particular, may present significant problems in the management of bacterial disease. Plasmids may also afford resistance to toxic ions such as copper, and may alter pathogenicity and metabolic activity of "carrier" bacteria. Plasmids are more frequently encountered in gram-negative bacteria but also occur in gram-positive bacteria. When apparent problems arise as a result of plasmids, they usually can be corrected by examining the sensitivity spectrum of the bacteria in question and making appropriate changes in therapy.

Regular (and sometimes unnecessary) use of antibiotics on fish farms or retail establishments has been documented to result in a large population of bacteria which contain plasmids for resistance to multiple antibiotics. In practical terms, the emergence of resistant bacteria can be avoided by employing antibiotics only when indicated, using a recommended dose (see further in this section), and continuing the treatment for at least three to four days.

The only certain way to determine the effectiveness of an antibiotic is to isolate the bacteria and test them for sensitivity to antibiotics, procedures which require expert laboratory assistance but may be arranged through a local veterinarian with access to a diagnostic laboratory. At the hobbyist level, the "shotgun" approach of simply trying different antibiotics may be practical. However, one should remember that antibiotics are not a cure-all. Some chronic bacterial diseases such as mycobacteriosis are not readily treated with antibacterial drugs, and antibiotics are ineffective against parasites.

Addition of antibiotics to water: Adding antibiotics to the water is the most common way aquarium fish are treated for bacterial infections. The advantages are that calculation of dosage is simple, uniform exposure of fish is assured, and any pathogens in the water or externally on the fish will be exposed to the antibiotic. Unfortunately, the adsorbability of antibiotics by tropical fish under differing water conditions has not been thoroughly investigated. Although some general guidelines can be given, the trial-and-error approach for any given water and antibiotic remains the best method of evaluation.

Water quality is a key factor in the adsorption of antibiotics by fish. Organic pollutants in water may bind antibiotics and decrease the dose available for adsorption by the fish. This suggests that water should be changed prior to the addition of an antibiotic. Water hardness also may affect antibiotic adsorption. For example, calcium ions in hard water bind to tetracyclines, resulting in failure of the antibiotic to be adsorbed. Solutions to this problem include either increasing the dosage or softening the water.

The pH of the water during therapy may also be of practical importance in antibiotic adsorption. Depending on the chemical composition of the antibiotic molecule, it will dissociate (ionize) at either high or low pH, and in this form it is less likely to be adsorbed by the fish. For example, a naturally acidic molecule such as naladixic acid

(Negram®) will remain non-ionized in slightly acidic water, and adsorption will be expected to be maximal if pH is adjusted to just under 7 (slightly acidic).

Previous studies suggest that selected antibiotics are adsorbed after four to five hours. Based on these studies, we would suggest a four- to five-hour exposure time followed by a complete water change. This will tend to eliminate any residual antibiotic and help to prevent the emergence of resistant bacterial strains. Short treatments followed by water changes will also tend to prevent any toxic effects on fish. Treatments should be continued on a daily basis until the fish appear cured. To prevent emergence of antibiotic-resistant strains, it is advisable to continue treatments for at least five days, even if fish appear normal three days after the initiation of the treatment.

Carbon filtration should be discontinued during treatments, since activated carbon will adsorb antibiotics. The effect on nitrifying bacteria in the filter bed also must be considered. Since many of the antibiotics used are bacteriostatic rather than bactericidal, nitrifying bacteria are inhibited only as long as the antibiotic is present. With a water change at the termination of the treatment, the bacteria should resume their normal function. Of course, foam filters or gravel could be removed from the filter bed during the treatment period. Alternatively, the treatment could be given in an aquarium without filters but with adequate aeration. If undergravel filters are used, remove air stems from the lift stack and place them in water for maximal aeration. Do not pull antibiotics through the gravel bed!

Addition of antibiotics to food: An alternative to water administration of antibiotics is to add them to the diet of sick fish. This method of administration has been used in food-fish production for many years, with some obvious advantages. Since antibiotics are mixed in with food, the dosage can be based on the average food intake of the fish. Additionally, this method affords a mechanism for gut absorption of antibiotics not suitable for water administration. Feeding also permits the use of less antibiotic than is needed for water treatment. A major shortcoming of mixing antibiotics with food is the fact that sick fish may not eat. Another serious disadvantage is that antibiotics mixed with feed may lose activity during long periods of storage. However, the practice of feeding antibiotics just prior to or after stress periods such as shipping makes good sense and can prevent bacterial infections from becoming established.

Medicated food can be purchased through commercial outlets, but the choice of antibiotics available in this form is limited. If sensitivity testing has been done or if other antibiotics are required, we suggest the incorporation of 0.75 percent of an antibiotic in a nutritionally complete gelatinized diet. Keep medicated food frozen between uses to avoid degradation of the antibiotics. Feeding should begin a few days before shipping and continue for at least five days after shipping.

Injection of antibiotics: A third means of administering antibiotics is by injecting them into fish. This method is used primarily with larger fish under conditions where

Common Antimicrobial Drugs for Treatment of Freshwater Ornamental Fish		
Compound	Dosage [1]Bath treatment	Long-term immersion
Chloramphenicol	10 – 50 ppm	12 –24 ppm (? absorption)
Tetracycline	10 – 20 ppm	12 – 24 ppm (absorbed)
Erythromycin	—	12 – 24 ppm (absorbed)
Furanace®	0.5 – 1 ppm, 5 to 10 min	0.01 ppm (absorbed)
Furadantoin	50 ppm, 1 hr	1.0 – 1.5 ppm (gut-absorbed)
Kanamycin	—	12 – 24 ppm (gut-absorbed)
Minocycline	—	6 – 12 (? absorption)
Metronidazole	—	5 ppm (absorbed)
Naladixic acid	—	10 – 15 ppm (gut-absorbed)
Oxolinic acid	—	12 – 20 ppm (? absorption)
Sulfamethozine	—	12 – 24 ppm (gut-absorbed)
Tribrissen®, Romet®	—	6 – 12 ppm (gut-absorbed)

[1] Unless otherwise noted, treat for no longer than four hours, and less if fish show stress.

fish may have been stressed from handling, hauling, or sorting. Injection also is the method of choice with larger aquarium fish with signs (such as hemorrhages or ulcers) suggesting bacterial disease. An obvious advantage is that the fish immediately receives the dosage needed, increasing its chances of survival.

Restraint and handling of fish is best done by netting. The antibiotic is injected intraperitoneally approximately 2 centimeters (about 0.8 inches) forward of, and slightly off to one side from, the anal area. Tuberculin or microsyringes with small (26- to 28-gauge) needles work well. Dosages of injected drugs such as chloramphenicol or gentamycin should be calculated according to the estimated weight of the fish.

Antimicrobial substances commonly used in fish: A variety of drugs have been used to treat fish for bacterial disease (see accompanying table). The antibiotic most extensively used is tetracycline. Approved for food fish, this compound is bacteriostatic in nature, preventing further multiplication of bacteria. Its extensive use in aquarium fish has led to problems of bacterial resistance.

The sulfa drugs, also approved for food fish, are bacteriostatic as well. Used extensively in the aquarium trade, they probably are most effective when used in slightly acidic water. Reports of therapeutic failure may be related to their use in high-pH water. One potentiated sulfa compound which has been approved for use in food-fish operations is Romet®. Whether this compound would be adsorbed from water by aquarium fish is not known.

Aminoglycosides, which include antibiotics such as kanamycin and gentamycin, are bactericidal and have some limited use for aquarium fishes. Kanamycin has been used to treat marine fish, and its reputed effectiveness may be due to the fact that marine fish drink water and presumably absorb antibiotics from the water. Neither kanamycin nor gentamycin are likely to be adsorbed by freshwater fish, and both are potentially toxic to kidneys. However, gentamycin could be used for injection of fish.

Chloramphenicol (chloromycetin) has a bacteriostatic action. It is not adsorbed by fish due to its insolubility in water. It is the preferred antibiotic for injection of larger fish.

Another group of chemical agents, the quinoline group, contains several compounds which

can be considered to fall in two groups. The first group contains the older derivatives, such as naladixic acid and oxolinic acid, all of which have relatively limited gram-positive antimicrobic spectra. Naladixic acid is better adsorbed by fish when water is slightly acidic. It has a broad spectrum against many bacterial pathogens, and to date, few resistant forms have arisen. The second group is comprised of fluorinated derivatives which have a broader antimicrobic range. Several of these currently are being examined for use in aquaculture.

Still another common group of chemical compounds are the furans, which include nitrofurantoin, furadextin, furicin, and furanase. All of these act as static compounds by blocking bacterial metabolism. Furanace® and nitrofurantoin are adsorbed by fish. Development of antibiotic-resistant strains has been minimal, but with extended usage these antibiotics can damage kidneys.

Another antibiotic used with aquarium fish is erythromycin. Its use should be limited to problems associated with gram-positive bacteria.

Diseases Caused by Fungi

The fungi are a large group of nucleated organisms which are plantlike but lack chlorophyll and are not differentiated into typical plant components such as roots, stems, and leaves. When seen on the surface of a fish, fungal infections appear as a cottonlike white mass. This mass is composed of filaments, known as hyphae, which may or may not branch. The entire mass of hyphae is called a mycelium. In the majority of fungi, the hyphae are divided into cells by cross-walls (septa).

Fungi use organic matter as a source of nourishment, and thus generally live in close association with other life-forms. Most consume dead remains and waste products of other organisms. Others live closely with other life-forms but do no harm. However, a third group of fungi are parasites, harming or injuring their host as they obtain organic nutrients from it.

Fungi typically reproduce by both sexually and asexually formed spores, but the latter are generally more important due to the greater number formed. Sexual reproduction involves the fusion of two nuclei, with the eventual formation of reproductive elements. Asexual spores are formed in special structures (sporangia) which form at the

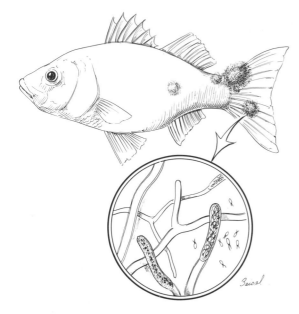

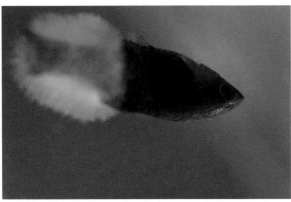

The tufts on this fish are typical of fungal infection, which is most often a secondary disease problem. Within the filamentous forms, developing spores are evident.

end of hyphae. Asexual reproduction can also occur through fragmentation of hyphae and subsequent dispersal of these fragments by wind or water. Under suitable conditions, these fragments will grow into new fungi.

Classification of fungi pathogenic for fish: The classification of fungi is complicated and exact identification as to genus and species is best left to experts. Identification of the fungi of concern to the aquarist has been confounded by a variety of problems, including failure to obtain the fungi in pure culture, failure to prove that a given isolate is truly pathogenic for fish, and failure to study the morphology of the characteristics of both asexual

and sexual reproductive organs.

Many fungi responsible for infections of fish as well as fish eggs belong to the family Saprolegniaceae, which includes a number of common freshwater molds often seen as a fuzzy, whitish growth on organisms that have died. A few genera predominate. *Saprolegnia parasitica* is the type species. Several other species of *Saprolegnia* also have been implicated in causing disease, but species cannot be differentiated by the characteristics of the disease which they induce. *Saprolegnia* infections are without doubt the most frequent fungal infections observed in ornamental fish. Other genera such as *Achlya* and *Aphanomyces* have also been implicated in infections of ornamental fish.

Predisposing factors for fungal infections: Many fish pathologists will agree that fungi of fish are rarely the primary cause of a disease episode. Spores are widespread in soil and water (especially water high in organics from uneaten food and accumulation of fish wastes), but it appears that a fish must be in a compromised state to become actively infected. The development of fungal infections in fish without obvious predisposing factors has been reported only rarely, and usually in these cases not all predisposing factors have been identified.

Temperature variation is considered to be a prime predisposing factor, with colder temperatures being most important. Florida ornamental fish farmers regularly fight fungal problems associated with water temperatures below approximately 50 degrees F (10 degrees C). (Conversely, higher-than-normal water temperatures have also been associated with outbreaks of fungal infections.) Lower water temperatures favor the growth of the fungus while at the same time lengthening wound-healing time in fish and depressing the ability of the fish immune system to resist fungal invasion.

The immune system of fish is depressed not only by temperature drops but by hormone imbalances and indeed, stress from any source. While open wounds induced by parasites, bacteria, or rough handling can serve as the initial point of invasion by a fungal spore, the immunological status of the fish plays a major role in the development of a disease. The high incidence of fungal infections in spawning salmonid fish is thought to be related to hormonal changes which reduce the effectiveness of the cellular component of the immune system to attack and kill invading organisms. Instances of fungal infection of breeding ornamental fish have been reported by commercial fish farmers.

Recognizing fungal disease: Most commonly, a fungal attack is seen as a skin or gill infection which may or may not be associated with a preexisting wound. The infection can be initiated by spores or mycelial elements. *Saprolegnia* lesions are focalized, circular, and have the appearance of cotton patches when viewed while the fish is in water. The distribution of lesions on the surface of the body may be random, but lesions often occur just forward of the dorsal fin. Frequently, the tufts of mycelia will appear brown to gray due to trapped debris. Upon removal of the fish from the water, the mycelial elements collapse, and the characteristic cottony growth pattern is not observed. Microscopic examination of the fungus will reveal a mass of elongate mycelia and sporangia containing motile spores. Although the fungus can penetrate to the muscular level, most cases involve superficial invasion of the dermis. Death is attributable to loss of body fluids and electrolyte imbalances. Superficial fungal infections can be complicated by bacterial pathogens.

A second syndrome is associated with the invasion of internal organs by both *Saprolegnia* and *Aphanomyces*. Such generalized infections have been reported in trout fry and in gouramis. In gouramis, we have found what appeared to be a species of *Aphanomyces* distributed in internal organs as well as in musculature. Histopathological analysis revealed a typical granulomatous reaction, and mycelial elements were demonstrated by special staining techniques. We suspect that with further investigation, other genera of fungi will be implicated in cases of generalized invasion. Such infections cannot be diagnosed by casual observation of the fish. In gouramis affected with *Aphanomyces,* the only signs of infection were granulomas noted on wet-mount preparations. Fungal elements were observed only after tissues were prepared for histopathological examination and stained with fungal-specific stains.

A third syndrome appears to be associated with body orifices such as the mouth, eyes, olfactory pits, and anus. Possibly tissues at these sites provide optimal conditions for spore growth in an already immunologically compromised fish.

Saprolegnia also invade fish eggs. At first, dead eggs are infected. Then the infection readily spreads to adjacent living eggs until the entire egg mass succumbs.

Control and treatment of external fungal infections: Fungal infections are closely associated with both environmental factors, which favor the propagation of the fungus (such as water temperature and organic load), and host factors (such as a predisposing disease, open wounds, or a compromised immune system). Fish producers must adjust management techniques to avoid or minimize infections and stress conditions. This "back-to-basics" approach may include water-temperature control, diet improvement, avoidance of overcrowding, more frequent water changes, improved handling procedures, quarantine to avoid parasitic diseases, and routine prophylactic treatments.

In general, established fungal infections in fish are difficult, if not impossible, to treat. Furthermore, since fungal infections generally are associated with a primary disease problem along with a management problem, therapy against other pathogens as well as the fungus must be initiated along with corrective management procedures. Additionally, the presence of an observed fungus on the surface of a fish implies that the skin has a break and is liable to bacterial infection.

Choice of drugs: At this writing, malachite green is used in aquaculture throughout the world as a fungicide that is highly effective, easy to use, and low in cost. Although allowable in ornamental-fish culture, its use in food-fish culture is not approved by the U.S. Food and Drug Administration, because it is known to be teratogenic in laboratory animals and can cause developmental anomalies when administered to eggs of rainbow trout.

Malachite green can be used as a short-term, high-dosage bath or as a longer, lower-dosage treatment. Short-term bath treatments are done in separate aquaria for individually affected fish or as a preventative for fungus development on fish eggs. Malachite green has been used in bath treatments for fish at 2 ppm for thirty minutes and for fish eggs at 5 ppm for sixty minutes. Since various ornamental fish vary in their susceptibility to malachite green, dosages and treatment times must be followed strictly.

For long-term treatments in home aquaria or in special-treatment aquaria, malachite green is added to give a final dosage of 0.1 ppm. Discontinue carbon filtration but maintain aeration during treatment. Remove air stems from lift stacks of undergravel filters to avoid dilution of malachite green by organics in the gravel bed. The treatment should be continued until signs of the infection are gone. Water changes (with care not to stress fish) at two- to three-day intervals will serve to maintain an effective dose. Antibiotics at 6 to 12 ppm can be given in conjunction with the malachite green if bacterial complications are suspected.

Commercially available formulations of malachite green should be used if available. If not, mix 10 grams (0.3 ounces) of zinc-free malachite green oxalate with 500 milliliters (about 2 cups) of distilled water. Adding the indicated amounts of this stock solution to 10 gallons (38 liters) of water will result in the following dosages:

0.2 milliliter to 10 gallons = 0.1 ppm (0.2 milliliter is equal to 4 drops)
3.0 milliliters to 10 gallons = 2.0 ppm
8.0 milliliters to 10 gallons = 5.0 ppm

It should be noted that formalin (37 percent formaldehyde) at a dosage of 250 ppm has been shown to be as effective in controlling fungus on fish eggs as malachite green at 5 ppm for sixty minutes.

Systemic fungal infections: Internal generalized mycotic infections in fish occasionally have been attributed to *Saprolegnia* and more frequently *to Aphanomyces*. Our experience suggests that systemic fungal infections in tropical fish are rarely seen.

Ichthyosporidium (*Ichthyophonus hoferi*) is frequently mentioned in the aquarium-fish-disease literature as a systemic fungus. Currently, the parasite has been grouped within the Microsporidea; consequently, the organism should be considered as a protozoan. Principally a problem with marine fish, it has been readily transmitted to freshwater species when fish meal contaminated with the organism has been used as a dietary component. Signs of the disease include invasion of the internal organs of the body, resulting in granulomas (whitish-appearing nodules) in the heart, liver, kidneys, spleen, and gonads. Skin infections result in roughened or "sandpaper" skin. Microscopic examination of wet-mount preparations reveals cystlike growths with buds. This disease can mimic systemic mycobacterial infections and can be differentiated by staining smears with acid-fast stains.

Ichthyosporidium should be suspected if fish have been fed diets containing uncooked marine "trash" fish. Incorporation of uncooked fish into diets can also spread a variety of other disease organisms, including *Mycobacterium* species. Obviously the best control of such infections is by avoidance through feeding fish uncontaminated diets.

Fungal infections of gills: Fungal infections of the gills are common and in most cases appear to be associated with *Saprolegnia* species. In freshwater fish, fungi of the genus *Branchiomyces* have been described growing within the blood vessels of the gill. Fungal spores are thought to enter the fish either by direct infection of the gill or by way of the intestine and bloodstream. While the causative agent of this disease has not been officially confirmed, within the gills of ornamental fish we have observed mycotic infections which closely mimic the condition described in carp. Infection with *Branchiomyces* species has been reported to be associated with high temperatures and water high in organic fertilizers with heavy algal blooms. The cause of death in fish is asphyxiation.

Viral Diseases of Aquarium Fish

Of all the pathogenic organisms associated with ornamental fish, the viruses are the least understood and the least studied. This is in large part related to cost restraints. The cost of establishing laboratories which have adequate equipment and personnel trained in virology is relatively high, and while the technology for virus isolation from fish has been available for thirty years, the funds required for isolation and study of potential virus-related problems in ornamental fish have not been forthcoming.

In his recent book, *Fish Viruses and Fish Viral Diseases,* Dr. Ken Wolf includes fifty-six viruses— eighteen viruses which have been isolated and have been associated with disease, five viruses of low virulence, ten viruses of unknown pathogenicity, sixteen viruses which have been observed by electron microscopy but not yet isolated, and seven instances where viruslike particles have been observed in fish. Not unexpected is the observation that the majority of the better-characterized viruses that have been isolated are associated with food fish.

What is a virus?: The definition of a virus is best approached by comparing its principal characteristics with those of other known groups of organisms, for these extremely small particles have some of the properties of living things but lack others.

A virus has no independent metabolism. It cannot live outside of a living cell, because it does not have the necessary components to generate energy or to produce basic components of cells such as amino acids, proteins, carbohydrates, or fats. A virus is composed solely of genetic material (either DNA or RNA) surrounded by a protective protein covering referred to as a capsid. The capsid consists of protein subunits called capsomeres. The organization of the capsomeres and of the capsid as an entity is useful in the classification of viruses.

Once the genetic material of a virus enters the cell of its host, it redirects the host's cellular machinery to produce copies of the viral nucleic acid and the protective proteins which are assembled into capsids. Viruses are released either from cells that burst open or from living cells that remain viable as they continue to shed viruses.

So small that they only became visible upon invention of the electron microscope, viruses are measured in nanometers. There are 25 million nanometers in an inch, and most virus groups range from 30 to 200 nanometers. (In contrast, bacteria usually measure 1 to 4 microns; 1 micron is equal to 1,000 nanometers.) The extremely small size of viruses led to the term "filterable virus," since filters which easily retained bacteria allowed viruses to pass.

Since viruses depend on a living cell for growth, they must contact a susceptible host before the viruses are inactivated by environmental factors. The host-to-host transfer of viruses has been well studied in mammals. Classical methods of spreading mammalian viruses have been via aerosol transfer, direct contact with infected body fluids, insects, or by infected food or water sources. In fish, transfer to a susceptible host is by direct exposure through the water. Gills are probably the initial organs of exposure.

Viral specificity and classification: Viruses show a very marked specificity for classes of animal life. Viruses are found to parasitize bacteria, fungi, plants, insects, amphibians, reptiles, and mammals. The term "species specificity" refers to the fact that viruses generally have a narrow host range. For example, the virus causing the disease hog cholera is found to infect only porcine species. One exception is the rabies virus, which can affect any mammal.

Fish viruses appear to have relatively narrow species specificities, although this has yet to be tested for many of the viruses that have been definitely associated with fish diseases. It is well known that viruses of salmonid fish have a range which is limited to other salmonids. Similarly, channel catfish virus will not affect trout or salmon. This type of specificity underlies the concept of "natural resistance" and has as its basis whether or not a virus can successfully be taken in by a cell, avoid the cell's enzyme systems, use the cell to reproduce itself, and finally assemble its component parts into what we know as a virus.

Viruses are classified into groups based on the presence of either DNA or RNA as their genetic material, presence of an envelope, structure of the proteinaceous capsid, number of capsomeres, site of intercellular development, and size. Presently there are fourteen main classes of viruses, but many viruses are still unclassified. Readers interested in the further study of viruses should consult other texts, such as Braude (1982). The classification of a virus is not based on which animals are infected.

Pathogenicity of viruses: Viruses can cause serious disease problems, moderately severe problems, or can infect a fish without obvious signs of disease. In many cases, the virulence of a virus is associated with other factors, such as age of the fish, and predisposing stressors, such as shipping, concomitant parasitic infections, water temperature, or nutritional status. In many cases, isolates of the same class of virus from an animal will differ markedly in virulence. Such virulence differences form the basis for the development of virus vaccines called "modified live viruses." Differences in virulence have been attributed to the manner in which a virus interacts (both quantitatively and qualitatively) with the various tissues of the infected animal. For instance, vaccine strains of poliovirus will not affect nervous tissue, yet will propagate and eventually stimulate the production of antibodies, which confer protection from further attack by the virus.

Some viruses are virulent. They can infect every organ of the body, resulting in death due to failure of vital life systems, or can cause a general depression of the immune system, resulting in secondary bacterial infections. Viral hemorrhagic septicemia of trout is a good example of a very virulent virus. Infectious pancreatic virus of trout is moderately virulent for fry but essentially avirulent for mature trout. Other viruses may not kill fish but are disfiguring. Lymphocystis virus produces massive enlargements of individual cells, which may resemble tumors. If such masses interfere with feeding, fish die of starvation.

Many fish viruses which have been observed by electron microscopy have not been isolated. The mere presence of a virus in tissues of a fish does not mean that it is causing a disease. In fact, several viruses isolated from a variety of fish produce no apparent disease condition. The isolation of viruses from apparently normal animals and fish has spawned the term "inapparent infection." The term "carrier" refers to an animal with an inapparent infection from which a virus can be isolated.

In many cases with well-studied animal viruses, animals can indeed be carriers of virulent viruses to which they have developed an immunity. In fish, the carrier state is also common in several well-studied viral diseases. This carrier state is one of the principal obstacles to viral disease control, especially when new stock are introduced into a breeding establishment.

Detection and isolation of viruses: Virological studies are complicated by the fact that a virus is a very sophisticated microorganism which can only live and grow in living cells, whether in the animal or in flask-grown cultures of cells from the animal.

Cell cultures can be established directly from fish as required, and some cell cultures can be developed into cell lines perpetuated indefinitely by subculturing. Many cell lines are used in the isolation of fish viruses. Some of these will not support the growth of any known fish virus; others will support a broader selection of known fish viruses. Because of potential specificity, it is generally considered important to use cell cultures which originate from a species closely related to the animal from which a virus recovery is attempted.

Inoculation of cell cultures with bacteria-free preparations of fish tissues is the standard technique for virus isolation. If a virus is present, the cells will begin to die. It is important to show that uninfected control cells remain healthy and that the changes in the cell cultures are not caused by contaminating bacteria. Virologists refer to the cellular changes as a cytopathogenic effect. Once a virus is isolated in cell cultures, it can easily be classified and used for further disease characterization. The isolation of a virus implies that a diagnostic system is available. This is of particular practical importance for detection of potential stock of uninfected breeding fish.

Fish viruses have been detected by direct examination of tissues with an electron microscope. However, while demonstrating the presence of a virus, this method does not establish whether the observed virus is actually causing the disease. To establish that, one must associate the virus with the disease on a regular basis. In addition, when given to unexposed fish, the virus isolated in cultures of fish cells must produce a disease similar to that seen in the field. The entire process of isolating a virus and proving that it is associated with a disease is complex, time-consuming, and expensive.

Diagnosis of viral diseases: Most fish viruses can only be definitely diagnosed by isolation and identification of the virus itself. (An exception is the lymphocystis virus of fish, which produces very characteristic lesions.) Laboratories specializing in fish pathology may be able to identify a virus isolate by the ability of specific antibodies to inactivate the isolate. Other tests include staining suspected infected cell cultures with a battery of fluorescein-tagged antibodies which will react with virus material, then detecting fluorescing cells by microscopy. Both of these tests assume that the virus has been isolated previously, has been well studied, and is one to which specific antibodies have been produced in laboratory animals.

Other techniques exist for detecting viruses directly in tissues. These rather sophisticated methods depend on the availability of specific antisera and/or molecular genetic techniques.

In practice, in most instances involving ornamental fish, a viral disease is suspected when all other possible causes of disease have been eliminated. Reaching this decision involves a detailed study of the fish as well as water quality.

Prevention, control, and treatment of viral diseases: The association between a virus and its host cell is an intimate one. A successful antiviral treatment must spare the life of the cell and inactivate the virus. The difficulty in reaching this goal is attested to by the fact that there are no antiviral drugs available to treat viral diseases of pets and domestic animals. In human medicine, drugs for cold sores and influenza are available and give some relief. Specific drugs for acquired immuno-deficiency syndrome (AIDS) apparently will prolong life in affected patients. At this writing, the potential of developing antiviral drugs for use in fish is poor due to low demand, high costs, and lack of suitable delivery systems.

Vaccines to prevent viral diseases of humans and animals are common. Most consist of strains of live viruses which have been modified so that they no longer produce a disease but will stimulate the production of antibodies against the virus. The presence of antibodies in the vaccinated host confers protection to invasion by the virulent wild-type virus. Vaccines using killed strains are also used, but their ability to confer immunity does not compare favorably with that of modified live vaccines.

In veterinary medicine, there is always a concern that some modified live-virus vaccines might revert to the native virulence. In fish medicine, the experimental use of modified live-virus vaccines suggests that trout can be immunized by exposure to modified infectious hematopoietic necrosis virus and to killed-virus preparations of infectious pancreatic necrosis virus. Although vaccines based on other methods might be developed, some serious questions remain unanswered. The age of the fish when it is most susceptible to the virus is a most important factor. If only very young fish are susceptible to the virus, administration of a vaccine may not confer protection because the very young fish may not have a sufficiently mature immune system to respond to the vaccine. A very serious consideration is the possibility of a modified live virus being virulent to nontarget species in the watershed where the vaccine is produced. Governmental approval of any vaccine would have to include tests showing that nontarget fish are not affected and that the vaccine cannot revert to virulence for the target fish. Another serious limitation is the route of vaccination. To be acceptable, any modified live vaccine would have to be given by adding it to the water. Killed-virus vaccines certainly would circumvent the problem of reversion of the virus, but they must be injected into each animal, which in present-day fish-culture practices is not practical. And last, the development and testing of a vaccine by a commercial vaccine producer would be done only after the market potential was considered.

Avoidance of viral disease is the most practical approach available to primary fish producers and to hobbyists. The first ground rule is that any fish is a potential carrier of a virus and that the virus may be virulent to similar (or possibly even other nonsimilar) species.

For hobbyists, an extensive quarantine period is the best available method for reducing the possibility that a newly introduced fish will spread a virus. The simple holding of a fish for a period of at least twenty-one days will provide an ample period for the fish to sicken and die, if a disease is present, or to develop an immunity to a possible virus. Naturally, routine treatments for other diseases can be initiated during this period.

As mentioned, fish may become virus carriers and may shed viruses without developing signs of disease. If this is a problem, test fish should be introduced into the quarantine tank for two weeks. If the test fish sicken, the quarantined fish should be suspected of carrying some type of pathogenic organism, including a virus. Quarantine procedures should be taken seriously. Aquaria holding quarantined fish should be in a separate room or preferably in an entirely different location. Pails, nets, and siphon tubes can easily carry enough virus to initiate an infection and should only be used for quarantine tanks.

Another way to avoid viruses is to purchase fish from hatcheries that are known to have healthy fish. The virus-free status of their fish may have been established by laboratory examination of fish or by a long history of having problem-free fish. Viral diseases in trout are avoided by purchasing eggs from certified virus-free hatcheries.

Known Viral Diseases of Ornamental Fish

Lymphocystis disease: Lymphocystis disease is a common malady in both freshwater and marine tropical fish. The DNA-containing iridovirus affects cells of fish, resulting in an increase in the size of individual cells up to 50,000 times their normal volume. Signs of the disease vary with the intensity of the infection. Initially, patches of fins may develop a slight opalescence where cells are beginning to enlarge. On the surface of the skin, small, whitish blebs give the skin a sandpaperlike appearance. In advanced cases, large tumorous growths can be found on any surface of the body. Close inspection of affected areas with a hand-held lens will reveal that the wartlike growths consist of enlarged cells. Involvement of eyes is not uncommon. Growths of cells on or immediately adjacent to mouthparts can lead to starvation. The virus can affect internal organs, but this is usually not a concern in ornamental fish.

A diagnosis of lymphocystis disease can be made by wet-mount preparations of affected tissues removed from the fish. Microscopic examination will reveal massive cells (0.5 to 1.0 millimeter across) with a thick capsule. It is generally thought that the virus is spread from fish to fish by contact of the virus with small openings in the skin caused by rough netting, fighting, or parasites. Once the virus becomes established, adjacent cells are infected.

The course of the disease in ornamental fish is variable, probably because of differences in individual immune responses. In some cases, the cells appear to be rejected by the fish. In other instances, the cells disappear, only to reappear at some later time.

Large tumorous masses which interfere with feeding can lead to starvation. We have successfully removed such masses surgically, then cauterized the exposed cut areas. Marine fish with lymphocystis disease have been observed to clear themselves of infected cells when placed in an aquarium with Pacific anemones. This suggests a possibility that anemones secrete a substance which stimulates the immune system of fish.

Goldfish iridovirus: In a routine survey of goldfish for the presence of viruses, researchers at Northeastern University isolated an iridovirus on two occasions from swim-bladder tissue of healthy goldfish (*Carassius auratus*). When fifteen goldfish were injected intraperitoneally with virus, eight fish died seven to twenty days later and showed hemorrhages within the peritoneal cavity. Attempts to reisolate the virus were unsuccessful. In a second trial, virus which had been passed for five and seven times in cell cultures caused no mortalities in test fish after fifty days of observation.

The presence of a virus in native goldfish is interesting. The apparent lack of pathogenicity under experimental conditions does not negate the possibility that the organism may be pathogenic for goldfish under natural conditions. The primary isolation of these agents from air-bladder tissues suggests a possible involvement with the common air-bladder problems in goldfish.

Spring viremia of carp: This acute disease is characterized by hemorrhages which affect carp during the spring months. The causal agent, *Rhabdovirus carpio,* is capable of killing carp of all ages. Common names of the disease (infectious dropsy of carp, acute infectious dropsy) reflect the common sign of ascites (bloat). The virus has never been isolated from North America, and research suggests that the common goldfish is not susceptible to the virus. Goldfish farmers rarely report massive spring die-offs of goldfish with hemorrhagic lesions, an observation which suggests that either the virus is not present or that these fish are not susceptible.

Ramirez dwarf cichlid virus: This virus was first observed when, between one and three days after importation from South America, all the fish in five different shipments of *Apistogramma ramirez* became ill, showing inactivity, inappetence, respiratory distress, and weakness as suggested by uncoordinated swimming. Fish appeared pale, with generalized hemorrhages in the skin and eyes. Notable internal signs included pale shrunken organs and an enlarged spleen.

Mortality ranged from 40 to 80 percent. The Ramirez dwarf cichlid virus was found in spleen cells of diseased fish, and examination of the fish failed to uncover other disease agents which could have caused the mortalities. Although virus isolation attempts were not made in this study nor were infectivity studies done, the complete pathological picture was highly suggestive that the virus particles observed by electron microscopy were associated with the disease.

In examining disease problems with dwarf cichlids, University of Georgia investigators have diagnosed systemic *Tetrahymena pyriformis* infections which resulted in 100 percent mortalities. We did not examine these fish for virus infections. However, it is possible that the virus described here depresses the natural defense mechanisms of the fish, rendering it susceptible to the parasite.

Rio Grande cichlid rhabdovirus: This virus was isolated from specimens of *Cichlasoma cyanoguttatum,* which died of an acute disease that killed all the fish in the shipment within a week. The disease has been experimentally transmitted to *Tilapia zillii, Cichlasoma cyanoguttatum,* and *Cichlasoma nigrofasciatum.* (The latter species is commonly known as the convict cichlid.) Rhabdoviruses are bullet-shaped viruses which have been associated with many species of fish. Recent studies by University of Georgia investigators suggest that rhabdoviruses are also associated with freshwater angelfish (*Pterophyllum scalare*). Whether cichlid viruses will infect any other fish species is an interesting but unanswered question.

Viruses associated with freshwater angelfish: During the period from 1987 to 1989, the tropical fish industry encountered an apparently new disease syndrome in angelfish (*Pterophyllum scalare*). Its principal signs appeared to be behavioral changes. Fish crowded together in either a head-up or a head-down posture and refused to eat. Thus they rapidly lost weight and died. Excessive slime seemed to be another prime characteristic of the disease. Some fish developed "injected" fins, which give a red or bloody appearance to finnage.

Reports from the field suggested that seemingly healthy fish developed the disease after shipping or following transfer to a different aquarium. Reports from fish producers indicated that breeding fish could transmit the disease to fry, but that fry might recover if unstressed. In some cases, exposed fry matured without finnage. It appeared that many fish are healthy carriers of the disease agent, and that the mixing of apparently healthy carriers with naive fish resulted in an increased death rate as unexposed fish became infected.

Research teams in the veterinary colleges at the University of Georgia and at the University of Florida began investigating what some producers were calling "angelfish plague" or "angelfish AIDS." (These names were based on the observation that the problem was both infectious and apparently incurable.) During the initial phase of our studies of sick angelfish sent to us from both domestic and foreign sources, we identified many problems that clearly were not viral in origin and could be contained by routine treatment and control measures. In some cases, for instance, very poor water quality was the problem. In other cases, poor nutrition or parasites were causing deaths. Sometimes the disease signs were quite similar to those of the so-called angelfish plague. In one case submitted by a producer, examination of intestinal tissues revealed a sporozoan closely related to the *Chloromyxum* group.

The virus hypothesis was strengthened by the observations of angelfish producers that the disease spread easily, that it weakened fish, making them susceptible to other diseases, and that adult fish could carry the disease without visible signs of infection. We had seen similar cases in the late 1970s and early 1980s where an obvious diagnosis could not be made but the possibility of virus involvement had been considered. The possibility that viruses were associated with angelfish also had been suggested by a finding of herpesviruslike particles in the spleens of dying fish (Mellergaard and Bloch 1988), but the virus had not been isolated.

As cases were presented (usually by air freight), we placed fish from each bag in a separate aquarium so that fish could be observed over a period of time. Living fish were examined for internal and external parasites as well as for bacterial infections, and whole fish were preserved in 10 percent buffered formalin for histopathological studies.

In studying suspect angelfish, we decided to look directly for viruses in tissues of sick fish with an electron microscope, in addition to using cell-culture techniques. Healthy fish were examined as experimental controls. This was a prudent step, for direct electron microscopic examination of internal tissues revealed the presence of parvoviruses, paramyxoviruses, and herpesviruses in both the healthy and the sick groups of fish. In addition, when using cell cultures derived from *Tilapia mossambica,* we successfully isolated both paramyxoviruses and parvoviruses.

While these results are proof that angelfish do carry viruses, proof that a particular virus is the actual cause of a disease lies in associating the virus with the disease on a regular basis. In addition, as stated earlier, a virus isolated in cultures of fish cells must produce the disease when given to unexposed fish, and the disease produced must be similar to that seen in the field. At this writing, infectivity tests are being conducted with viruses isolated from cell cultures.

Control measures for viral angelfish infections: Research will eventually provide means by which fish can be easily tested for suspected viruses. This will provide the basis for selection of healthy breeding stock and monitoring hatcheries for suspected disease agents. However, because antiviral therapy and vaccines are not a viable option at this time, standard approaches to avoid viruses should be employed. In particular, breeders of angelfish or discus should not purchase new breeding stock from outside sources where problems have developed.

If it is absolutely necessary to acquire new breeding stock, new fish should be placed under strict quarantine until at least one spawning has taken place and fry have been reared successfully to one-quarter of their adult size. Another way to determine whether adult fish are carriers of a virulent virus is to add fry to the quarantine tanks. Death of the added fry should serve as a potential "virus alert" in the absence of other well-known disease agents. While such methods may seem time-consuming and troublesome, they are the safest way to introduce new fish into a hatchery.

Diagnosis and treatment of angelfish problems: Since many diseases of angelfish elicit identical signs in the fish, one either must diagnose and treat accordingly, or medicate in a broad manner for external and internal parasites. During the quarantine period, treat fish with 3 to 5 ppm of metronidazole in water or 0.25 percent in a gelatinized diet to rid fish of *Hexamita*. Gill flukes (and tapeworms in the intestine), if present, will be eliminated by using one of the following treatments: 3 to 6 ppm of praziquantel (Droncit™) in water, 25 ppm of formaldehyde in water, or 0.25 ppm organophosphates in water.

Bacterial fin-rot problems, associated with parasites or more commonly with bacteria, may be an important sequel to the so-called angelfish plague. Consequently, addition of antibiotics to water or food may reduce mortalities.

While these recommendations for treatment during quarantine will help solve many problems, a true viral infection is not treatable. From case history studies, it appears that fish which have recovered from the infection will become carriers and may infect their own young as well as other fish. The wise breeder or hobbyist will be very wary of mixing new fish, even after quarantine and treatment. In addition, it is easy to spread viruses from tank to tank by nets, sponge filters, or even wet hands.

Where did the angelfish plague agent come from, will it go away, and can it return? Reports suggest that healthy angelfish are being produced, a situation which may indicate that the causative agent has somehow mysteriously disappeared. From experiences with other diseases such as rabies in wildlife, however, scientists know that disease cycles are common. These often peak every three to seven years, depending on the virus. During the low periods of such cycles, the disease agent has not disappeared but is present in an inapparent form in some animals. As young susceptible fish appear, the virus may have ample time to mutate and cause a new episode of disease. Thus, the chances are that if the suspected viral agent does wane, it will return in the future. However, by that time, research groups may be able to better understand the biology of the disease and be in a better position to suggest effective control measures.

Selected References

Andrews, C.; Excell, A.; and Carrington, N. 1988. *The Manual of Fish Health.* Tetra Press.

Anne, W., ed. 1980. *Fish Diseases. Third COPRAQ Session.* New York: Springer-Verlag.

Berry E. S.; Shea, T. B.; and Gabliks, J. 1983. Two iridovirus isolates from *Carassius auratus* (L.) *J. Fish Dis.* 6: 501–10.

Braude, A. 1982. *Microbiology: Basic Science and Medical Applications.* Philadelphia: Saunders.

Hoffman, G. L., and Meyer, F. P. 1974. *Parasites of Freshwater Fishes.* Neptune City, N.J.: T.F.H. Publications.

Mellergaard, S., and Bloch, B. 1988. Herpesvirus-like particles in angelfish, *Pterophyllum altum. Dis. Aquat. Organisms* 5:151–55.

Reichenbach-Klinke, H., and Elkan, E. 1965. *The Principal Diseases of Lower Vertebrates. Disease of Fishes.* Neptune City, N.J.: T.F.H. Publications.

Roberts, Ronald J., ed. 1978. *Fish Pathology.* London: Bailliere Tindall.

Wolf, K. 1988. *Fish Viruses and Fish Viral Diseases.* Ithaca, N.Y.: Cornell University Press.

Zabata, Z. 1985. *Parasites and Diseases of Fish Cultured in the Tropics.* London: Taylor & Francis.

Diseases of Ornamental Marine Fishes

George C. Blasiola

Less is known about the diseases of ornamental marine fishes than about those of economically important marine and freshwater species. Parasites clearly are of major importance, and nearly all marine fish sold in the aquarium trade harbor them. Bacteria and fungal infections often accompany infestations by parasites. The successful control of fish diseases requires an enhanced ability to recognize the problem, pinpoint the cause, and implement appropriate corrective measures. Though not all disease outbreaks can be averted, the use of preventative measures can minimize infectious disease outbreaks.

Quarantine

Preventative measures are essential to avoid the development and transmission of diseases in marine aquaria. One of the most important of these is the procedure of quarantine. Newly captured fish invariably harbor disease agents which may be introduced to established aquatic systems. In the natural environment, mildly parasitized fish generally are able to maintain their defense system against invaders very successfully. Insofar as microbial diseases are concerned, fish can be actively infectious or the fish can be a carrier, harboring the disease in a latent stage in equilibrium with its own physiological state without the overt clinical signs often associated with the disease. Either way, the host is still capable of spreading the disease agent.

Quarantine measures are defined as the isolation of new animals that are suspected of harboring infectious disease for specific time intervals required for the completion of life cycles by various parasitic agents, in an effort to prevent introduction of pathogens to disease-free aquatic systems. In the case of marine ornamental species, one should assume that all newly acquired fish may harbor disease agents and should be quarantined accordingly.

Quarantine facilities (also known as hospital tanks) are essential for averting the transmission of marine fish diseases to established aquaria. All new fish must be placed into quarantine facilities for specific periods of time to ascertain whether they are carrying a transmissible disease. During the quarantine process, preventative treatments can be administered to eradicate any developing infestations and/or infections.

The quarantine facility in its simplest form is an isolated container, either an aquarium, bowl, or vat not connected to the main aquatic system. The capacity of the quarantine facility can range from 10 to 20 gallons (38 to 76 liters) to hundreds of gallons or liters, depending on the number of fish involved. The tank should be equipped with a standard filtration system, including heater, airstone, and other required items. The bottom of the tank should have an adequate layer of aquarium sand or gravel and enough coral or rock to provide ample hiding places.

Water conditions in the quarantine tanks should be adjusted to approximate those of the aquatic system to which the fish will be transferred after the isolation period. This will require a regular system of water tests and record keeping.

As they are placed in the quarantine facility, all fish must be examined for frayed fins, open lesions, and ulcers, which could be indicative of an infection. Any signs of abnormal behavior which would be indicative of parasitic infestations should also be noted. The examination should be repeated the next day, after the fish have begun to adjust to their new environment. At this time, watch particularly for signs of increased respiration, abnormal presence of white spots, excess mucus secretion, or scratching, all of which could indicate the presence of various external parasites.

Before introducing new specimens to the quarantine tank, test the water temperature, salinity, and pH, both in the shipping container and in the tank, and adjust the tank conditions accordingly. Dim the light over the aquarium during specimen introduction to minimize shock.

As a general rule, all new marine fishes should be isolated in quarantine for at least twenty-one days. The older recommendation of ten to fourteen days has been shown to be inadequate for certain diseases. The twenty-one-day period is based on the time required for most piscine parasites to complete their life cycles. During this time, careful attention must be paid to general overall conditions and feeding behavior. All fishes must be quarantined, without exceptions, if one is to avoid the possibility of disease agent introduction.

Medication during quarantine: During the quarantine period it often will be necessary to administer chemical treatments to control common parasites as well as any existing bacterial or fungal infections. The medications selected will depend upon the specific disease agent to be eradicated, the species of fish, and other factors. The chemicals selected must be labeled specifically for aquatic system use.

Chemicals and drugs which have a long history of usefulness include acriflavine, formalin, malachite green, copper compounds, trichlorfon, and nitrofurazone.

Caution should be exercised with any new chemical treatment, especially those which are relatively new for use in treating marine fishes. Never expose large numbers of fish to new chemicals without prior testing of chemicals with a small group of fish, as some fish species may be highly sensitive to particular chemical treatments.

Standard preventative procedures are recommended for use on the most common marine fish parasites. New marine fishes should receive a minimum of a twenty-one-day treatment with copper or other appropriate medications to eradicate external parasites, including *Cryptocaryon* and *Amyloodinium.* In addition, they also should be treated with other parasiticides, such as formalin for eradication of flukes and copepods.

Antibacterials can also be used to treat fish showing signs of secondary bacterial infections. Antibacterial medications should be selected carefully, as some commercially available ones such as tetracycline preparations are not suitable for use in marine systems.

The most common method for treatment of aquarium fishes is the addition of chemicals directly to the water. Less frequently, medications may be added to food or injected.

The administration of drugs to water is often referred to as the immersion, or bath, method. Fish may be immersed in short-term baths or dips using drugs at fairly high concentrations for thirty seconds to several minutes. Or they may be subjected to long-term baths, immersion treatments in which the treated fish are exposed to a reduced concentration of the drug for hours or indefinitely.

Disinfection: As a final point, it is worth noting that disease agents can spread from one aquarium to another through contaminated equipment such as nets, unwashed aquarium rock, reused plastic bags, or unwashed hands. Proper disinfectants should be used to destroy potential disease-causing organisms. Those that commonly have been used are formalin, chlorine compounds such as bleach, potassium permanganate, and benzalkonium chloride solutions.

Benzalkonium chloride solutions are highly

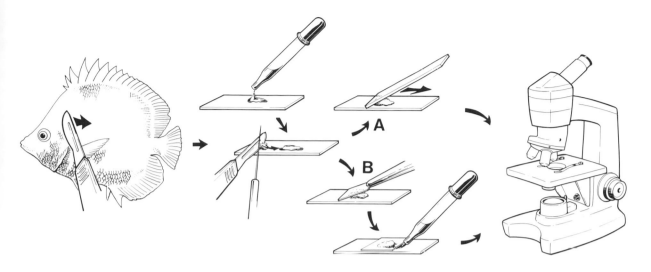

Procedure for making a skin smear. Place a drop of salt water on a microscope slide. Add sample taken from fish. A. For a dry-mount preparation, spread material on slide and allow to dry in air. B. For a wet-mount preparation, place a coverslip on the slide and add additional water if necessary.

recommended. These compounds are colorless, tend to be odorless, and have a marked antimicrobial activity. They are sold under various trade names and have been used widely on poultry farms, in laboratories, zoos, public aquaria, and veterinary hospitals. For disinfecting nets, benzalkonium chloride is generally used at 10 to 12 ppm.

Fundamentals of Disease Identification

One must become somewhat proficient in the diagnosis of marine fish diseases in order to treat them effectively and control them properly. Disease diagnosis becomes easier if one is already a good observer with some prior familiarity with common fish diseases.

Although many disease-causing agents are visible with the naked eye, a light microscope is an important tool for the definitive diagnosis of diseases, particularly parasitic ones. For this you will also need glass microscope slides and coverslips.

To ensure that poor water quality is not the basic cause of the poor state of health of the fish, water tests must be made. Water-quality testing is always the first step in ascertaining the cause of a disease problem. If the test results are within acceptable parameters, then one can proceed to attempt to identify a biological agent responsible for the disease.

Each disease or condition, whether it be related to water quality or to a biological agent, has its own associated clinical signs. Some signs readily pinpoint a particular cause of the condition. Many others are nonspecific. In order to be interpreted accurately, such nonspecific signs require additional information.

When a fish is suspected of being diseased, begin by making careful notes of its general behavioral patterns and any external abnormal body characteristics. Abnormal actions such as scratching on the bottom of the aquarium, heavy respiratory rates, or lack of appetite are important to consider. Abnormal signs such as ulcers, protrusions, fin ray atrophy, exophthalmia, raised scales, body lumps, or reddened areas must also be noted. Do not overlook historical data or the background information. "When did the problem start?", "How long has it been going on?", and "When were new fish added?" are questions, among others, that should be asked.

Next, obtain a fish that has just died or some of those that are ready to do so. It is best to remove as many diseased fish as possible in order to make a series of multiple skin smears. Fish which have been dead for several hours generally are useless for disease identification, particularly if attempting to identify certain protozoans.

Amyloodinium on the clownfish (*Amphiprion percula*). Infested fish have an increased respiratory rate and look as though fine powder were sprinkled on their body. *Source:* Tetra Archives.

Net a fish from the aquarium and place it on a flat surface. Moving from the head region just behind the gill cover (operculum) and toward the tail, use a scalpel or coverslip to make an even and rapid scrape on the skin surface. The pressure should be even and uniform, but not so hard as to remove scales. If scales are found in the smear, undoubtedly too much pressure was applied to the body surface. If performed properly, mucus will be apparent on the scalpel. Place this material on a slide. Add a drop of salt water, then a coverslip. Blot away excess water on the slide or add additional salt water, if necessary. Examine the slide immediately under the microscope. A dry mount is made in a similar manner, except that it is air-dried prior to examination.

After preparation of skin scrapings, a more detailed overall examination of the fish should be made to note any lumps, discolored areas, frayed fins, embedded parasites, or other abnormal conditions. Then the operculum should be removed. Note the condition of the gills and then remove a portion of the gill. Place this on a slide with a coverslip and examine it under the microscope, noting any abnormalities or parasites.

For an internal examination, lay the fish flat on a surface. Open it from just midway between the pectoral fins toward the anus. Then carefully cut upward in a semicircle toward the dorsal fin, making sure not to cut the intestinal tract. Continue to make a semicircle as you move forward, finally meeting just behind the operculum and then down to the point of the original cut. The flap can then be removed easily, exposing the organs.

Gross examination of the internal organs should be made, looking for any abnormal growths, discoloration, and encysted parasites such as nematodes, as well as mycobacterial granulomas or other abnormalities.

Once all information has been gathered, it is possible to make a diagnosis. An initial hunch is known as a tentative diagnosis or a best guess. It must include all relevant information that has been gathered, for this will aid in making the definitive diagnosis.

Arriving at a proper definitive diagnosis may not be an easy matter. Many diseases have non-specific clinical signs. For this reason, simplified keys for diseases sometimes may be useless, misleading, and/or confusing. An accurate diagnosis of a disease sometimes requires years of experience of working with the diseases of aquatic animals.

Infectious Diseases of Marine Fishes

Infectious diseases of marine fishes are certainly the most serious maladies one encounters, since they can be transmitted easily from one fish to another. (This is in contrast to noninfectious diseases, which are not transmissible.) Diseases that normally are not a problem in the natural habitat can quickly cause extensive mortalities in captive closed systems. The crowding of fish in aquatic systems aids in the rapid transmission of disease agents. Prevention is far easier to implement than chemotherapy, particularly in the case of parasitic diseases.

Parasites are the most common disease-causing agents in marine aquaria. This broad group includes the protozoa, platyhelminths, crustacea, and other metazoans. Various abiotic and biotic factors in the aquarium affect their development, life cycle, and transmission, including temperature, salinity, crowding, availability of intermediate hosts, and deterioration of water quality.

Protozoa

By far the most serious parasites are the protozoa, which account for extensive and often rapid mortalities of marine fishes. Most protozoa are microscopic, although some are visible to the naked eye, and undergo simple or complex life cycles. Protozoan species affecting marine fishes include both obligate parasites requiring a host for their development and facultative parasites, which will attack marine fishes only under certain circumstances. Facultative parasites do not require a host to reproduce.

Amyloodinium ocellatum (common names: saltwater velvet, coral reef disease)

Amyloodinium ocellatum, often referred to as *Oodinium,* was the first marine protozoan known to be responsible for massive mortalities of marine fishes in aquaria. It was reported in 1931 by Eleanor Brown from an epizootic at the Zoological Society of London Aquarium. In the United States, epizootics were reported from the New York Aquarium by Nigrelli in 1936 and by Dempster from Steinhart Aquarium after 1951.

Clinical signs: *Amyloodinium* primarily parasitizes the gills, but will attack other portions of the body, including the fins, causing moderate to severe infestations. Although rare, it has been reported to parasitize the internal organs of marine fish. In one report, trophonts were found in the pharynx and kidney of the pork fish, *Anisotremus virginicus.*

The parasites are visible with the naked eye and appear on the body as a fine powder with a velvety sheen, prompting the name "velvet" for the disease. The parasites are most readily seen on the transparent portions of the fins or on dark-pigmented portions of the body. The greatest concentrations of parasites occur on the gill epithelium. Ulceration and hypersecretion of mucus are also evident. Hemorrhage, inflammation, and cellular necrosis are common pathological consequences of this infestation. Other signs include pallid color, respiratory distress, lethargy, irregular opercular beat, and frequent scratching (flashing) on the aquarium bottom or on objects such as coral. Parasitized fish frequent areas of high oxygen content such as near airstones or near surface turbulence.

Epizootiology: *Amyloodinium* is infectious for all tropical and temperate teleost (bony) fishes, although elasmobranchs (sharks and rays) appear to be immune. The disease spreads rapidly, particularly in overcrowded aquatic systems.

A parasitic dinoflagellate in the family Blasto-

diniidae, *Amyloodinium ocellatum* has a life cycle with three stages: the nonmotile parasitic trophont stage, the encysted or palmella stage, and the dinospore stage. The dinospores are free-swimming, flagellated, and capable of infecting new hosts. In general, they must find a host within twenty-four to thirty-six hours or they perish. The dinospores attach to the host, lose their flagella, and are then transformed into the feeding trophont stage. After a period of growth and maturation, they drop off the host and fall to the substrate, where they undergo vegetative divisions. The de-

Close-up views of *Amyloodinium.* Top: Tomont with developing dinospores. Bottom: Dinospores. *Source:* Tetra Archives.

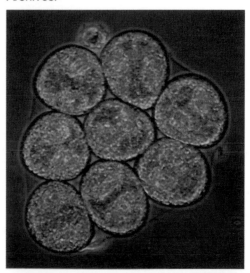

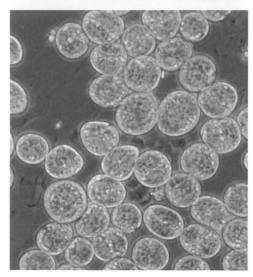

velopment of the cysts is influenced by various factors, including temperature and salinity. Above 25 degrees C (77 degrees F), development of the cysts and release of the dinospores is usually accomplished within three days. In temperatures from 10 to 20 degrees C (50 to 68 degrees F), development is reduced. Below 10 degrees C (50 degrees F), development is inhibited.

Pathogenesis: Parasitization of the gills causes tissue ulceration and hypersecretion of mucus. The mucous cells of the gill epithelium may be partially or completely destroyed in severe infestations. Hemorrhage, inflammation, and cellular necrosis are common pathological consequences. Hyperplasia and filament adhesions are not uncommon.

The parasite attachment causes severe cellular damage, for it derives all its nutrients form the host by a specialized attachment organ comprised of numerous rootlike processes which penetrate host cells and absorb tissue fluids.

Diagnosis: A presumptive diagnosis is based on observation of clinical signs associated with the disease, including the presence of diffusely distributed spots with a golden, yellow-brown cast. Skin and gill scrapings must be made and examined. Live fish can be examined after anesthetizing them with a suitable anesthetic such as tricaine methanesulfonate or quinaldine sulfate.

Under the microscope, the parasite appears oval to pyriform, with a large vesicular nucleus. The cytoplasm is filled with numerous starch granules. A conspicuous eyespot (stigma) is also present. The attached parasitic stage varies in size from 20 to 120 microns or more.

The free-swimming dinospores are highly motile, and have flagella, an eyespot, and a visible constriction called an annular furrow extending across the body. Dinospores measure approximately 12 microns in length when mature.

Prevention and treatment: Epizootics can be prevented by use of quarantine procedures. The treatment of choice for *Amyloodinium* infestations is use of copper-based medications. Other chemotherapeutics, including quinine compounds, have had a mixed history of success.

Copper-ion medications should be maintained at a concentration of 0.115 to 0.18 ppm for not less than ten days but preferably fourteen days. Higher dosages of free-ion copper are unnecessary and can be harmful to copper-sensitive fishes such as *Amphiprion*. Caution must also be

exercised when adding copper to tanks with juvenile fishes, which can be sensitive. Severe pathological damage can result if fish are maintained in higher-than-recommended copper concentrations. Sublethal effects of copper include a disruption of osmotic and ionic homeostasis and accumulation of copper in the internal organs.

Chelated coppers, that is, those complexed with chelating agents such as EDTA, can also be used, but generally must be used at substantially higher concentrations than ionic copper. Dosages of chelated copper formulations used in chemotherapy often exceed 2.0 ppm. Due to their inherent stability, chelated copper formulations have the advantage of remaining in solution for longer period than ionic copper solutions.

A copper-ion test kit is necessary to monitor the proper ionic copper concentration. In new systems, an initial dose of copper will decrease rapidly, and booster doses will be required shortly after the first dosage. Copper ions will be removed from water by various factors, including precipitation, binding to organics, binding to carbons, and adsorption to substrates. Studies have recently demonstrated that adsorption by coral, dolomite, or oyster shell is the primary route by which copper ion is removed from circulating aquarium water. Tests should be done daily, and additional copper- ion solution added to the tank if necessary.

Since copper ion is extremely toxic to invertebrates, they must be removed from the tank before commencing the treatment. Upon termination of the treatment period, invertebrates must not be returned until the concentration drops below 0.03 ppm.

Brooklynella hostilis (common name: anemonefish disease)

Brooklynella hostilis was first reported in the scientific literature in 1970 as a causative agent responsible for mortalities of aquarium fishes at the New York Aquarium. The first popular account of the problems caused by the parasite appeared in 1980. Less well known than other parasitic diseases of marine fishes, *Brooklynella* is capable of causing rapid mortalities of marine fishes.

Clinical signs: *Brooklynella hostilis* parasitizes both the skin and gills of fish. Clinical signs of affected fish include lethargy, lack of appetite, hypersecretion of mucus, and respiratory distress. Body lesions originate as small, diffuse, discolored foci which involve larger portions of

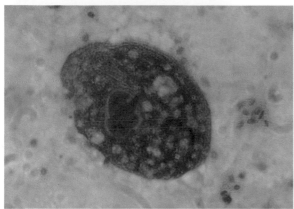

Brooklynella infestation. Top: Appearance on a seahorse (*Hippocampus kuda*). Note abnormal body coloration and sloughing of epithelium. Above: Dried and stained smear.

the fish's body. In advanced stages, the epithelium sloughs off the fish's body. The characteristic sloughing is an important diagnostic sign associated with *Brooklynella* infestations.

Epizootiology: *Brooklynella* is infectious for all tropical teleost fishes and can affect temperate species as well (Blasiola, unpublished). Currently, no parasitism of elasmobranchs has been reported. *Brooklynella* is a "debility parasite," affecting fish that have been severely stressed and maintained in crowded conditions. Clownfish appear to be particularly susceptible, as do seahorses (*Hippocampus*). Affected seahorses exhibit similar clinical signs, including the characteristic

epithelial sloughing.

A ciliated parasite in the family Dysteriidae, *Brooklynella hostilis* is an obligate parasite of fishes. The life cycle of *Brooklynella* is similar to that of its freshwater counterpart, *Chilodonella.* Reproduction occurs by simple cell division with transmission of the parasites directly to other hosts.

Pathogenesis: Severe damage to the host results from the presence of large numbers of parasites and their associated feeding and locomotor activities. The most serious area of damage is the gill epithelium, which is often extensively destroyed. *Brooklynella* feeds on epithelial and blood cells of the host. Death is primarily attributed to loss of epithelium and the subsequent impaired osmoregulatory capabilities of the host.

Diagnosis: A presumptive diagnosis is based on observation of clinical signs and epithelial sloughing. The parasite is not visible with the naked eye. Skin and gill smears from moribund fish examined microscopically can confirm the presence of the parasite. Only live fish are suitable for examination. (Frozen fish are useless for diagnostic work.) *Brooklynella* is highly ciliated and mobile. The parasites occur in large numbers and are easily found on the body and on gills. They range in size from 58 to 80 by 40 to 48 microns. Living parasites are heart-shaped or kidney-shaped, with an oval macronucleus, several micronuclei, and numerous food vacuoles. Notable diagnostic structures include the posterior-ventral adhesion organ used for attachment to the host and the basketlike cytopharyngeal tube.

Prevention and treatment: A combination of formalin and malachite green solutions is recommended for rapid eradication of *Brooklynella.* Combination liquids of formalin and malachite green are readily available commercially. Enough of the solution should be added to produce 15 to 25 ppm of formalin and 0.05 ppm of malachite green. Usually the treatment must be repeated every other day for a minimum of three treatments. Partial water changes should be made between treatments. Freshwater dips are also useful, but should be followed by the malachite green treatment of 0.10 ppm or with the formalin and malachite green combination. Formalin dips must be avoided in cases where fish have sustained severe skin damage.

Brooklynella is resistant to copper treatments and will reproduce in systems treated with cop-

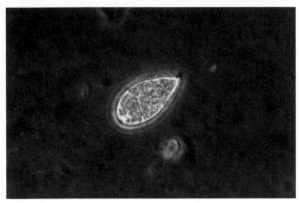

Uronema marinum infestation. Top: Ulceration, hemorrhage, and skin pitting are evident on this maroon clownfish (*Premnas biaculeatus*). Above: Isolated organism.

per. In many cases, the control of parasites must be followed with antibacterial treatments to control topical or systemic bacterial infections that may have developed during parasitization of the host.

Uronema marinum (common name: uronema)
Normally a free-living ciliate, *Uronema marinum* is known to parasitize and cause extensive damage to captive marine fishes. The parasite was first reported in 1980 from fishes in the New York Aquarium. The freshwater counterpart of *Uronema* is *Tetrahymena,* often responsible for the dreaded "guppy killer" disease.

Clinical signs: *Uronema marinum* initially does not produce readily diagnostic lesions. Small discolored areas eventually spread, resulting in ulcerations. In advanced stages, lesions can easily be misdiagnosed as a topical bacterial infection. Sloughing of the epidermis is similar to that of fish parasitized with *Brooklynella.* However, a pro-

nounced pitting of the skin is often evident. Not always limited to the skin, the protozoans can also be found in the internal organs. Some species of parasitized fishes, such as seahorses, may not exhibit external lesions.

Parasitized fish are generally listless, anorexic, and demonstrate abnormal respiratory distress. They can appear pale in color, and secondary bacterial infection is quite common.

Epizootiology: *Uronema marinum* rapidly kills tropical marine teleost fishes, but has not been reported from elasmobranch fishes. A ciliate in the family Uronematidae, it normally occurs as a free-living species but can become parasitic on fishes under certain conditions, often accompanying episodes of trauma. It is usually found on the skin and gills but can become invasive in the internal organs.

The life cycle is uncomplicated, with the parasite reproducing by simple binary fission. The ciliates reproduce rapidly, and large numbers are often found on infested fishes.

Pathogenesis: Parasitization of the gills and epithelium of the body causes ulceration. The musculature is also involved and can be hemorrhagic. Cellular necrosis is evident. *Uronema* can invade internal organs, including the kidney and urinary bladder. Ciliates can be found in capillaries of the gill lamellae, obstructing normal blood flow to the distal portions of the lamellae.

The parasite causes extensive damage to the fish tissue by its feeding activity. Secondary infection almost always accompanies infestation by *Uronema.* Impairment of normal osmoregulatory processes are suspected to contribute to death of the host.

Diagnosis: A presumptive diagnosis is based on observation of clinical signs, including ulcerations, hemorrhage, and sloughing of skin. Skin and gill scrapings should be made and a muscle biopsy obtained to examine for ciliate invasion. Smears can be made from the skin and gills. Only live fish should be used for diagnostic work.

Under the microscope, the ciliates appear tear-drop-shaped, with a pointed anterior and rounded posterior. Ciliates measure approximately 32 to 38 by 13 to 20 microns. A single oval macronucleus is present, as well as a single micronucleus. The parasite is highly motile.

Prevention and treatment: *Uronema* can be controlled with use of parasiticides in combination with freshwater dips. Prepare a freshwater

Saltwater ich (*Cryptocaryon irritans*) is readily apparent on this lionfish (*Pterois volitans*). *Source:* Tetra Archives.

dip with a pH equal to the pH of the water into which fish will be transferred after treatment. Dip new fish for three to fifteen minutes, depending on species. Then twenty-four to thirty-six hours afterward, treat the fish either with formaldehyde at 15 to 25 ppm or with a formalin/malachite green combination. Commercial solutions of formalin/malachite green are available that produce a final concentration in the water of 15 to 25 ppm formalin and 0.05 to 0.10 ppm of malachite green. A minimum of three treatments is required. Additional treatments can be required, particularly if the disease is in the advanced stage and the parasite has burrowed under the skin. *Uronema* tends to be more difficult to eradicate than *Brooklynella hostilis*, due to the invasive nature of the former.

Additional adjunct treatments to control topical secondary bacterial infections are required with fish that have already contracted the disease.

Cryptocaryon irritans (common names: saltwater ich, white spot disease)

As with *Amyloodinium*, *Cryptocaryon irritans* has been responsible for mass mortalities in marine aquaria and oceanaria. The incidence of *Cryptocaryon* infestations has become more of a prob-lem over the past decade than *Amyloodinium*. Outbreaks of cryptocaryonlasis are correlated with adverse conditions, including overcrowding, extremes of water temperature, and induced stress during transport.

Cryptocaryon was first named by Brown at the Zoological Society of London in 1951. However, the disease and the parasite were first reported from infested fishes by Sikama in Japan in 1938. He described the parasite in 1961, naming it *Ichthyophthirius marinus,* unaware that the parasite had already been described by Brown.

Clinical signs: *Cryptocaryon irritans* produces white opaque to grayish papules on the eyes, gills, and skin of the host. The ciliates are found within the papules. The lesions produced are characteristic of the disease and similar to those caused by its freshwater counterpart, *Ichthyophthirius multifiliis.* The lesions are considerably larger than the fine dustlike spots observed on fish infected with *Amyloodinium ocellatum*. Macroscopically, the papules are readily seen on transparent portions of the fins on darkly pigmented areas of the body. In addition, the fins may appear to be torn and ragged. In moderate to severe infestations, the papules are often clustered and

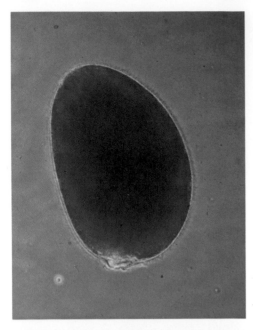

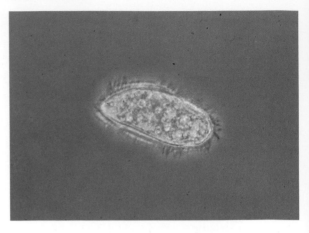

Close-up views of *Crytocaryon*. Top left: Trophont. Below left: Tomont. Above: Tomite (the infective stage). *Source:* Tetra Archives.

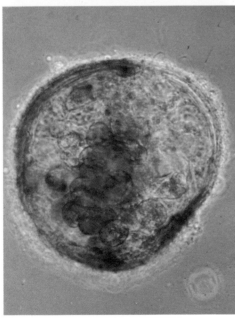

can coalesce. Epithelial tissue can be observed to fall off in stringlike masses.

Parasitized fish are restless, dart suddenly, and exhibit marked respiratory distress. In the early stages of the infestation, the fish occasionally scratch on the substrate or on objects such as coral or rock. As the disease progresses, the scratching becomes more frequent and normal body coloration is lost, with turbid skin often appearing. Death ensues rapidly

without immediate treatment.

Epizootiology: All tropical and temperate teleost fishes are susceptible to *Cryptocaryon irritans.* Elasmobranchs tend to be resistant to infestations. *Cryptocaryon* can spread rapidly in crowded systems.

Cryptocaryon irritans is a holotrichous ciliate of the family Ichthyophthiriidae in the order Hymenostomatida. Its life cycle and morphological characteristics are similar to the freshwater ciliate *Ichthyophthirius multifiliis,* but it differs in cytological characteristics and host specificity.

The life cycle of *Cryptocaryon irritans* involves three stages: The tomite or infective stage, the trophont or feeding stage, and the tomont or encysted stage. Free-swimming tomites locate a suitable host and burrow into the epithelium of the gills or into the epidermis, after which they transform into the trophont stage. Trophonts are active feeders subsisting on the host's cellular debris and tissue fluids. After a period of growth and maturation, the trophonts fall to the substrate and encyst, becoming tomonts. After a series of multiple divisions and maturation, the free-swimming tomites are released and seek new hosts. Developmental time of the tomont is strongly dependent on temperature and salinity. Above 37 degrees C (98.6 degrees F) and below 7 degrees C (44.6 degrees F), the parasite cannot encyst.

Pathogenesis: *Cryptocaryon irritans* causes severe tissue irritation, resulting in epithelial hyperplasia and hypersecretion of mucus by the fish. In

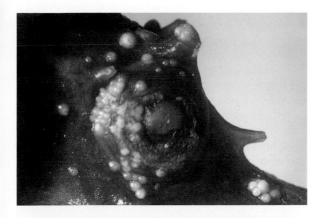

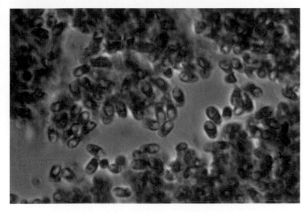

Glugea heraldi. Top: cysts on the seahorse (*Hippocampus erectus*). Above: spores as they appear under phase microscope.

advanced cases of the disease, the epithelial tissue becomes inflamed and hemorrhagic. The ciliate's presence is accompanied by hypersecretion of mucus, cellular hyperplasia, petechiae, and lamellar tissue erosion. Parasites frequently are known to invade the corneal epithelium, causing opacity of the eyes, and on occasion, permanent blindness.

Diagnosis: A presumptive diagnosis is based on the observation of diffusely distributed white papules on the gills and skin. Skin scrapings should be made and examined under a microscope to confirm the disease. The diagnostic features of the parasite include a large four-lobed macronucleus and several micronuclei. Both the macronucleus and micronuclei are readily observed in the tomite, but tend to be obscured by vacuoles in the trophont. Trophonts are oval to spherical, and move by means of short, uniformly distributed cilia. Close observation discloses a

buccal cavity and well-developed feeding apparatus. The cytoplasm contains food vacuoles and many dark granules. Trophonts vary in size from 160 to 454 microns.

Tomites are pear-shaped and have longer cilia than do trophonts. They are highly motile compared with the slower-moving trophont. Numerous vacuoles, dark granules, and ingested food materials are observable in the cytoplasm. Tomites measure approximately 30 to 50 microns along the major axis.

Prevention and treatment: The treatment of choice for eradication of *Cryptocaryon* involves copper compounds. Other chemicals such as quinine compounds may also be used, but may not be as consistently effective as copper. Quinacrine hydrochloride has shown promise as an alternative to copper, and can be used directly in a tank. A combination of quinine HCl (2.64 milligrams per liter) and chloroquine (10.6 milligrams per liter), used in conjunction with hypersaline (45 ppm) treatment for twenty minutes prior to treatment, has proven to be successful.

Copper should be used in the same manner as outlined for the treatment of *Amyloodinium ocellatum.* Extended treatments, perhaps for up to four weeks, are sometimes necessary. Recent studies have indicated that a ten- to fourteen-day treatment period may not be long enough to fully eradicate the parasite. *Cryptocaryon* tends to be more difficult to eradicate than *Amyloodinium.* Chelated compounds are not recommended for treatment of fishes parasitized with *Cryptocaryon* due to their relative ineffectiveness compared with ionic copper medications.

Microsporea and Myxosporea

Once grouped in the Sporozoa with other microorganisms, these microbes are all obligate parasites. All species in these groups produce spores, and many have complex life cycles. Numerous species of both orders parasitize fishes. Only a few representative species will be discussed in the following sections. In general, these parasites are secondary in importance to the protozoans previously discussed.

Microsporea (common name: boil disease)
The Microsporea are comprised of some of the smallest and most widely distributed parasites infecting fishes. Many are no larger than a bacterial cell. They are intracellular parasites which

cause marked host-cell hypertrophy and the formation of cysts. *Glugea* and *Pleistophora* are two of the most important genera parasitizing marine fishes.

Clinical signs: Lesions generally appear as small, pale opaque or white swellings, found externally or internally. They can be found on the gills, body, connective tissue, liver, and musculature.

Behavior signs of the host can vary from little alteration in behavior to pronounced behavior changes. When the seahorse (*Hippocampus erectus*) is infested with the microsporidan *Glugea heraldi,* it becomes lethargic, anorexic, and emaciated as the disease progresses. Normal locomotor ability becomes impaired in later stages of the infestation as the parasite destroys cells while encysting in the connective tissue.

Epizootiology: The Microsporea are infectious, although the exact mode of transmission of these parasites is not known in fishes.

A generalized life cycle of the Microsporea involves the release of spores from a dead and decaying host. The spores are taken up by a host, either directly or possibly indirectly through an intermediate host. In the intestinal tract, they attach to the gut epithelium via the polar filament. At this time, the sporoplasm emerges from each spore and migrates to the infection site. Once the sporoplasm reaches the site of infection, the sporoplasm (now called trophozoite) enters a host cell and undergoes multiple cellular divisions. This process is followed by the formation of spores (sporogony). During sporogony, a maturation of young spores or sporoblasts results in development of mature spores. Autoinfection by the vegetative stages developing during the multiple cellular division stage can also occur. During the development stages swellings occur, the result of the enlargement of single parasitized cells. With species such as *Glugea,* the "cyst" which forms in response to the increasing number of parasites and the cellular response is referred to as a xenoma.

Pathogenesis: Parasitism by Microsporea has various pathological consequences. During initial infestation, the cysts will increase in size, involving larger areas of the host's body. Cellular responses include the infiltration and/or proliferation of migratory cells and formation of multinucleate giant cells. Connective tissue encapsulations are readily evident in many infestations. With some microsporean species, only slight cellular response is evident.

Infestation of host musculature causes destruction of the muscular fibers, with accompanying congestion, hyalinization, and paralysis. Infestation of the ovaries interferes with egg development. Invasion of the host's gills by Microsporea results in epithelial hyperplasia and lamellar fusion. Parasitization of other organs can cause metabolic dysfunctions.

Diagnosis: A presumptive diagnosis is based on the appearance of small cysts or swellings which gradually enlarge and proliferate. This can be evident on skin, gills, or internally in the musculature during necropsy. Possible infected fishes should be anesthetized, the cysts examined and lanced, and the material placed on a microscope slide for examination. The use of phase microscopy is recommended for detection of microsporidean spores. Additional tissues should be fixed for routine histological sectioning.

Mature spores are identifiable primarily on the basis of their morphology. The spores vary in shape and can be oval, tubular, spherical, or pyriform. The oval form is the most commonly observed. Spores can vary in length from 1.5 to over 10 microns. At high magnification, clear areas will be observable at the ends of the spore. The spores are surrounded by a limiting membrane which tends to be refractive and usually can be observed in fresh wet mounts.

In cases where mature spores are absent, immature stages of the parasites can be observed, but classification of the parasite is not possible without the presence of mature spores.

Prevention and treatment: No known chemotherapeutic control is available to eradicate Microsporea from fishes. Thus one must isolate the parasitized fish or destroy it to avoid infecting other fishes. The use of ultraviolet light at 35,000 microwatts per square centimeter on a continual basis has had some success in destruction of spores in contaminated water systems. Because of the infectious nature of many microsporidians, all equipment that comes in contact with the infected aquatic system or with the infected fishes must be thoroughly disinfected with sodium hypochlorite or other disinfectant agents.

Myxosporea

As protozoan parasites of lower vertebrates, the myxosporeans consist of numerous coelozoic (living in the body cavity) and histozoic (living in tissues) species. Like the microsporidans, the myxosporeans are very small parasites. The mature spore is very distinctive and easily identified as a myxosporean. Various species of a number of genera, including *Kudoa, Myxobolus, Henneguya, Myxosoma,* and others, parasitize marine fishes.

Clinical signs: These parasites may live in tissues or in the body cavity. Histozoic myxosporean parasites affect various fish tissues and organs, including gills, cartilage, and musculature. Coelozoic species are found primarily in the gallbladder. Gross lesions appear as cysts or swellings visible in tissues and organs of the host. Cysts can be found on the fins, skin, musculature, or in internal organs.

Fish infested with myxosporeans may demonstrate a multitude of abnormal behavior signs, including lethargy, emaciation, dropsy, whirling behavior, and increased respiration rate.

Epizootiology: Like the Microsporea, Myxosporea are infectious, but their mode of transmission has not been established. The life cycles of many of the myxosporeans are virtually unknown.

A generalized life cycle begins with the release of spores into the water after the decay of an infested host. External cysts in the gills or body can also rupture while the host is alive, thereby releasing spores. The spores may be ingested directly or via an intermediate host. In the digestive tract, gastric secretions cause the spores to extrude their polar filaments, anchoring the spore in the host's gut. The sporoplasm emerges, migrates to the infection site, and transforms into a feeding trophozoite, which either subsists on the absorption of the host's body fluids or is saprozoic. After undergoing shizogony, sporonts are formed in which distinct cell types appear and which differentiate into specific parts of the spore.

Pathogenesis: Parasitization of the host by histozoic myxosporeans has serious consequences for the host. Musculature invasion generally causes degeneration and liquification of the muscle fibers. The liquification is believed to be caused by enzymes secreted by the parasites.

A new myxosporean was recently described from the collared butterfly fish (*Chaetodon collare*). The fish were in captivity for two months. No ulcerations or any other external signs were apparent. However, a marked atrophy of the dorsal musculature was noticed. On examination, the musculature was soft and mushy. Smears made from the tissue showed numbers of cysts in the muscle fibers. The parasite has been described as *Pentacapsula muscularis,* a species which is characterized by the presence of five polar capsules.

Parasitism of the gallbladder results in organ inflammation and enlargement. Parasitism of the gills is very serious, interfering with normal respiration. The lamellae can thicken and fuse as cysts of the parasites develop. Normal blood circulation through the capillaries can be obstructed, causing necrosis.

Diagnosis: A presumptive diagnosis is based on the appearance of cysts, swellings, and ulcerated or light-colored areas of the body. The light-colored areas tend to be soft to the touch. Cysts should be lanced and the exudate examined microscopically.

Examination of wet mounts confirms the presence of Myxosporea. Spores will contain characteristic polar capsules grouped at one end or at opposite ends of the spore. Phase microscopy, if available, is useful in distinguishing these, especially if slides can be stained with Giemsa or Trichrome. Stained spores will show distinct stained dark polar capsules. The sporoplasm can be seen in the proximity of the polar capsules. In immature spores, sporoplasm nuclei may be distinguishable.

Tissues sampled during necropsy should be fixed in standard 10 percent buffered formalin fixative solutions for histological sectioning.

Myxosporean spores are considerably larger than those of Microsporea. Depending on species, their size varies from as little as 5 to over 40 microns. The shape of the spores will vary and can include oval, fusiform, spherical, and stellate forms. Some species such as *Henneguya* possess long characteristic tall-like spore extensions.

Prevention and treatment: Currently no known chemotherapeutic agent will control Myxosporea, although furazolidone has been claimed to be moderately successful in controlling some species. Infested fish must be isolated or destroyed to prevent possible spread of the parasite. Ultraviolet disinfection of water is useful in destroying spores.

Platyhelminthes

The phylum Platyhelminthes includes both free-living and parasitic species. The majority of these flatworms are parasitic, and a large number have complex life cycles which require intermediate hosts. The group is comprised of three classes: the Turbellaria (free-living flatworms), Trematoda

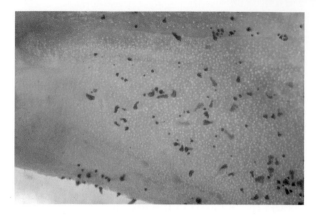

Turbellarians which give rise to the condition
sometimes called "black ich;" top: on the skin
of a yellow tang (*Zebrasoma flavescens*);
above: removed from infested tang and
stained. Note prominent eyespots.

(flukes), and Cestoda (tapeworms).

The turbellarians are largely a free-living class
of worms. However, a few notable exceptions
parasitize fish under certain conditions. The most
common is a small turbellarian infesting species
of Acanthuridae, Chaetodontidae, and Labridae
but not restricted to those families.

The class Trematoda is divided into three main
orders. Two of these, the Monogenea or monogenetic trematodes, and the Digenea or digenetic
trematodes, contain numerous species of parasites affecting marine fishes.

Members of the Cestoda, the most specialized
class of the Platyhelminthes, are segmented, covered by a nonliving cuticle, and lack a digestive
system. Deriving their nourishment directly from
their host, they attach by means of a specialized
organ called a scolex. Cestodes are not generally
a serious problem for ornamental marine fishes.

Most cestode species require one or more intermediate hosts to complete their life cycle.

Ichthyophaga (common names: tang turbellarian, black ich)

At the writing of this chapter, the taxonomic position of the tang turbellarian is questionable but
under study. In 1976, this author first reported the
occurrence of the turbellarian from the yellow
tang (*Zebrasoma flavescens*), sailfin tang
(*Z. veliferum),* imperator angelfish *(Holacanthus
imperator*), and the lemon peel angelfish (*Cen-
tropyge flavissimus*). Condé independently reported a small turbellarian parasitizing two
species of Caribbean wrasses, *Halichoeres bivit-
tatus* and *Thalassoma bifasciatum*, and a species
of scarid, *Scarus croicensis.* Both infestations
undoubtedly were caused by the same turbellarian species.

Clinical signs: The turbellarian parasitizes the
skin and gills of fishes. The worms appear externally as minute black spots randomly distributed
on the host's body, but mainly on the body proper
and rarely on the fins. In moderate to severe
infestations, inflammation of the skin is readily
apparent.

Behavioral signs include frequent scratching
on the aquarium bottom and on objects, cessa-
tion of normal feeding patterns, general listlessness, and pallid body coloration.

Epizootiology: The tang turbellarian is infectious
to teleost fishes. It is not known to parasitize
elasmobranch fishes. The life cycle is direct, with
the young worms developing within the adults.
The worms are believed to be parthenogenic.
After approximately six days on the host, the
worms drop off. On the substrate, the juvenile
worms continue to mature and then are released
by rupture of the body wall. As many as 160
juvenile worms per adult are released. The free-
swimming larvae seek other hosts, where they
attach and mature into adults.

Pathogenesis: Infestation is primarily on the
body surface, although worms can be detected
in the opercular cavity and on the gill filaments.
Lesions and diffuse dermal hemorrhaging are
caused by the parasites' movement and the feeding of the worms on the cellular debris of the skin.
Untreated fishes become emaciated and die with
heavy infestations.

Diagnosis: A presumptive diagnosis is based on
the appearance of small black spots on the fish,
with accompanying listlessness. Fish should be

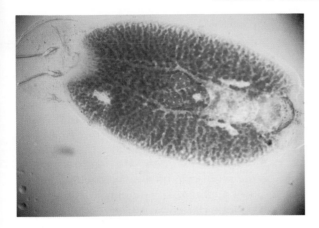

The eye fluke (*Neobenedenia*). Note oval attachment organ, opisthohaptor, with anchors, and oral sucker.

anesthetized and examined under a microscope. The worms are small and confirmed as those which measure approximately 110 to 115 microns in length and 70 to 78 microns in width. The worms appear oval or leaflike, with two prominent eyespots and numerous cilia. Developing young can be observed within the body of mature turbellarians.

Prevention and treatment: Infestations can be controlled by the use of organophosphates, formalin dips, or freshwater dips. Formalin is effective when used at 1.0 milliliter per gallon (3.8 liters) for a twenty- to thirty-minute bath. Several treatments may be required. However, this method is not the most suitable one for established aquaria, as formalin is toxic to nitrifying bacteria and to invertebrates. In addition, the entire volume of the aquarium has to be changed after treatment. Alternative treatments are therefore recommended for eradication of turbellarians.

Organophosphates (for example, Masoten™, trichlorfon) are effective when used at the rate of 0.80 to 1.0 milligram (active) per liter of water. They must not be used in aquaria with crustaceans, because organophosphates are quite toxic to shrimp, lobsters, and crabs.

Freshwater dips are effective if used when fish are lightly infested. Secondary infection by bacteria can occur and will require adjunct chemotherapy with appropriate antimicrobial drugs.

Monogenea (common name: flukes)

The Monogenea are by far the most serious of the trematode parasites affecting fish. They can account for large numbers of aquarium mortalities and are often small enough to go unnoticed. Flukes are ectoparasitic and only require one host to complete their life cycle. Almost all fishes harbor flukes. The worms usually vary in size from 0.4 to 1.0 millimeter in length. Although some species exceed 2.0 millimeters in length, most of the common species are too minute to be seen with the naked eye.

Clinical signs: Monogenetic trematodes are parasites of the skin and gills. Unless the worm is a large species like *Neobenedenia* (the eye fluke) or *Microcotyle,* common on the gills of butterfly fishes and angelfishes, they are not easily detected. Behavioral signs include frequent scratching on objects, pale body color, and respiratory distress. In moderate to severe infestations, mechanical damage and ulceration will be evident. This is most often accompanied by a secondary bacterial infection.

Epizootiology: Monogenetic trematodes are parasites of both teleost and elasmobranch fishes. The genus *Dermophthirius* is represented by several species parasitic on sharks, including the lemon shark (*Negaprion brevirostris*) and the dusky shark (*Carcharhinus obscurus*).

The life cycle is direct, with the parasites laying eggs that develop into larvae which reinfect the host or infest other susceptible fishes. Members in the Gyrodactylidae bear their young alive, some with two generations developing within the uterus of the worm.

Pathogenesis: Parasitism of the gills and skin causes serious tissue and cellular damage to the host. The movements of the parasite cause damage by a special attachment organ, the opisthohaptor, which consists of either anchors, clamps, or hooklets. Trematodes feed directly on the blood, mucus, and tissue fluids of the host. This damage opens the way for secondary infections which can develop into systemic infection when not treated promptly. In freshwater fish, flukes can act as vectors for bacteria. Microcolonies of bacteria have been found on parasites and on the site of opisthohaptor attachment. It is plausible that the same situation could exist with marine fish flukes, particularly with regard to the bacterium *Vibrio.*

Diagnosis: A presumptive diagnosis is made from observation of clinical behavioral signs and appearance of worms and ulcerations or reddened areas on the skin. Confirmation of disease requires observation of the worms in smears from the skin and gills of the fish.

Monogenetic trematodes are generally either elongate or oval flatworms which lack a ciliated epidermis. (The young do, however, have a ciliated epidermis.) A characteristic attachment apparatus will be observed on the posterior portion of the body. This organ is often elaborate and composed of suckers, anchors, clamps, and hooks. Anterior attachment suckers will also be evident.

Prevention and treatment: Freshwater dips, formalin dips, or organophosphate compounds are effective in control of monogenetic trematodes.

New fish can be treated with a standard freshwater dip for five to fifteen minutes, depending on species. Generally, however, freshwater dips are not sufficient to eradicate trematodes completely, and should be followed by either formalin dips or organophosphate treatments within thirty-six to forty-eight hours.

Organophosphates are recommended for eradication of flukes. The dosage is dependent on the pH and temperature. Recommended concentrations range between 0.75 and 1.0 ppm. Severe infestations require more than one treatment. A series of three treatments, spaced a week apart, is a suggested regime. Apparent resistance developed by flukes to organophosphates is not a problem with marine fish species as compared with freshwater species. However, repetitive treatments of marine fish with organophosphates, such as found in public aquaria conditions, could possibly induce resistance.

Treatment with a combination of mebendazole (0.2 milligram per liter) and trichlorfon (0.9 milligram per liter) for twenty-four hours has been shown to be successful in controlling freshwater *Gyrodactylus.* The use of this combination could also be useful in controlling *Gyrodactylus* in marine environments.

Formalin is also an appropriate treatment. However, the nature of the chemical makes it hazardous to use and caution must be exercised. Formalin must never be used on fish that have just been received or handled, or when ulcers are evident on the fish. Traumatized fish are very sensitive to formalin treatments, and not all species can withstand treatment episodes. Bath treatments for twenty to thirty minutes are recommended for most fishes. However, the treatment must be terminated at any point at which the fish begin to appear unduly stressed.

Formalin also is known to reduce dissolved oxygen levels in water. Supplementary aeration should always be provided during treatments.

Digenea (common name: digenetic trematodes)
The Digenea require one or more intermediate hosts in order to complete their life cycle, with a mollusk being one of the intermediate hosts. The final host can be a fish, bird, or carnivorous mammal. Unlike the monogenetic trematodes, all digenetic trematodes are endoparasitic. Their attachment organs are simple disks without hooks or anchors. The digenetic trematodes are less serious parasites of marine fishes than are the monogenetic trematodes, and are of secondary importance as causes of captive fish mortalities.

Clinical signs: Digenetic trematodes can be found on marine fishes either as adults or as the larval forms, called metacercariae. The adults are easily seen and can be found in the intestine, esophagus, stomach, circulatory system, or internally in other areas of the fish's body. Metacercariae can be found in the skin, eyes, and muscles. Often, metacercariae are encysted and appear as spherical melanin-pigmented cysts. Nonmelanized cysts are white and will be present on internal organs. Virtually no unusual behavioral signs will be observed in fishes parasitized with digenetic trematodes.

Epizootiology: Digenetic trematodes are fairly species-specific. Life cycles differ accordingly. A typical life cycle is that of *Sanguinicola,* a blood fluke that parasitizes the gill arches of various fish species. Eggs develop in the capillaries, and small larvae called miracidia break through the gills. Miracidia then invade an intermediate host, in this case a snail of the genus *Oxytrema.* In the snail, the miracidia metamorphose through various other larval stages, and emerge as cercariae. The cercariae parasitize a fish and develop into adults to complete their life cycle.

In another common life cycle, metacercariae encyst and remain in the host until the host is consumed by another animal. Within the next host, the parasites may continue their life cycle or the metacercariae may remain encysted. In general, this cycle involves the same larval stages. When cercariae leave the snail, they infect fish, where the larvae encyst.

Pathogenesis: Damage to the host fish occurs when large numbers of larvae leave the gills, causing extensive hemorrhagic and tissue damage. Eggs of trematodes can also interfere with normal circulation in the capillaries of the gills, liver, kidneys, and other organs. Metacercariae encysted in the eye will cause extensive pathology and permanent blindness.

Diagnosis: A diagnosis is based on the finding of adult worms or metacercariae in the fish. Adults will be found anywhere in the body internally. The worms vary in size, depending on species, but are visible with the naked eye. Their attachment organs are simple disks without accessory hooks or anchors. The oral sucker is located anteriorly and an acetabulus (abdominal sucker) is located at the posterior position of the parasite or near the center of the body. When metacercariae are found on the body, they appear as small to large gray to black eruptions.

Prevention and treatment: Treatment for digenetic trematodes is more difficult than for monogenetic trematodes. A few metacercariae on fish have little effect on the health of the fish. No known chemotherapy for treatment of metacercariae has been found, and it is best to leave affected fish alone.

Di-N-tin-butyl oxide was used in the past to eradicate digenetic trematodes. However, since the parasites do not cause significant mortalities in marine fishes, such treatments are unnecessary. Under aquarium conditions, the life cycles of digenetic trematodes cannot be completed due to absence of other required intermediate hosts.

Cestoda (common name: tapeworms)

Cestodes can appear in marine fishes in either an adult or a larval form. Adults inhabit the intestine or pyloric cecae. Larval forms (plerocercoids) are typically found encysted or free in the liver, muscle, and body cavity.

Clinical signs: Parasitized fish generally demonstrate no abnormal behavioral or physical signs except in cases of severe infestation. Severely parasitized fish tend to be lethargic, and can show abdominal enlargement due to the presence of adult or larval forms in the abdominal cavity.

Epizootiology: The life cycles of cestodes vary, depending on the species. A typical life cycle is illustrated by a trypanorhynch cestode, *Grillotia erinaceus,* whose definitive hosts are elasmobranch fishes. The adult cestodes shed eggs which pass out of the host via the feces. An intermediate host becomes infested, in this case a copepod. Within the copepod, the parasite de-

velops into a procercoid form. When the copepod is eaten by a bony fish, the second intermediate host, the procercoid develops into a plerocercoid. These larval forms inhabit the pyloric cecae, intestine, and stomach. The cycle is complete when the bony fish is eaten by the definitive host, in this case a ray.

Pathogenesis: Damage to the host occurs by the presence of the adults and the larval forms. Migrating forms especially can cause extensive damage to the host's body organs by compression of the organs, adhesions, and a proliferation of fibrous connective tissue. Damage to the reproductive organs is quite common and impairs normal spawning.

Adult cestodes tend to live in the intestine and pyloric cecae, causing damage to the intestinal walls by their attachment and by direct absorption of nutrients. Severe infestations are accompanied by anemia and peritonitis. When parasites are present in large numbers, obstructions of the intestinal tract can cause death of the host.

Diagnosis: A diagnosis is based on the confirmation of adult cestodes or larval forms. Adults are segmented, ribbonlike, and attach by means of a scolex to the host. Plerocercoids tend to be white or cream-colored, with a superficial fine segmentation. They are visible to the naked eye.

Prevention and treatment: The treatment of cestodes in marine fishes is very difficult. For all practical purposes, the condition is not treatable. However, it is unlikely that treatment of marine fishes will ever be necessary. Some success has been shown in the administration of various anthelmintics such as Yomesan®. A recommended starter dose is 1.0 milligram per 90 grams (0.2 pounds) of fish weight. Generally only one dose is required. Usually adult cestodes are shed within twenty-four hours. Caution must be used, as fish are sensitive to this drug.

A new anthelmintic, praziquantel, has been shown to be effective in controlling freshwater cestodes in immersion treatments. It is likely that it could also be used for treatment of marine fish.

Nematoda

The nematodes, or roundworms, comprise a large group of both free-living and parasitic forms. Nematodes are elongated, cylindrical worms tending to taper toward the body ends. They frequently are red, reddish-orange, or white and opaque. It is quite common to find numerous free-living nematodes in aquarium gravel filter beds. They are generally harmless. Parasitic nematodes are encountered from time to time in marine fishes. However, they are insignificant as a cause of diseases in marine fishes. When found, they tend to parasitize the intestine, internal organs, eyes, mesenteries, and other areas. Immature forms are found in mesenteries and internal organs, with adults primarily in the digestive tract. One or two intermediate hosts are required before development in the definitive hosts. Nematodes are not considered serious parasites of marine fishes in aquaria. Most parasites come in via new fishes and cannot complete their life cycle, as they usually require an intermediate host.

Crustacea

The class Crustacea is a large one which includes parasitic and free-living species. Three major groups having species parasitizing fishes are the Branchiura, Copepoda, and Isopoda. The first two groups include the most serious crustacean parasites of fish in captivity. Isopods are less frequently encountered.

The crustaceans affect their hosts by causing pressure atrophy to the soft tissues of the host, by damage caused by their attachment, and by damage inflicted by their feeding on the host.

Branchiura

The Branchiura include various species exclusively parasitic on fishes. *Argulus* is the major genus in the group and the only genus that has marine representatives. As an obligate parasite, it cannot survive without its host.

Clinical signs: *Argulus* is an external parasite found on the body surfaces of fish. Affected fish tend to scratch repeatedly on the aquarium bottom and on other objects. Inflammation and congestions are evident on the skin of parasitized fishes. Fish can be observed to dart, causing abrasions that can develop secondary infections.

Epizootiology: Argulus is easily transmitted due to its mobility and its ability to move from one fish to another. It can reproduce rapidly in closed systems. On submerged objects, the females deposit eggs which develop into larvae that reinfect the hosts or new hosts. No intermediate host is involved. A well-known Atlantic species is *Argulus bicolor,* which parasitizes the redfin needlefish (*Strongylura notata*) and the barracuda (*Sphyraena barracuda*).

Pathogenesis: Parasitization of the skin or gills causes epidermal inflammation and subsequent ulceration. Secondary infection accompanies this damage. The parasites pierce the body of the host with their stylet, release a toxin, and feed on hemolymph and tissue fluids. Digestive secretions are used to aid in ingestion of blood. Inflamed lesions are inevitable on the fish during prolonged attachment of the parasites.

Diagnosis: Live fish must be examined to locate small, dorsoventrally flattened parasites on the skin. The parasites are equipped with a feeding apparatus consisting of a proboscislike mouth, suckers, and a piercing stylet. The shieldlike carapaces of various species of *Argulus* tend to be pigmented and appear as dark areas on the body of the parasitized fish.

Prevention and treatment: All new fish should be quarantined prior to introduction into the aquarium system. The parasite is very susceptible to organophosphate compounds. Formalin treatments are also effective.

Copepoda

The copepods are by far the largest group of crustacean parasites affecting marine fishes. Copepod crustaceans have evolved free-living and parasitic forms with accompanying bizarre morphology to adapt to their diverse ecological niches. Of the various taxonomic orders in the Copepoda, the largest number of species that are parasitic on fishes are in the orders Caligoida and Cyclopoida.

Clinical signs: In many cases, very few behav-

The copepod (*Serpentisaccus magnificae*) on the firefish (*Nemateleotris magnifica*). Trailing yellow egg strings are visible just above the pelvic fins.

ioral or physical signs are evident on parasitized fish. Only in severe cases of parasitism do ulcerated areas appear, accompanied by secondary infection.

Parasites are seen on the body or gills. The easiest diagnostic sign is the presence of trailing egg strings. These may be straight, coiled, or serpentine. The copepod's cephalothorax is embedded into the fish's body, and only the trunk and egg string of the parasites are usually seen.

Epizootiology: Species of copepods affect virtually every species of marine fish, including bony fishes and elasmobranchs. Many are host-specific. Others involve intermediate hosts to complete the life cycle. Only the females attach to the host. Attachment of some copepods is superficial. Other species burrow quite deeply into the host. After maturing on the host, the females produce eggs which subsequently develop with the release of larvae.

Pathogenesis: Copepods are capable of severe damage to the host tissues, integument, gills, eyes, muscles, and internal organs. Those on the surface cause erosion of the epithelium and hyperplasia. The site of attachment is almost always ulcerated. Attachment to the gills by copepods can cause hypertrophy of both the epithelial and connective tissues of the lamellae, impairing normal blood circulation and respiration. Species which burrow deeply in the body can cause extensive damage. For example, *Cardiodectes* burrows in to attach its holdfast to the heart of the host fish. The area of attachment appears as a reddened depression.

Diagnosis: The diagnosis is based on external examination of the fish for attached parasites, which are recognizable by a body which is either dorsoventrally flattened or laterally compressed, jointed appendages, a cephalothorax, and egg strings. Some species move freely on the body. Others are permanently fixed by their attachment processes. The attachment area has a raised ulcerated ring, and is hemorrhagic and inflamed.

Prevention and treatment: The free-moving forms are more easily controlled than are attached forms. Treatment is aimed at controlling any further attachment by larvae. Organophosphates or formalin are useful for treatment. Repeated treatments are necessary. When using organophosphates, the concentration must be at least 0.60 milligrams per liter. The chemical can be added to an aquatic system once a week for

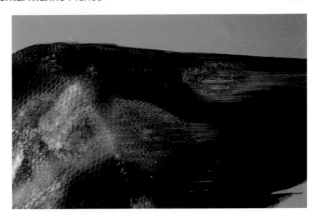

Large lesions caused by *Vibrio* on the batfish (*Platax*).

a period of at least three weeks.

Bacterial Diseases

Bacteria are ubiquitous in the marine environment and tend to cause disease only under conditions favoring their development and invasion of a stressed host. Fishes are subject to stress brought on by a variety of abnormal environmental conditions, including low dissolved oxygen, high carbon dioxide, elevated temperatures, and high concentrations of ammonia.

The majority of bacterial infections are initiated by stress factors such as are caused by parasitic infestations or deterioration in water quality. Bacteria encountered in infections of marine fish include species of *Vibrio, Mycobacterium,* and *Pseudomonas.*

Vibrio

Vibrio is implicated in many infections, primarily in marine fishes but also in brackish-water species. It is a significant cause of bacterial diseases of ornamental species. Known species include *V. anguillarum, V. damsela,* and *V. carchariae,* the latter species virulent to carcharhinid sharks.

Clinical signs: Affected fish are listless and have body ulcerations and inflammation of the skin and fins. Petechiae are visible on the mouth, opercula, and ventral body surfaces. Hyperemia of skin and fins occurs, with congestions of the median and paired fins. Hemorrhagic lesions are notable, and exophthalmia may be exhibited. Lesions on fins cause necrosis and exposure of spines and rays.

Epizootiology: *Vibrio* is infectious for all marine teleost and elasmobranch fishes by contact. It also has been postulated the infection can occur

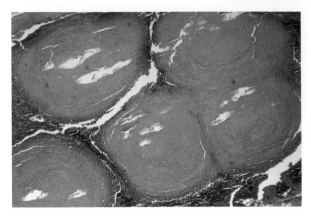

Granulomas in the liver of the triggerfish (*Balistoides*) caused by *Mycobacterium marinum*.

when fish are fed previously contaminated foods.

Pathogenesis: It is assumed that *Vibrio* releases an endotoxin responsible for the observed pathology. Transmission appears to be by direct contact in environmental conditions favoring its development. Elevated water temperatures are thought to favor the initiation of *Vibrio* infections.

Diagnosis: One can obtain preliminary evidence from external clinical signs. A definitive identification of the organism is best accomplished by using a sterile inoculating loop to obtain a sample from the desired organ. Only moribund fish should be selected for examination. Dead fish should never be used due to rapid postmortem changes and invasion by other bacteria. A sampling of these fish could give an inaccurate picture of the flora that caused the condition. The kidney, liver and heart are the recommended choices, although any other organs can be selected for sampling. First, sterilize the desired organ with a heated scalpel, then insert the loop into the organ, and streak the inoculum on a culture plate. The inoculum should be cultured on TSA agar supplemented with blood. Generally, finding a gram-negative, polar-flagellated carbohydrate fermenter indicates a species of *Vibrio*.

Prevention and treatment: Prompt treatment is necessary. *Vibrio* is sensitive to various nitrofurans such as nitrofurazone and other broad-spectrum antibacterial drugs. Nitrofurazone can be used at 3 to 9 milligrams per liter (active). Treatment with potentiated sulfonamides is also very useful in control of *Vibrio*. Nifurpirinol has proven very effective in controlling infections in fishes. When used in a bath, therapeutic blood

levels have been attained within one hour. The absorption route is primarily through the gills. Preventative measures must also include avoidance of crowding in holding tanks and aquaria, and maintenance of good water quality.

Mycobacterium marinum (common names: mycobacteriosis, piscine tuberculosis)

Mycobacteriosis, one of the most well known systemic diseases of marine fish, is caused by an acid-fast bacterium, *M. marinum*. The disease is also referred to as piscine tuberculosis. However, due to the differences in pathology between tuberculosis of other animals and of fish, the term is not technically correct and should be avoided. The infection is classed, in most cases, as a chronic disease.

Clinical signs: Affected fish swell and may become dark. Other signs are variable, depending on the stage of the disease. Fish can become emaciated, demonstrate exophthalmia, have cloudy eyes, and exhibit degeneration of the fins. In advanced stages, hemorrhage and formation of ulcers can appear.

Epizootiology: Mycobacteriosis is infectious for all marine fishes. The disease can be acquired by direct ingestion of the bacteria, such as in feed that contains animal matter. In the aquarium, it can be acquired by fish picking on dead fish that have had the disease.

Pathogenesis: Mycobacteria produce necrotic lesions in the internal organs of the affected fish, causing abnormal function of the organs. Over time, the disease causes mortalities, which tend to be sporadic. Tubercules can be found in virtually any internal organ, but usually occur in the

Lymphocystis on the rockfish (*Sebastes*). Nodules can be seen on the pectoral fin.

kidney, spleen, or liver.

Diagnosis: Live fish should be used for identification. Squash preparations should be made from the intestine, liver, spleen, heart, or other organs and examined under 100x to 400x magnification. The Ziehl-Nielsen method is necessary for staining and identifying acid-fast bacteria. With this procedure, acid-fast bacteria stain red. Other bacteria and cellular debris stain blue. Bacteria tend to be straight or curved bacilli found in nests. The bacteria are usually nonmotile rods.

Prevention and treatment: Although kanamycin has shown promise in controlling the disease, no practical treatments are currently available. Claims that isoniazid is effective as a cure are still unsubstantiated. Prevention is the only method of curtailing the spread of the disease. Good sanitation in holding aquaria is important. Presence of this disease in aquaria can indicate poor environmental conditions.

Viral Diseases

Viral infections are caused by organisms smaller than bacterial cells that are essentially parasitic on living cells. Few marine viruses have been identified. This is not to imply that there are only a few marine viruses, only that current research has not been oriented toward marine ornamental fish but rather to more commercially important species.

Lymphocystis (common name: lymphocystis disease

Lymphocystis is without a doubt the most well known of fish viruses. It is also the oldest known, dating back to when it was first described from a flatfish in 1874. The virus affects not only marine fish but also freshwater fish species.

Clinical signs: The virus produces chronic skin lesions, but seldom is the cause of death. Normal fish behavior is not affected in most cases. The lesions are white to pink in appearance, nodular, and may form a mulberrylike growth. They commonly are found on distal ends of fins and on the body. The nodules occur singly or in groups. Enlarged cells average 100 microns in diameter.

Epizootiology: The virus is infectious for all teleost fishes, but infection of elasmobranchs is unknown. The virus infects cells and makes them produce additional viruses by combining with their nuclear component. The transmission of the virus is direct. Sloughing or rupture of the infected

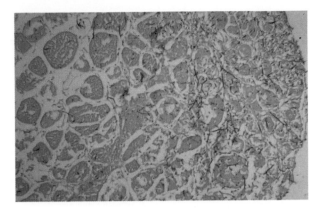

Section through the muscle of a marine fish infected with *Exophiala*. Numerous darkly stained fungal hyphae can be seen throughout the muscle.

cells releases the virus into the water. Upon death of the host, there is also a release of viruses. It has been suggested that damaged skin can predispose a fish to infection by lymphocystis disease. In one study it was observed that the blennioid fishes *Hypsoblennius jenkinsi* and *H. gentilis* developed an infection at damage sites after territorial disputes during the breeding season.

Pathogenesis: Infection of the skin and fins causes appearance of nodules with a hyaline capsule. The disease is benign and seldom causes death of the host.

Diagnosis: The disease is diagnosed grossly by the appearance of nodular, hard, mulberrylike growths on body, fins, or lips. Confirmatory diagnosis must be from histological sections and ultrastructure studies.

Prevention and treatment: No effective treatment is known for lymphocystis. Sometimes the lesions will slough off and not reappear. Surgical removal is sometimes effective. Care must be used to avoid rupture of infected cells around the lesion that could reinfect the site. Fish that have undergone this surgical procedure must be treated with an antimicrobial drug for three to five days to prevent secondary infection. Care should be taken in disinfecting all equipment used near infected areas. *Lymphocystis* virions will survive drying and retain their infectivity for long periods. In one study, dried viruses retained infectivity for fifteen years. The reintroduction of the virions into the aquarium can cause lymphocystis infection.

Recently a nonlymphocystis virus was suggested during studies of lesions from a flounder,

Starvation is not uncommon in marine fish. Note the sunken and apparently enlarged head of this clownfish.

Pseudopleuronectes americanus. The fish showed characteristic papilloma lesions on its dorsal surfaces. There were irregular swellings with a blister-like appearance similar to lymphocystis. Further examination showed the presence of viral particles.

Fungal Diseases

Fungal diseases are quite uncommon in marine fishes, despite accounts in various popular texts of *Saprolegnia* fungal infections of marine fishes, complete with pictures. While *Saprolegnia*-type infections are common in freshwater fishes, there is no such counterpart in marine fishes. Popular accounts of *Saprolegnia* infections of marine fishes should for the most part

Erosion of the head region in this sailfin tang can be attributed to a dietary imbalance. *Source:* Tetra Archives.

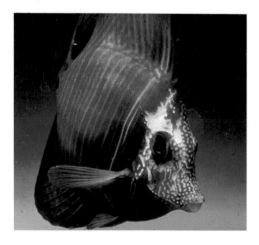

be considered erroneous.

Another commonly mentioned and supposedly common fungal infection is that caused by *Ichthyophonus.* In older texts on fish diseases, the accounts of this fungus are pages in length. The organism is uncommon as an infection of ornamental fish in marine aquaria, but has affected clupeid fishes in the wild, causing extensive epizootics. Many of the descriptions of the fungus occurring in ornamental marine fishes are probably due to misdiagnosis.

One fungus, *Exophiala,* is an occasional parasite of ornamental marine fishes. This fungus is pigmented and appears as a black tuft on the body, often in an area which has sustained damage. The fungus is invasive, affecting the musculature and the internal organs.

In the rare instances where fungi such as *Exophiala* are present, standard treatments with formalin or malachite green prove useful for control.

Noninfectious Diseases

In addition to diseases which are infectious, maladies and problems which occur in marine aquaria may be directly linked to a group of noninfectious diseases. These problems are often caused by a multitude of factors, such as poor nutrition, toxic water conditions, tumors, and genetic anomalies. Discussion of a few of the most common noninfectious diseases follows.

Nutritional Diseases

Three major problems can occur in this category in marine aquaria: starvation, imbalance of nutrients, and an excessive intake of lipids or carbohydrates.

Starvation is a serious problem with captive marine fishes if prolonged. While it is common for some fish to refuse food during trauma, usually they should begin to eat within four to six days after being moved to an aquarium. After this period, the longer the animal refuses food, the poorer its chances of recovery. Starvation can be related to various factors. A major factor with some species such as some butterfly fish and angelfish is their stringent requirements for a specific type of food. Obviously, such species should not be maintained in aquaria unless their food requirements can be met. Other causes for starvation can include anorexia, parasitism, infection, incompatibility with other fishes in the aquarium, and other factors.

Fishes require proper intake of protein, carbohydrates, vitamins, and minerals. Low protein or incomplete protein levels affect normal growth, tissue repair, and disease resistance. Excess lipids in the diet cause abnormal buildup of them in internal organs, resulting in severe pathological consequences, such as fatty infiltration of the liver and kidney. Excess carbohydrates can cause liver glycogen deposition and liver degeneration.

Vitamins, the catalysts for biochemical transformation of other nutrients, are essential in all diets. A deficiency of any of the fat-soluble or water-soluble vitamins can cause weight loss, slow growth, exophthalmia, anemia, scoliosis, and other conditions. Vitamin C, for example, is required for normal tissue repair and maintenance of disease resistance. It is also required for the production of collagen, a component of connective tissue. A deficiency in vitamin C can manifest itself in spinal abnormalities such as scoliosis or lordosis, abnormal cartilage production, and hemorrhage of the skin, liver, intestine, muscle, and kidney.

Mineral deficiencies are unknown in marine fishes. However, iodine deficiency can result when fish are fed a poor diet or when water quality has deteriorated. The development of hyperplasia, or enlargement of the thyroid, has been reported in marine fishes.

Providing a variety of foods ensures that a proper supply of nutrients is available. Use of dry foods and frozen foods, supplemented with brine shrimp, algae, clams, and fish, is a safeguard to increase resistance to disease. Reliance on dry prepared foods alone is not recommended. If at all possible, the types and variety of foods should be matched closely with the natural diet and feeding habits of the fish species in the wild.

Diseases Caused by Toxic Environmental Conditions

High ammonia concentrations, low oxygen, low pH, and presence of toxic metals such as zinc or mercury can all affect fish health. Municipal water supplies are often treated with chlorine and recently with chloramines. Such water can also contain toxic quantities of copper, aluminum, or fluoride, which can cause fish mortalities.

Ammonia: This is the most toxic of the nitrogen

Gas-bubble disease. Top: Note the air in the gills. Above: Involvement of the eye of a squirrelfish (*Holocentris*).

compounds found in aquaria. Ammonia actually exists in two forms in water, one which is ionized (NH_4^+) (ammonium) and one which is not (NH_3). The latter is the toxic form. Its toxicity is related to an increase of ammonia in the blood and tissues. As ammonia concentration increases, normal excretion rates are reduced. It also affects the osmoregulatory mechanisms and the normal transport of oxygen to the tissues due to damage of the gills and red blood cells.

Ammonia accumulation in a system initially occurs during the conditioning of an aquarium, when it is caused by excretion by the animals and by decaying foods. The toxicity of ammonia depends on various factors, primarily pH and temperature. Generally, there should be less than 0.01 milligram of NH_3 per liter in marine aquaria. Ammonia concentrations can be monitored in aquaria by use of commercially available test kits.

Nitrite: Though less deadly than ammonia, ni-

Malignant tumor of the thyroid which has spread to the gills, causing large nodules.

trite is still toxic to marine fishes. High concentrations of nitrite are common in new tanks. Affected fish show respiratory distress. The physiological response of the fish to nitrite concentration is methemoglobinemia. This condition occurs when nitrite chemically binds with oxygen and prevents hemoglobin from taking up oxygen. Experiments on the effects of nitrite with the sea bass (*Dicentrachus*) have demonstrated that at high concentrations of nitrite, methemoglobinemia begins at once. After twenty-four hours, hemoglobin concentration declined. Fish began dying after sixty hours, at which time the hemoglobin level dropped to 50 percent of the control values. The experiments were done at 27 degrees C (80.6 degrees F) and 36 percent salinity. Nitrite levels in aquaria should never exceed 9.1 milligrams per liter as nitrite ion (NO_2).

Nitrate: Nitrate, the least toxic of the three nitrogen compounds found in water, accumulates continuously. It can have a profound effect on proper growth and survival of juvenile marine fish. Experiments with clownfish (*Amphiprion*) showed a reduction in larval growth, metamorphosis, and survival when they were maintained in 100 milligrams of NO_3-N per liter. The presence of green algae in the aquarium plays an important role in reducing the level of nitrates in recirculating aquatic systems. It is generally accepted that nitrate should be less than 20 milligrams per liter as nitrate ion in aquaria.

Chlorine/chloramine: Municipal water supplies have traditionally treated water using the chlorination process for purification. Chlorine removers, mostly based on sodium thiosulfate and water conditioners, have been used to condition water prior to introduction of fish, for chlorine and related compounds are extremely toxic to aquatic life.

Recently, chloramines have been introduced as an alternative for water purification. Chloramines are basically a combination of ammonia and chlorine. Chloramines are also very toxic to aquatic life. As little as 0.05 milligrams per liter can kill fish. Chloramines differ from chlorines in that: 1) they are not as easily dispersed from water; 2) their decomposition yields ammonia, also a toxic product; 3) the molecule is more stable; and 4) chloramines readily pass through gills.

Chloramines are now being used worldwide, particularly in the United States, Canada, and Australia. To render chloramines nontoxic, specific water conditioners can be used. However, it may be necessary to remove the ammonia using a specific ammonia remover or activated carbon.

Gas-bubble disease: The so-called gas-bubble disease can be initiated by a variety of causes. These might include a leak in a hose, causing supersaturation of gas in the aquarium, an imbalance in the enzyme system of the fish, or inadequate decompression of fish when captured. The appearance of a swollen eye or eyes, referred to as exophthalmia, is a common sign of gas-bubble disease. When caused by supersaturation of gases, gas-bubble disease causes skin lesions, which can develop secondary bacterial infections. Upon close observation, gas bubbles can be found in the skin and gills. They are most readily seen in capillaries of the gills, where the gills take on a silvery appearance.

Neoplasia: Tumors can be external or internal, benign or malignant. Benign tumors tend to develop slowly. Malignant tumors or cancers proliferate rapidly and are invasive, involving other organs. The appearance of tumors on marine fishes can be caused by other factors, including viruses, pollutants, imbalance of nutrients, and hormonal imbalances. Thyroid tumors are relatively well known and can be caused by inadequate intake of iodine. They are rare in aquaria when fish are being fed well-balanced diets. Tumors which appear on fins or other parts of the body can be removed in cases where they are determined to be benign.

Genetic and induced anomalies: Most aquarists will not encounter fish that have anomalies, as fish have already been sorted and selected during capture and before being sent to stores. Genetic anomalies such as deformed bodies or fins are uncommon. However, fish acquired when in the juvenile stage may develop anomalies as a result of poor nutrition or exposure to chemicals. Care must be exercised when raising young fish to make sure they are not exposed to chemicals which are known to cause anomalies. Such chemicals as trichlorfon can result in permanent nervous disorders if used at high concentrations with juvenile fish.

Selected References

Blasiola, G. C. 1976. Ectoparasitic turbellaria. *Marine Aquarist* 7(2): 53–58.

———. 1979. *Glugea heraldi*, a new species of microsporida from the seahorse, *Hippocampus erectus* Perry. *J. Fish Dis*. 2(6): 493–500.

———. 1980. *Brooklynella hostilis,* a protozoan parasite of marine fishes. *Freshwater and Marine Aquarium* 3(3): 18–19, 82–83.

———. 1984. Protecting aquarium and pond fish from the dangers of chloramines. *Freshwater and Marine Aquarium* 7(4): 10–12, 78–80, 82–83.

Blazer, V. S., and Wolke, R. E. 1979. An *Exophiala*-like fungus as the cause of a systemic mycosis of marine fish. *J. Fish Dis*. 2: 145–52.

Cheung, P.; Nigrelli, R. F.; and Ruggieri, G. D. 1980. Studies on the morphology of *Uronema marinum* Dujardin (Ciliata: Uronematidae) with a description of the histopathology of the infection in marine fishes. *J. Fish Dis*. 3: 295–303.

———. 1981. *Oodinium ocellatum* (Brown, 1931) (Dinoflagellata) in the kidney and other internal tissues of pork fish, *Anisotrema virginicus* (L.). *J. Fish Dis*. 4: 523–25.

———. 1983. *Pentacapsula muscularis* sp. nov. (Myxosporea: Pentacapsulidae): a histozoic parasite of butterflyfish. *Chaetodon collare* Bloch. *J. Fish Dis*. 6: 393–95.

Cheung, P. J., and Ruggieri, G. D. 1983. *Dermophthirius nibrelli* n. sp. (Monogenea: Microbothriidae), an ectoparasite from the skin of the lemon shark, *Negaprion brevirostris. Trans. Am. Microscop. Soc.* 102(2): 129–34.

Colornia, A. 1985. Aspects of the biology of *Cryptocaryon irritans,* and hyposalinity as a control measure in cultured gilt-head sea bream *Sparus aurata. Dis. Aquat. Org.* 1: 19–22.

Condé, B. 1976. Parasitisme de Labrides de la region Caraibes par une Planaire. *Aquariol. Herpetol.* 3: 23–24.

Cusak, R., and Cone, D. K. 1985. A report of bacterial microcolonies on the surface of *Gyrodactylus* (Monogenea). *J. Fish Dis. 8:* 125–27.

Emerson, C. J.; Payne, J. F.; and Bal, A. K. 1985. Evidence for the presence of a viral non-lymphocystis type disease in winter flounder, *Pseudopleuronectes americanus* (Walbaum), from the north-west Atlantic. *J. Fish Dis*. 8: 91–102.

Frakes, T., and Hoff, F. H., Jr. 1982. Effect of high nitrate on the growth and survival of juvenile and larval anemonefish, *Amphiprion ocellaris. Aquaculture* 29: 155–58.

Goven, B. A., and Amend, D. F. 1982. Mebendazole/trichlorfon combinations: a new anthelmintic for removing monogenetic trematodes from fish. *J. Fish Biol.* 20: 373–78.

Goven, B. A.; Gilbert, J. P.; and Gratzek, J.B. 1980. Apparent drug resistance to the organophosphate dimethyl (2,2,2,-trichloro-1-hydroxyethyl) phosphonate by monogenetic trematodes. *J. Wildl. Dis.* 16(3): 343–46.

Gratzek, J. B., and Reinert, R. 1981. Physiological responses of experimental fish to stressful conditions. *Symposium on the Use of Small Fish Species in Carcinogenicity Testing.* Natl. Institutes of Health, Bethesda, Md.

Grimes, D. J.; Gruber, S. H.; and May, E. B. 1985. Experimental infection of lemon sharks, *Negaprion brevirostris* (Poey) with *Vibrio* species. *J. Fish Dis.* 8: 173–80.

Huff, J. A., and Burns, C. D. 1981. Hypersaline and chemical control of *Cryptocaryon irritans* in red snapper, *Lutjanus campechanus,* monoculture. *Aquaculture* 22: 181–84.

Kabata, Z. 1970. *Crustacea as Enemies of Fishes.* Neptune City, N.J.: T.F.H. Publications.

Keith, R. E. 1980. Disease prevention and control. *Freshwater and Marine Aquarium* 3(1): 20–23, 74.

Kent, M. 1981. The life cycle and treatment of a turbellarian disease of marine fishes. *Freshwater and Marine Aquarium* 4(11): 11–13.

Lawler, A. R. 1977. The parasitic dinoflagellate *Amyloodinium ocellatum* in marine aquaria. *Drum & Croaker* 17(2): 17–20.

Lom, J., and Nigrelli, R. F. 1970. *Brooklynella hostilis* n.g., n. sp., a pathogenic cyrtophorine ciliate in marine fishes. *J. Protozool.* 17(2): 224–32.

Love, M.; Teebken-Fisher, D.; Hose, J. E.; et al. 1981. *Vibrio damsela,* a marine bacterium, causes skin ulcers on the damselfish, *Chromis punctipinnis. Science* 214: 1139–40.

McCosker, J. E. 1969. A behavioral correlate for the passage of lymphocystis disease in three blennioid fishes. *Copeia* 3: 636–37.

Nigrelli, R. F., and Ruggieri, G. D. 1966. Enzootics in the New York Aquarium caused by *Cryptocaryon irritans* Brown, 1951 (=*Ichthyophthirius marinus* Sikama, 1961), a histophagous ciliate in the skin, eyes and gills of marine fishes. *Zoologica* 51: 97–102.

Paperna, I. 1980. *Amyloodinium ocellatum* (Brown, 1931) (Dinoflagellida) infestations in cultured marine fish at Eilat, Red Sea: epizootiology and pathology. *J. Fish Dis.* 3: 363–72.

———. 1984. Chemical control of *Amyloodinium ocellatum* (Brown, 1931) (Dinoflagellida) infections: in vitro tests and treatment with infected fishes. *Aquaculture* 38: 1–18.

Pearse, L.; Pullin, R.S.V.; Conroy, D. A.; et al. 1974. Observations on the use of Furanace for the control of *Vibrio* disease in marine flatfish. *Aquaculture* 3: 295–302.

Scarano, G.; Saroglia, M. G.; Gray, R. H.; et al. 1984. Hematological responses of sea bass, *Dicentrarchus labrax,* to sublethal nitrite exposures. *Trans. Am. Fish. Soc.* 113: 360–64.

Shotts, E. B. 1981. Bacterial disease of fish. Proceedings, Republic of China – U.S. Cooperative Science Seminar on Fish Diseases. *NSC Symp.* Series no. 3: 7–9.

Sindermann, C. J. 1966. *Diseases of Marine Fishes.* Neptune City, N.J.: T.F.H. Publications.

Sniesko, S. 1974. The effects of environmental stress on outbreaks of infectious diseases of fishes. *J. Fish Biol.* 6: 197–208.

Stagg, R. M., and Shuttleworth, T. J. 1982. The accumulation of copper in *Platichthys flesus* L. and its effects on plasma electrolyte concentrations. *J. Fish Biol.* 20: 491–500.

Wilkie, D. W., and Gordon, H. 1969. Outbreak of cryptocaryoniasis in marine aquaria at Scripps Institute of Oceanography. *Calif. Fish and Game 55(3): 227–36.*

Wolf, K. E.; Quimby, M. C.; Carlson, C. P.; et al. 1979. Lymphocystis virus: infectivity of lesion preparations stored after lyophilization or simple desiccation. *J. Fish Dis.* 2: 259–60.

Checklists, Quarantine Procedures, and Calculations of Particular Use in Fish Health Management

John B. Gratzek and George C. Blasiola

Where does one begin when faced with a sick fish? How does one begin to determine the causes of the illness? How does one decide what to do first? Where—even in this book—does one begin in the search for information relevant to a problem?

It was in response to such questions that this appendix was developed. It is intended as a brief, nonexhaustive, but hopefully helpful, guide to some types of information of particular use in fish health management. Here the reader will find a diagnostic guide to help the aquarist determine the cause of the fish problems he or she is facing, an explanation (with examples) of the calculation of various medicinal dosages, and a guide to the quarantine procedures which are essential to preventing fish disease from spreading.

A Brief Guide to Diagnosing Fish Health Problems

When one or more fish in a tank are dying or dead, panic is understandable. Before immediately deciding that the problem must be an infectious disease or parasite, it is worthwhile to consider the possibility of noninfectious causes. Refer to the index to locate further information about possible noninfectious causes of problems outlined below.

Is the problem related to the aquarium water?

A. Check temperature. It should be 75 to 85 degrees F (about 24 to 29.5 degrees C) for most tropical fish. Goldfish and other cold-water species tolerate lower temperatures and can easily overwinter in frigid water.

B. Check for ammonia and nitrites. Test results should be negative in a well-established aquarium.

C. Check pH. The optimum for freshwater fish is close to neutrality (pH 7.0); the acceptable range is between 6.8 and 7.8. For marine systems, a pH of 7.8 to 8.3 is acceptable.

D. Check for presence of toxins.

    1. Was water dechlorinated properly?

    2. Have medicaments such as copper been added? Accidental spills? Any unusual items added to aquarium?

    3. Source of water? Municipal water may have chloramines. Shallow wells can be contaminated with bacteria. Water taken directly

from rivers or lakes could introduce parasites or contain pesticides.

E. *Check hardness of water.* About 100 ppm minerals is desirable. Avoid excessively soft (less than 57 ppm minerals) or distilled water. Extremely hard water may create excessively high pH.

Is the problem related to basic aquarium setup and management?

A. *Is aquarium size adequate for the number and size of the fish?*
B. *Is there adequate filtration and aeration?*
   1. *Are filters periodically rinsed or replaced?*
   2. *Is detritus removed from gravel periodically?*
C. *Is aquarium covered to prevent jumping?*
D. *Have adequate shade and escape room been provided?*
E. *Is water changed periodically? How frequently? Amount?*
F. *Have plants been disinfected prior to introduction?*

Is the problem related to choice of fish?

A. *Are the fish species compatible?*
B. *Is stocking density appropriate for the species?*
C. *What is the age of the fish? Might they be at the end of their expected life-span?*
D. *Were the fish quarantined and treated prior to addition to aquarium? If so, for how long? Which medicaments were used, if any?*
E. *Were fish treated previously for problems? How? Was the treatment method effective?*

Is the problem related to food or nutrition?

A. *Is the food choice nutritionally balanced?*
B. *Is the food fresh? How long in storage?*
C. *Is the feeding frequency appropriate?*
D. *Are sinking pellets being fed to bottom feeders?*
E. *Are live foods fed? What is their source?*
F. *Is food medicated? If so, with what?*

After noninfectious causes have been ruled out, one can begin the search for other possible reasons for illness. Careful examination of the death pattern, fish behavior, and external and internal lesions (such as spots, blemishes, etc.) will provide valuable clues. Check each of these in turn. Refer to the index in this volume to locate further information about the problems outlined below.

How many fish have died? Over what time period?

A. *Majority of fish died within a very short period of time:*
   1. Toxic problem. Check water quality.
   2 *Ichthyophthirius multifiliis.*
   3. Overcrowding, with lack of oxygen.
B. *Gradual death rate over long period:*
   1. Old age, perhaps complicated by *Mycobacterium* or tumors.
   2. Poor food quality.
   3. Low-level toxicity.
   4. Immunological failure associated with poor water or poor food quality, leading to bacterial diseases.
C. *Approximately 20 to 60 percent of fish sick or dying:*
   1. Acute parasitic infection following shipment or addition of disease-carrying fish to aquarium. (See *Ichthyophthirius; Chilodonella; Ichthyobodo; Tetrahymena.*)
   2. Acute bacterial infection. Check water quality.

Do dying fish show unusual swimming patterns?

A. *Fish at surface near water outlet:*
   1. Low oxygen.
   2. Gill parasites.
   3. Gill damage.
B. *Sluggish movements, fish at bottom:*
   1. Parasites.
   2. Bacteria such as *Cytophaga.*
   3. Poor water conditions.
C. *Circling, twirling, or erratic motion:*
   Chronic bacterial problem. (See *Streptococcus; Edwardsiella; Eubacterium.*)
D. *Flashing, scratching:*
   Skin irritation; check water, parasites on body or gills.

Do fish show external clinical signs of disease?

A. *White spots on body and fins.*
   1. Spots less than 2 millimeters (0.08 inches) in diameter. Parasites. See *Ichthyophthirius* (freshwater fish) or *Cryptocaryon* (saltwater fish).
   2. Small, white, focalized areas. Cysts of vari-

ous sizes may be elevated to form small nodules. Fish do not appear to be clinically sick. (See Sporozoans.)

3. White tufts resembling cotton balls. May be seen on mouth, eye, or body. Can be up to 10 millimeters (0.4 inches) in size. Common on fish eggs. Fungal infection (frequently following an injury) or bacterial infection.

4. Small white tufts. Smaller than fungal growths. Frequently are colonies of *Heteropolaria,* a stalked protozoan.

5. "Saddleback"— whitened area on fish's back. (See F, below.)

B. *Fine, dusty golden or "velvet" appearance.* Best seen with incident light from above. Cysts of *Oodinium,* a parasitic dinoflagellate for both freshwater fish and marine species.

C. *Tumorlike cellular masses. Lymphocystis* virus causes enlarged cells on surface of skin, tumor-like masses on lips or eyes, and masses of cells resembling grape clusters on tips of fins.

D. *Large (3 to 4 millimeters, or 0.1 to 0.15 inches) white, yellow, or (rarely) black lumps on skin.* These are usually metacercariae of digenetic trematodes.

E. *Excess slime on skin.* Best seen with incident light from above.

1. Check pH.
2. Can be caused by excessive medication.
3. Frequently associated with heavy parasitic infestations from *Ichthyophthirius, Chilodonella, Ichthyobodo,* or monogenetic trematodes.

F. *Fin and body rot.* Fins may appear white, incomplete, or frayed. Eyes may be cloudy, and mouthparts may be affected. Lesions on body may appear as whitened areas over dorsal part of body, referred to as "saddleback" disease. (See *Cytophaga; Flavobacterium; Aeromonas;* and other species of bacteria.)

Are parasites themselves visible on fish?

A. *Elongated white parasites attached to skin.* May protrude as much as 1 centimeter (0.4 inches), depending on maturity. Anchor worms. (See *Lernaea, Ergasilus;* a closely related species parasitizes gills.)

B. *Disc-shaped parasites that move freely about the surface of fish.* Their size, up to 1 centimeter (0.4 inches), allows them to be seen easily. Fish lice (see *Argulus*).

C. *Elongated isopods up to 1 centimeter (0.4 inches) in length.* They are freely mobile and fre-

quently burrow a hole in the fish, where they reside. (See *Livoneca.*)

D. *Oval "worms" whose bodies can elongate up to 2 centimeters (0.8 inches) in length upon being disturbed.* In addition to being seen on fish, they may be found on plants or on the surface of gravel. (See Leeches.)

E. *Small white worms 2 to 3 millimeters (0.08 to 0.1 inches) long.* May also be found on glass. (See Turbellarians.)

F. *Intestinal worms protruding from anal opening.* (See Nematodes; Tapeworms.)

Are bloody or reddened areas visible?

A. *"Injected" blood vessels.* Handling fish will result in a reddening of fins, caused by the dilation of blood vessels. "Injected" vessels can also frequently be seen during the initial phases of a systemic bacterial disease or severe stress.

B. *Hemorrhage.* Bloody areas of the skin can be pinpoint to brushlike in character.

1. Usually associated with parasitic bacterial or viral infections. (See *Tetrahymena; Uronema; Aeromonas.*)
2. Subcutaneous hemorrhaging about the mouth, throat, and base of fins. Enteric red mouth disease. (See *Yersinia.*)
3. Red necrotic lesions on skin, mouth, vent, base of fins, coupled with bloat. (See *Vibrio; Pseudomonas; Mycobacterium; Aeromonas.*)

C. *Ulcerations.*

1. Deep ulcers with circumscribed hemorrhagic areas are commonly associated with bacterial infections.
2. May be seen as a result of *Tetrahymena; Uronema; Pseudomonas.*
3. Ulcer disease, common in goldfish and koi. (See *Aeromonas salmonicida.*)
4. "Hole-in-the-head" disease, lateral line erosion. Shallow ulcerations seen over lateral line area, extending to head. May note small white blebs prior to onset of necrosis. Long strands of exudate may resemble worms. Etiology unknown. (See *Hexamita; Edwardsiella.*)

Are there problems in the musculature and/or deep skin areas?

A. *Deep ulcerations.* (See Bacteria.)

B. *Diffuse whitening of muscles.* (See Sporozoans.)

C. *White foci in musculature.* (See Sporozoans; Digenetic Trematodes; encysted Nematodes.)

D. *Lumpy, uneven musculature.* (See *Pleisto-phora.*)

Are the fish's eyes affected?

A. *Exophthalmia, or "popeye."* May occur in one or both eyes. Can be caused by tumors, bacterial diseases, or gas-bubble disease. May follow handling of fish.
B. *Cloudy eye.* May involve one or both eyes. Can be initiated by attacks from other fish. (See *Myxobacterium;* columnaris disease.)
C. *Opacity of lens.* (See Digenetic Trematodes; nutritional deficiencies.)
D. *Area surrounding eye is white.* (See *Tetra-hymena; Heteropolaria; Lymphocystis* virus.)
E. *Missing eye.* Result of injury, infectious disease, or tumor.

Are there abdominal problems?

A. *Abdominal distention (bloat, dropsy).*
  1. Internal tumors.
  2. Parasitic infestations of kidneys. (See *Mitraspora.*)
  3. African/Malawi bloat. (See *Aeromonas; Clostridium.*)
  4 Cystic kidneys. Possibly inherited or due to toxic metals.
  5. Mycobacterial infections. (See *Mycobacterium.*)
  6. Tapeworms. May protrude from anal opening.
  7. Pseudokidney disease. (See *Lactobacillus.*)
B. *Emaciation/wasting, "hollow belly."*
  1. Nutritional problem.
  2. Mycobacterial infection.
  3. Chronic parasitism. Intestinal parasites, *Hexamita,* migrating nematodes within abdominal cavity.
  4. Internal tumors.

Quarantine and Treatment of Freshwater Ornamental Fish

To quarantine an animal means to isolate it from healthy animals for a period of time. Historically, the word "quarantine" meant a forty-day isolation period. The basic concept of quarantining fish for a period of time is to ensure that the fish will not introduce disease organisms into an aquarium full of healthy fish. During the holding period, a carrier fish may in fact develop a disease and die. Alter-natively, a carrier fish may shed a particular parasite during the quarantine period. Routine treatment should be instituted during the quarantine period to rid the fish of any parasites.

Aquarists with large investments in fish realize that the introduction of new fish into a breeding colony without quarantine leads to problems. Parasites such as *Ichthyophthirius, Ichthyobodo, Chilodonella, Oodinium, Hexamita,* and monogenetic trematodes can be introduced into aquaria by carrier fish which appear to be healthy. Routine quarantining of fish prevents many common and highly dangerous diseases from being introduced into an aquatic system. However, one must note that there are groups of parasites and bacteria which may not be affected. For example, sporozoan parasites or mycobacterial infections are not treatable and may be introduced even though a fish is treated during the quarantine period.

How to quarantine fish: Fish must be held in an aquarium which is supplied with good water

Generalized Quarantine Procedure for Fish.

Prepare quarantine facilities. Make necessary temperature, salinity, and pH adjustments of water.

⇓

Add fish to quarantine holding facilities. Allow fish to acclimate twenty-four to forty-eight hours before treatment.

⇓

Assess the fish's condition. Note any serious problems requiring immediate attention.

⇓

Perform required water tests throughout the quarantine period.

⇓

Conduct frequent inspections of quarantine facility. Remove dead fish promptly.

⇓

Administer recommended chemical treatments to control common disease agents.

⇓

After fourteen to twenty-one days, transfer fish to permanent display aquarium.

Source: G. C. Blasiola.

Quarantine and Treatment Record

Date: _____

Fish Quarantined:

Scientific Name: _____

Common Name: _____

Quarantine

Aquarium No(s): _____   Purchased from: _____

Date of Arrival: _____   DDAs: _____

Required Quarantine Dates:

From: _____   To: _____

Clinical Signs upon Arrival:

_____

_____

Preliminary Diagnosis: _____

_____

Treatments

Dates: From: _____   To: _____

Chemicals Used: _____

Dosages: _____   Duration of Treatment _____

Administration Method: ( ) Dip ( ) Bath ( ) Oral ( ) Injection

Results of Treatment: _____

_____

_____

Remarks:_____

_____

Example of a quarantine and treatment record form.
Source: G. C. Blasiola.

and/or where the filtration system maintains good water quality with respect to pH, ammonia, and nitrites. This can be done in various ways, and a genralized procedure is given in the flow chart on the previous page. It is important to maintain records on any quarantined fish; the sample form above is used for keeping track of quarantine and treatment.

A flow-through system can be installed where fresh, dechlorinated water is dripped slowly into an aquarium, with provision for overflow. However, in this situation, water must be heated and dechlorinated, and this can involve complex water-handling systems. If a flow-through system is not practical, one can quarantine fish in a suitable aquarium (10 to 30 gallons, or 38 to 114 liters, depending on size and number of fish to be quarantined) in which aquarium water is maintained at about 75 to 80 degrees F (24 to 27 degrees C) and pH is adjusted to 6.8 to 7.2. Place plastic pots and/or plants in the aquarium to provide shelter and hiding areas. Provide conditioned filter substrate (such as gravel) within a filter. Conditioned gravel can be placed in mesh bags for this purpose. Also, conditioned foam filters can be used in a quarantine tank. Periodically test water for ammonia, nitrites, pH, and temperature in order to gauge when water changes should be made.

Quarantining fish in an aquarium with an unconditioned filter is possible if water is changed regularly to avoid ammonia and nitrite buildup. Water should be tested periodically for pH, ammonia, and nitrites. Ammonia toxicity can be reduced by using ammonia-adsorbing clays in filters, by maintaining a neutral pH, and by water changes. When changing water, it is important to avoid stress upon the fish by making sure that the water temperature does not fluctuate by more than a few degrees. A water temperature between 75 and 80 degrees F (about 24 to 27 degrees C) is adequate. Chlorine can be removed by addition of sodium thiosulfate (2 drops per gallon or per 3.8 liters of a 13 percent solution), and pH should be kept at approximately 7.0 by use of commercially available buffers. If nitrites are detected (a situation which usually occurs after three to seven days in an unconditioned aquarium), water should be changed. Addition of 1 teaspoon of salt per gallon (3.8 liters) will interfere with nitrite-ion uptake in some nitrite-sensitive fish. Combine the addition of salt with water changes if nitrites are a problem.

The longer the quarantine period, the greater the chance that fish will have shed any parasites or recovered from other infections. For absolute safety, a period of thirty days is recommended. A fourteen-day period is minimum. During this period, water changes alone may serve to rid the fish of parasites by diluting their numbers and minimizing reinfection, as in the case of *Ichthyophthirius multifiliis.* In some cases, fish may die of known or unknown causes. Unfortunately, clients may lay the blame for fish deaths on the quarantine procedure; this emphasizes the importance of maintaining and testing for good water quality. Treatment of fish during the quarantine period is essential since, in most cases, the resident population of parasites cannot be determined and many will remain on or in the fish. In cases where many fish are to be quarantined and a few can be spared, the results of a routine necropsy examination may uncover parasites toward which specific therapies can be directed. Although quarantine could be done without any routine administration of parasiticides, the incidence of parasitism in ornamental fish is enough reason to routinely medicate fish during quarantine.

How to medicate quarantined freshwater fish safely: Not all parasitic conditions are readily treatable, and even with the best of available medications, some parasites may kill the fish during quarantine or survive quarantine altogether. However, from a clinical approach, one can attempt to rid fish of known highly infectious problems which are readily treatable and which are the primary agents of disease.

Medicaments which aquarists have traditionally used include salt, methylene blue, and acriflavine. The following suggestions for an increased drug arsenal (see accompanying table) are based on: 1) the availability of the drug, 2) the efficacy of the drug for a broad spectrum of parasites, and 3) the safety of the drug.

A summary of the indications and use of the most efficacious drugs for routine antiparasite treatment of freshwater fish during quarantine.	
Formaldehyde or formaldehyde–malachite green mixtures	
Use indications	External protozoans, monogenetic trematodes.
Dose	1 milliliter of formaldehyde (25 ppm) or 1 milliliter of formaldehyde–malachite green mixture, for no longer than twelve hours.
Precautions	Preparations of formaldehyde will kill severely sick fish. If fish are of a species judged to be sensitive to either formaldehyde or malachite green (scaleless fish, neon tetras), terminate treatment after one to two hours by water changes or by removal of fish to nonmedicated water.
Metronidazole	
Use indications	Effective against flagellated protozoans such as *Hexamita* and *Spironucleus*. May be effective against *Ichthyobodo necatrix* and species of *Oodinium*. Presently used against internal flagellates.
Dose	250 milligrams per 10 gallons (38 liters) (6ppm) for twenty-four hours. In food , at a concentration of 0.25 percent.
Precautions	This medicament does not appear to be toxic to fish at the levels used. Terminate medication at twenty-four hours.
Praziquantel	
Use indications	Effective against monogenetic trematodes and tapeworms. May kill digenetic trematode metacercariae and larval tapeworms. Its efficacy against adult tapeworms in fish has been demonstrated when drug is administered via water.
Dose	The drug has been shown to remove external trematodes at 2 ppm after twenty-four hours and will remove intestinal tapeworms within an hour.
Precautions	Toxicity problems have not been encountered at 2 ppm.
Ivermectin	
Use indications	Nematodes in fish (highly toxic).
	(continued)

Dose	Used as an injectable solution in mammals, but addition of the drug to water will remove nematodes. A common stock solution is available to veterinarians as a 1 percent injectable solution. One part of this solution diluted with 19 parts of water will yield a stock solution. Add 0.7 milliliters of the stock solution per 76 liters (20 gallons) of water, and give as a split dose over a four-day period (0.2 milliliters on days 1 and 2, and 0.3 milliliters on day 3). Change water on day 4.
Precautions	Ivermectin is a very effective drug for nematodes, but should only be used on an experimental basis because of its toxicity.

Panacur™

Use indications	Nematodes. Possibly the broadest spectrum nematocide for fish.
Dose	In food, at a concentration of 0.25 percent.

Sodium chloride

Use indications	Sodium chloride has been used for many years, most often as a "tonic" for fish. While not mandatory for raising fish (as some aquarists believe), it is advantageous under certain circumstances. Obviously sick or stressed fish may benefit from added salt by the replacement of sodium or chloride ions that are lost to the water. Salt has been shown to be antiparasitic. Low levels of salt (10 ppm) will block the uptake of nitrites in some fish.
Dose	For use as a parasiticide, a solution of 2.5 percent salt has been used as a dip. Fish are placed in a well-aerated solution until balance cannot be maintained. Many parasites of freshwater fish will be killed by placing the latter into water suitable for marine fish (specific gravity from 1.017 to 1.023) for a period of ten to fifteen minutes. Fish should be removed at the first signs of stress, regardless of time. Many aquarists believe that routine use of added salt is beneficial to live-bearing fish and some cichlids. All agree that salt is not tolerated by some catfish such as *Corydoras.* On an experimental basis, we have successfully used as much as 0.3 percent salt (115 grams [4 ounces] per 10 gallons or 38 liters of water) in aquaria.
Precautions	If using salt as a parasiticide, remove fish as soon as they show signs of stress. Some species may be sensitive to salt. Some aquarium plants may not tolerate salt if higher concentrations (0.3 percent) are used.

Acriflavine

Use indications	Acriflavine, a yellow dye, has both antibacterial and antiprotozoan activities. It has been used to treat fish with external protozoan parasites and has been used for surface bacterial infections of fish. Acriflavine is not as effective as formaldehyde as a general parasiticide and has been largely replaced by antibiotics for treatment of bacterial infections.
Dose	2 to 3 ppm.
Precautions	This medicament will turn water yellow and can be toxic to fish. Other antiparasiticides and antibiotics have been shown to be more effective without affecting the color of the water.

Methylene blue

Use indications	Methylene blue was one of the first aquarium medications used primarily for treatment of external parasites. Other parasiticides have been shown to be more effective. This drug is relatively nontoxic to fish and has been used to treat weak fish soon after arrival. The use of methylene blue with 0.1 to 0.3 percent salt represents a mild treatment for recently transported fish which are under severe stress.
Dose	5 ppm.
Precautions	Methylene blue has been shown to inactivate nitrifying bacteria. The drug should not be allowed to permeate gravel beds. It is possibly best used in circumstances where biological filters are not present.

Potassium permanganate

Use indications	Potassium permanganate is an oxidizing agent. It is used primarily in aquaculture for algae control and as a clarifying agent. It also will kill external parasites and possibly externally located bacteria. At this writing, it is one of the most frequently used parasiticides in ponds, although it is not approved for food fish. For aquarium use, it has been used as a clarifier and as a parasiticide. However, other parasiticides and antibacterial drugs have been shown to be more effective.
Dose	1 to 3 ppm in ponds, depending on the organic load.

(continued)

Precautions	Potassium permanganate can oxidize and burn tissues of fish. If water is exceptionally clear, a dose of 3 ppm could damage gills, resulting in deaths. If water contains high plankton levels, a dose of 2 ppm may not be enough to kill parasites. Tests for effectiveness and proper dosage should be done in vats prior to treating entire ponds. The drug initially turns water red and will oxidize any living materials. If used on already stressed or severely parasitized fish, expect deaths from the added stress of the treatment.
Copper sulfate	
Use indications	Copper sulfate is frequently used for weed and algae control in ponds. It is also an effective parasiticide when properly administered.
Dose	0.1 to 0.2 ppm of copper ion (hydrated copper sulfate, $CuSo_4 \cdot 5H_2O$ is 25 percent copper ion).
Precautions	The proper dosing of copper sulfate is complicated by the chelation of the copper ion by carbonates and other anions in water. In freshwater systems, the amount of copper sulfate to be added will depend on the hardness level. It is always best to determine the effect of hardness on the amount of free copper ion prior to addition of copper sulfate to an aquarium or fish culture system. Accurate measurements of copper ion may be obtained with a copper test kit. Copper can be very toxic to fish and plants. Its use in freshwater systems is dangerous. Chelated copper forms are safer than using copper ion, but also less effective. Most copper test kits will detect chelated copper, leading the aquarist to the erroneous conclusion that the copper is biologically active.

In fish therapy, a wise adage states, "Know your fish, the chemical, and the water." First, some fish are more sensitive to a medication than others. For example, some species of ornamental catfish such as *Corydoras* do not tolerate salt. Second, the nature of the water may affect medication. For example, the effective therapeutic dose of a drug may differ with the ionization and pH of water. Organophosphates degrade more quickly at higher water pH levels. Organic substances in water may bind medicaments and reduce their efficacy. Unfortunately, these idiosyncrasies have not been cataloged, especially with the appearance of new parasiticides. Third, the route of medication must be tailored to the situation. When medicating fish, it is often impractical to add medicaments to feed since sick fish will not eat. One might add the medicament to the water in the hope that sufficient adsorption will result in a clinical effect. However, while saltwater fish drink copious amounts of water for osmoregulatory purposes, freshwater fish drink little or none. Obviously this behavior alone could influence dosage, toxicity, and efficacy. At this writing, there is very little hard information on such questions. Presumably, many medications added to fresh water are adsorbed via gills.

Safety can be maximized by using correct dosages and by limiting the time of treatment to minimize toxicity. In all medication schemes, aeration should be maintained by agitation of water (filters, air bubblers), but activated carbon must be removed since it will remove medicaments. Air-stems should be removed from lift stacks of undergravel filters to avoid pulling the medicament through the gravel substrate while providing aeration. Termination of the treatment is best done by water changes, or in the case of saltwater systems, by filtration through activated carbon.

Suggested treatment for external trematodes and/or protozoans: Formaldehyde at 25 ppm (1 milliliter [20 drops] per 10 gallons, or 38 liters, of water) is considered a long-term treatment for parasites such as *Ichthyophthirius, Chilodonella, Ichthyobodo,* and monogenetic trematodes. At this dosage, formaldehyde is considered to be an indefinite treatment and could be left in the aquarium to dissipate gradually. Since most parasites will be killed within minutes or hours, we suggest treatment in the morning, followed by a 70 to 90 percent water change after six to eight hours of exposure. Maintain aeration, remove activated carbon from filters, and remove air-stems from undergravel filters, if used. This general treatment can be repeated at three-day intervals if infections of ich are suspected.

In some cases, increased levels of formaldehyde can be administered for shorter periods of time. Thus, at a 75 ppm level, treatment time may be reduced to not more than eight hours or until fish begin to show signs of stress. Such treatments are best done as baths in special treatment aquaria. If this approach is used, the display aquarium should be treated with a lower dose (25 ppm) for a few hours, followed by a complete water change. Failure to do this may result in reinfection of the fish when returned to the aquarium. Short baths (ten to fifteen minutes) in 250 ppm formaldehyde have also been used in treatment aquaria, but this may represent too severe a stress for sensitive species of ornamental fish.

Mixtures of formaldehyde and malachite green have been shown to be superior to the independent use of either medicament. Our experience suggests that formaldehyde has a wider efficacy than malachite green when either chemical is used alone. A stock solution can be made by adding 1.4 grams of zinc-free malachite green to 380 milliliters of formaldehyde solution (0.49 ounces in a gallon of solution). The dose per 10 gallons (38 liters) of water is 1 milliliter (20 drops), resulting in approximately 25 ppm of formaldehyde and 0.01 ppm of malachite green. This formulation should not be used on food fish since malachite green has been shown to be carcinogenic. Treatments can be as short as five hours and can extend to twelve hours. Water changes to avoid toxicity to fish are suggested at the termination of the treatment.

Organophosphates at 0.25 ppm have been used to remove monogenetic trematodes from ornamental fish, but these drugs appear to yield no better results than formaldehyde. Furthermore, their repeated usage for removal of trematodes from goldfish has resulted in the emergence of organophosphate-resistant forms. Organophosphates have no effect on external protozoan parasites, but are particularly effective for the control of parasitic copepods, *Argulus,* and leeches.

Results from our laboratory suggest that praziquantel (Droncit™) added to water at 2 ppm will remove monogenetic trematodes from both gills and skin of infested goldfish. This drug has been used on a variety of freshwater and marine ornamental fish without problem, and is effective in removal of tapeworms and may kill larval forms of digenetic trematodes. We suggest adding this drug during the final two or three days of quarantine. Our results suggest that trematodes will be gone twenty-four hours after treatment. At 2 ppm there appears to be no effect on the biological filter and no toxicity to fish. The drug is quite expensive, but may be the drug of choice for removing external trematodes and larval forms of digenea and tapeworms.

Suggested treatments for internal parasites: To treat fish for *Hexamita,* add metronidazole at 6 ppm directly to the water. Our experience suggests that a single treatment is adequate to rid fish of parasites. The drug is apparently adsorbed via skin or gills and appears to be nontoxic even

at 20 ppm. We have noted no effect on biological filters, but as a precaution one should avoid pulling medicament through filters. Metronidazole can also be added to food at 0.25%.

Nematode removal can be approached by incorporating drugs such as fenbendazol (Panacur™) or piperazine in food at a level of 0.25 percent. Ivermectin has been used at 0.7 milliliters (14 drops) of an injectable formulation (0.05 percent active compound) per 76 liters (20 gallons) to give a calculated dosage of approximately 0.005 ppm. The total dose was given over a period of four days (0.1 milliliter [2 drops] on the first day, then 0.2 milliliter [4 drops] on each of the following three days). Products such as Ivomec™, which are supplied as sterile 1 percent solutions, would have to be diluted 1 part to 19 parts of water to obtain a solution containing 0.05 percent active compound. This drug must be protected from light. As the drug is very toxic to fish, its use should be preceded by ample biological testing.

Using combinations of drugs during quarantine: In quarantine situations, it is best not to administer any drugs until the fish have adapted to the quarantine tank and are feeding. This may take three to four days. We have used formaldehyde (25 ppm), metronidazole (6 ppm), and praziquantel (2 ppm) in combination for twelve- hour treatments without harm to the fish. In practice, the use of formaldehyde and metronidazole toward the beginning of the quarantine period, followed by praziquantel toward the end of it, would represent a more conservative and possibly safer use of these drugs. In all cases, we suggest that medicaments be removed from water after treatment to avoid a possible toxic effect on the fish. This removal can be done by water changes or by filtration using activated carbon.

Quarantine and Treatment of Saltwater Fish

Because of the higher cost of saltwater fish and the cost of synthetic sea salts for water preparation, the marine aquarist is more likely than the freshwater aquarist to quarantine fish, especially if he or she has had disease problems in the past. Traditionally, treatment during quarantine has been directed toward removing external parasites (see accompanying table). Purchasing saltwater fish from dealers who are aware of disease prob-

---

A Method for Ridding Saltwater Fish of External Protozoans and Trematodes During the Quarantine Period

1. Make a 0.75 percent solution of copper sulfate-penthydrate ($CuSO_4 \cdot 5H_2O$). Use 5 milliliters (0.17 fluid ounces) of this mixture per 38 liters (10 gallons) of water to give a copper sulfate dose of approximately 0.25 ppm. The objective of the treatment is to keep the copper-ion level at 0.1 to 0.2 ppm for ten days. Because the initial dose will tend to be chelated, readings on a copper test kit will be lower than expected. Test water daily. In some cases, no copper ion will be detected and it may be necessary to add an additional half-dose on the first day. If the copper-ion reading is below 0.1 ppm, add a half-dose and retest. Eventually, the level of copper ion will stabilize, and no additional doses may be needed.

---

2. On the next-to-last day of the quarantine period, add 2 ppm of praziquantel to remove trematodes and kill larval forms.

---

3. On the last day of quarantine, bathe fish in pH 8.3 fresh water for fifteen to thirty minutes or until fish begin to appear stressed. Formaldehyde can be added at the rate of 100 ppm (4 milliliters per 10 gallons or 38 liters of water). Maintain vigorous aeration during this bath treatment.

---

lems is important. Such dealers may have initiated their own quarantine systems and may have central filtration systems where copper levels are maintained at between 0.1 and 0.2 ppm. Many knowledgeable retailers routinely expose saltwater fish to a half-hour dip in fresh water at pH 8.3 to remove external trematodes and other protozoans. Many people purchase a fish and keep it under observation within the retailer's aquarium for a period of time. In effect, this serves as an ersatz quarantine period which, in relation to a strict quarantine, may be likened to playing Russian roulette.

It should be noted that maintaining copper-ion levels at 0.1 to 0.2 ppm will control *Cryptocaryon* and *Oodinium,* but may not "cure" carrier fish if they are sold prior to the time when all trophonts have left the fish and the fish has developed some degree of immunity. Our experience suggests that fish from some such systems may still carry monogenetic trematodes, and if they have not been kept under copper treatment for a sufficient time period, they may still carry the two previously mentioned protozoan parasites.

Method: Depending on the size and number of fish to be quarantined, set up a 10- to 50-gallon (38- to 190-liter) aquarium with sufficient conditioned gravel in a filter to oxidize ammonia and nitrites. Use commercially available salts with a pH from 7.8 to 8.3 and specific gravity from 1.017 to 1.023, and maintain a temperature of approximately 73 to 77 degrees F (about 23 to 25 degrees C). Provide plenty of aeration using bubbling stones and/or outflow from a filter. Provide hiding areas for fish using plastic pots, pipes, or coral. While fish are in quarantine, continue to feed them whatever they were eating in the store (frozen brine shrimp, flakes, etc.). To prevent ammonia accumulation, do not overfeed, and periodically remove any uneaten food from the aquarium. Throughout the quarantine period, pH, ammonia, and nitrite levels must be monitored daily or every other day, and water changes must be made if ammonia and/or nitrite levels go over 0.1 to 0.2 ppm.

Treatment during quarantine should be directed toward ridding fish of external protozoans and trematodes. As with freshwater fish, internal parasites (nematodes, larval forms) may be a problem. In experiments at the University of Georgia, we have maintained fish at a 0.1 to 0.2 ppm copper-ion concentration for at least ten days, then treated them with 2 ppm of praziquantel toward the end of the fourteen-day quarantine period. Before placing fish in the display aquarium, they have been given a freshwater dip (with or without formaldehyde) as a final insurance measure for trematode removal.

When reintroducing fish into the main display tank after quarantine, rearrange coral or other landmarks in conjunction with a routine water change and cleaning. This will serve to disorient older inhabitants from territorial behavior and tend to spare the newcomer(s). Introducing new fish at night may also reduce fighting. In some cases, dominant fish may have to be removed to avoid deaths from biting.

Disinfection to Prevent Disease Spread

In any wholesale, retail, research, or home facility where multiple tanks are used, sharing of nets, hoses, or other objects between aquaria may spread pathogenic organisms such as parasites, bacteria, and viruses.

How to disinfect nets and solid objects: Many

disinfectants have been used. All should be changed at least once weekly. It is very important to rinse items in clear water after disinfection, since there can be a carryover problem resulting in death of sensitive fish. This is especially true in small aquaria.

A. Air drying: Drying eventually will kill parasites and other organisms, but this process is not strictly disinfection. Spores and cyst forms of such parasites as *Ichthyobodo necatrix* can withstand drying. In establishments with multiple tanks, air drying would necessitate the use of many nets.

B. Chlorine: Chlorine is an excellent disinfectant, but will destroy nets. Chlorine is best used for disinfection of solid objects such as aquaria or hoses. Since organic films will protect bacteria from the effects of chlorine, the surfaces of the objects being cleaned should be scrubbed prior to addition of chlorine. Follow instructions on the bottle for normal disinfection purposes. If scrubbing is not feasible, as in the inside of aquarium piping, 300 ppm of active chlorine may be required.

C. Quaternary ammonia compounds: Various surfactants for general disinfection purposes are available under a variety of trade names, such as Roccal™. These disinfectants are particularly useful as net dips. Follow dilution instructions given on the bottle. Depending on use, the solution may have to be changed two or three times a week. It is important to rinse nets in clear water after disinfection, since carryover of disinfectant may kill small fish.

D. Formaldehyde: Used at 75 to 100 ppm (3 to 4 milliliters, or 0.1 to 0.14 fluid ounces per 10 gallons or 3.8 liters of water), formaldehyde is a good parasiticide. However, it is not recommended due to generation of formaldehyde fumes.

E. Potassium permanganate: Although effective at 50 ppm, since it is an oxidizer and will stain hands, its use is not recommended.

F. Salt: At 3 percent, salt works as a disinfectant for parasites, but in a multiuse situation surfactants have been shown to be more effective.

How to Calculate Water Volume and Medicinal Dosage

When it becomes necessary to medicate fish for health problems, some mathematical figuring becomes essential if the matter is to be done properly and safely. As the following examples illustrate, the calculations involved are much simpler when one uses the metric system. However, in many cases the English system will be included because of its familiarity to North American aquarists.

Safety considerations, both for the fish and for the aquarist, require special mention any time medication is involved. All drugs should be kept under lock and key. They should be handled carefully to avoid skin contact or inhalation contact. If liquid formulations are to be dispensed, never perform mouth pipetting. Inexpensive pipettors are available, or syringes can be attached to the end of a pipette using a small piece of rubber tubing.

Safety of drugs for fish also is a matter of serious concern. Dosages of drugs must be very accurate to avoid poisoning of fish. For example, both formalin (at 25 ppm) and malachite green (at 0.1 ppm) can be toxic to selected species of fish. Smaller fish of any species will be more sensitive to these drugs. Fish with fine scales or scaleless fish will be more sensitive than their larger-scaled relatives. These more sensitive species include eels, loaches, knife fish, and catfish such as *Pimelodella* species and shovel-nose catfish. These species should be treated conservatively by using alternative treatments covered in the text.

Biotesting refers to the trial treatment of a few fish to determine safety and effectiveness of a specific dose of a drug. It is always an advisable procedure before treating large quantities of fish, and is particularly essential if using a treatment which is relatively untested.

Dosages of Common Medicines Used in Water.[1]		
Drug	**Use**	**Dose (ppm)**
Formalin	External parasites	25 to 100
Copper sulfate	External parasites in marine systems	0.1 to 0.2
Metronidazole	Hexamitiasis	3 to 6
Praziquantel	Tapeworms, external trematodes	1 to 3
Antibiotics	Bacterial infections	0.1 to 12[1]

[1] See text for suggested treatment schemes.

A number of common fish medicaments are given in water (see acccompanying table). To provide an accurate dosage when medicine is added to water, one must carefully calculate both the volume of water to be treated and the amount of active drug required (which often differs from the amount of formulated compound to be used).

How to measure the volume of a rectangular aquarium: This seemingly simple procedure is the key to all water-based fish treatments.

A. English system. Measure the inside dimensions of the tank in inches. For height, measure from the middle of gravel, if present, to the top of the water. Multiply the length x width x height in inches. Divide product by 231 = U.S. gallons.

Example: Aquarium is 30 inches long, 14 inches from front to back, and measures 18 inches from middle of gravel to top of water. 30 x 14 x 18 = 7,560 cubic inches. 7,560/231 = 32.7 gallons of water.

B. Metric system. Measure the inside dimensions of the tank as above, but in centimeters. Multiply length x width x depth. Divide product by 1,000 = liters.

Example: Aquarium is 75 centimeters long, 35 centimeters from front to back, and depth of water from middle of gravel to top of water is 45 centimeters. 75 x 35 x 45 = 118,125 cubic centimeters. 118,125/1,000 = 118.1 liters of water.

How to measure the volume of a cylindrical tank or vat: Fall back upon your knowledge of the volume of a cylinder to determine the water it contains.

A. English system. Measure diameter of base and height of water column in inches. Divide diameter by 2 to obtain radius. Square this number, and multiply by 3.14 and by water column height. Divide by 231 to obtain U.S. gallons.

Example: What is the volume of a cylindrical tank with a 24-inch diameter base and a water height of 36 inches?

Solution: 24/2 = 12-inch radius. Applying the formula, 3.14 x (12 x 12) x 36 = 16,277.7 cubic inches and 16,277.7/231 = 70.5 U.S. gallons of water.

B. Metric system. Measure diameter of base and height of water column in centimeters. Divide diameter by 2 to obtain radius. Square this number, and multiply by 3.14 and by water column height. Divide by 1,000 to obtain liters.

Example: What is the volume of a cylindrical tank with a 30-centimeter base and a water height of 35 centimeter?

Solution: 30/2 = 15 centimeter radius. 3.14 x (15 x 15) x 35 = 24,727.5 cubic centimeters. 24,727.5/1000 = 24.7 liters.

How to calculate how much drug to add to water to obtain a specific dosage: Dosages are most easily calculated in parts per million (ppm). A part per million equals 1 milligram of chemical in 1,000 milliliters of water. It also equals 3.8 milligrams in one U.S. gallon of water, so 0.0038 is the conversion factor to change from metric units to gallons, since 38 milligrams per gallon results in 1 ppm.

One cannot assume that a drug is 100 percent pure. In many cases, especially in working with bulk powders, the drug may be mixed with various "carrier" substances. This will be indicated on the drug label. One compensates for this lack of purity by adding an increased amount of chemical. To determine how much of an increase, a "purity factor" term is added into the formula for calculating dosage.

A. English system. Dose in grams = U.S. gallons x desired dosage in ppm x 0.0038 x "purity factor."

Example: You are asked to treat a goldfish pond with Masoten™ (an organophosphate used to treat monogenetic trematodes, anchor worms, and fish lice). The label states that the drug is 80 percent pure. The owner has calculated the volume of water in the pond to be 1,500 gallons. You want to obtain a dosage of 0.25 ppm.

Solution: You note that in the formula, dose is in grams, and recall that 1.0 gram = 1,000 milligrams, 0.1 gram = 100 milligrams, and 0.01 gram = 10 milligrams. Because the drug has inactive ingredients in it, you will need to use more of the chemical than if it were fully active. Convert 80 percent to 100/80 (the "purity factor") to figure out how much more. Now, use the formula. Compound needed for a 0.25 ppm dosage of the drug = 1,500 gallons x 0.25 ppm x 0.0038 x 100/80 = 1.78 grams.

B. Metric system. Follow the same basic procedure as above, but no conversion factor is needed. Dose in grams = liters of water x desired dosage in ppm x "purity factor."

How to calculate dosage when a medication is available in a specified formulation for some

other use: Occasionally, useful medications for fish are available in existing formulations for non-aquatic species. For example, many liquid formulations of organophosphates used to control grubs and lice on pigs and cattle are suitable for treatment of parasitic copepods such as anchor worms, fish lice, and monogenetic trematodes. While their use for food fish is prohibited, such drugs may be used for aquarium species. Of course, prior to using any such drug, preliminary testing should always be done to establish safety.

Example: You have a commercial preparation of a stabilized organophosphate solution containing 8 percent active drug, and you wish to treat goldfish in a 100-gallon vat for *Argulus* using 0.5 ppm of organophosphate.

Solution: Quantity of preparation to use in order to have 0.5 ppm of active drug = 100 gallons x 0.0038 x 0.5 ppm x 100/8 = 2.38 milliliters.

How to calculate dosage when using preweighed tablets or capsules: Many commercial medications are provided with full instructions for use. Other useful medications such as antibiotics, Flagyl™, praziquantel, and nematocides are supplied as preweighed tablets or capsules. When the following amounts of any active drug are added to 10 gallons of water, the following dosages are obtained:

50 milligrams = 1.3 ppm; 100 milligrams = 2.6 ppm; 150 milligrams = 3.9 ppm; 200 milligrams = 5.2 ppm; 250 milligrams = 6.5 ppm.

How to calculate the dosage of specific commonly used chemicals: Because they are in such common use, calculation of dosages for formaldehyde, copper sulfate, and sodium chloride are outlined below.

A. *Formaldehyde:* When added to 10 gallons (38 liters) of water, the following quantities of formalin (37 percent formaldehyde) will result in the following concentrations: 1 milliliter = 25 ppm; 2 milliliters = 50 ppm; 3 milliliters = 75 ppm; 4 milliliters = 100 ppm.

Always keep formalin in a dark bottle. Formalin with a white precipitate at the bottom of the bottle should not be used.

B. *Copper sulfate:* Copper is available as powdered copper sulfate with 5 waters of hydration ($CuSO_4 \cdot 5 H_2O$). The formula weight of the copper sulfate molecule is 249.5 and the atomic weight of copper is 63.5. Therefore, every gram of copper sulfate with 5 waters of hydration contains just over 25 percent copper. The "purity factor" is 100/25, or 4.

Example: You have a 10,000-gallon central salt-water system in which you would like to maintain a copper level of 0.2 ppm. You have purchased powdered copper sulfate with 5 waters of hydration.

Quantity of copper sulfate needed to achieve a 0.2 ppm copper level = 10,000 gallons x 0.0038 x 0.2 ppm x 100/25= 30.4 grams.

Note: Copper sulfate will chelate with hard water. Daily testing of copper-ion levels will determine the need for addition of more copper. Eventually, the dose will stablize, depending on the hardness of the water. As with any solid chemical, copper should be dissolved prior to addition to a water system. Invertebrates are highly sensitive to copper.

C. *Sodium chloride (salt):* Common noniodized kitchen salt is frequently used as an aquarium treatment. A level kitchen tablespoon measure holds about 15 grams of salt.

Salt is known to inhibit *Chilodonella* at concentrations between 0.1 to 0.2 percent (1,000 to 2,000 ppm). Adding 38 grams (about 2 tablespoons) to 10 gallons (38 liters) of water will establish a dose of 1,000 ppm, or 0.1 percent. Maintaining salt concentrations is best done by use of a refractometer.

Salt has been used to compete with the uptake of nitrites, and may provide replacement of sodium and chloride ions in stressed or injured fish. Baths using 2.5 percent salt can be established by adding 95 grams (6 to 7 tablespoons) of salt to a gallon (3.8 liters) of water. Fish should be immersed for fifteen to thirty minutes or until they appear stressed.

How to establish small dosages when your scale weighs only grams: If it is necessary to establish small dosages of a powdered drug without the benefit of an analytical balance, one can make up a greater quantity of solution than would otherwise be used, then subdivide this solution to obtain the necessary dosage. Check the solution's stability in liquid form or in a frozen state if unused portions are to be stored.

Example: You wish to add 20 milligrams of an active drug to a food preparation, but the smallest your scale will weigh is 1 gram. The drug is available in a formulation which, according to its label, has an activity of 10 percent.

Solution: Weigh out a gram of the material to

be used. Add this gram (1,000 milligrams) to 100 milliliters of water. Now, because 100 milliliters of water contain 1 gram, 1 milliliter of water contains 10 milligrams of chemical, which includes both active drugs and inactive drug carriers. If the activity is 10 percent, then this 1-milliliter solution contains 9 milligrams of inactive substances and only 1 milligram of active drugs. Thus 20 milliliters of the solution is needed to provide 20 milligrams of active drug. Similar procedures can be followed using the English system of measurement.

How to Incorporate Drugs in Fish Food

For treatment of some internal parasites and for the prevention of bacterial diseases after a stress situation such as shipping, some fish breeders find it easier and more economical to medicate food rather than water. Drugs can be incorporated into commercially available foods by binding the drug to the food with oils, albumin, or gelatin. Some suggested drugs, the rationale for their use, and dosages in foods are given in the accompanying table. Medicated feeds should not be given to apparently healthy fish. The following steps show how to prepare a fish diet which can be used for incorporation of medicaments.

A. *Combine these ingredients:*
    35 grams canned sardines, salmon, or tuna
    30 grams finely ground vegetables, fresh or canned (choice of peas, squash, spinach, or carrots finely ground; baby-food preparations work well)
    30 grams cooked oatmeal or other grain
    5 milliliters cod-liver oil, unflavored, food grade
    500 milligrams B-complex vitamins or 2 to 3 grams brewer's yeast
    250 milligrams vitamin C
    50 units vitamin E
    5 to 10 grams gelatin as a binder
B. *Add warm water and blend to make a slurry which is just pourable.*
C. *Add medicaments as appropriate.* Drugs should be predissolved in warm water before they are added to the food slurry.
D. *Dissolve the gelatin in one or two cups (about 100 milliliters) of boiling water.* Allow it to cool for a few minutes, then mix it into the food slurry.
E. *Pour medicated feed mixture into plastic bags and close.* Refrigerate until firm, then freeze.
F. *To feed fish, shave off a portion of the frozen block with a food grater, vegetable peeler, or knife.*

How to Determine Dosages When Treating Fish by Injection

When fish are large and have obvious signs of a systemic bacterial disease such as ulcers or hemorrhages, injection of antibiotics by the intraperitoneal route is indicated. Fish can be restrained in a net and injected through the netting material.

The following dosages (in milliliters) have been calculated to deliver an amount of drug proportional to the normal dose used for small animals in veterinary medicine. Repeated injections may be required, depending on the clinical response of the fish.

Chloramphenicol sodium succinate: Reconstitute each gram of antibiotic with 10 milliliters of sterile water. The resulting stock solution, 100 milligrams per milliliter, will be stable for thirty days at room temperature. For use in smaller fish, add 1 milliliter of the solution to 200 milliliters of sterile water or sterile saline solution. This second dilution will result in a solution of 0.5 milligrams per milliliter. Inject 0.5 milliliters (1 cubic cen-

Useful Medicaments Added To Food			
Drug[1]	Use Indication	Dose in food (percent)	Feeding time (days)
Metronidazole	*Hexamita Spironucleus*	0.25	3 – 7
Praziquantel	Tapeworms	0.25	3
Panacur[TM]	Nematodes	0.25	3 – 7
Antibiotics[2]	Bacterial infections Preshipment conditioning	0.25	7 – 10

[1] Dosages with the listed drugs have been shown to be effective under controlled conditions.

[2] Refer to section on antibiotics for choice of antibiotics.

timeter [cc] is identical to 1 milliliter) for every 10 grams of fish. For larger fish, dilute 1 milliliter of stock in 100 milliliters of water and use 0.05 milliliters per 10 grams of fish. Thus, for a 500-gram fish use 2.5 milliliters of diluted antibiotic.

Gentamycin sulfate: Dilute 50 milligrams (1 milliliter) of liquid drug in 1,000 milliliters of sterile distilled water or sterile saline solution to make a stock solution of 50 milligrams per milliliter.

For smaller specimens, inject 0.5 milliliters per 10 grams of fish. For larger fish, make a more concentrated stock solution (50 milligrams to 100 milliliters of a diluting agent) and inject 0.05 milliliters per 10 grams of fish body weight. Thus, a 500-gram fish would be injected with 2.5 milliliters of the diluted antibiotic.

Contributors

JOHN B. GRATZEK received a bachelor of science degree in biology and chemistry at St. Mary's College in Minnesota, where he studied the parasites of muskrats. Pursuing his interests in animal disease, he was awarded the Doctor of Veterinary Medicine degree from the University of Minnesota in 1956 and a Ph.D. in the study of animal virology from the University of Wisconsin in 1961. Dr. Gratzek presently heads the Department of Medical Microbiology in the College of Veterinary Medicine at the University of Georgia. He is past president of the American College of Veterinary Microbiologists and the Interna- tional Association for Aquatic Animal Medicine, and serves on the aquaculture committee of the American Association of Animal Health.

RICHARD E. WOLKE received his Doctor of Veterinary Medicine from Cornell University and his Ph.D. in pathology from the University of Connecticut. He has been employed as a diagnostic and research pathologist at the Comparative Aquatic Pathology Laboratory, University of Rhode Island, for twenty years. Dr. Wolke's experience with fish has included freshwater and marine species, and both cultured and wild populations. Most recently, his work has centered upon environmental biomarkers and diseases in winter flounder. Dr. Wolke has written on fungal, nutritional, bacterial, and neoplastic diseases found in public aquaria, commercial hatcheries, and hobbyists' tanks.

EMMETT B. SHOTTS, JR., received a bachelor of science degree from the University of Alabama and master of science and Ph.D. degrees from the University of Georgia. For five years , Dr. Shotts was a member of the Epidemic Intelligence Service, a highly specialized group of "disease troubleshooters" at the Centers for Disease Control in Atlanta, Georgia. Dr. Shotts currently is a professor in the Department of Medical Microbiology at the University of Georgia College of Veterinary Medicine. He has written over 200 scientific articles and numerous book chapters on bacterial diseases of both aquarium and food fishes, and presently is researching the pathogenic mechanisms of fish disease bacteria at a molecular level.

DONALD L. DAWE received a bachelor of science degree in animal science from the University of Wisconsin, a Doctor of Veterinary Medicine from Iowa State University of Science and Technology, and a master of science and Ph.D. degrees from the University of Illinois. A professor at the University of Georgia College of Veterinary Medicine, Dr. Dawe's research interests are in immunity and disease resis- tance in animals as varied as chickens, swine, and channel catfish, work which has included studies of fish resistance to and immunization against *Ichthyophthirius* (ich). Dr. Dawe is the author or coauthor of sixty-six research publications, nineteen of which relate to fish immunology.

GEORGE C. BLASIOLA received a bachelor of science degree in biology from the University of Miami, Coral Gables, and a master's degree in marine biology from San Francisco State University. From 1973 to 1980, he managed the Water Analysis and Pathology Laboratory at the California Academy of Sciences' Steinhart Aquarium. From then to 1987, he was a research biologist and the AquaVet division manager for Novalek Inc., and from 1987 to 1991 he was the director of research and development for The Wardley Corporation. Mr. Blasiola is a well-known specialist in the diseases of ornamental marine fishes. His articles on fish biology, health, and disease control have appeared in journals and magazines in the United States and internationally.

Index of Scientific Names

Subject Index